MENTAL HEALTH THROUGH WILL-TRAINING

ABRAHAM A. LOW
Founder of Recovery, Inc.

MENTAL HEALTH
THROUGH WILL-TRAINING

A SYSTEM OF SELF-HELP IN PSYCHOTHERAPY
AS PRACTICED BY RECOVERY, INCORPORATED

BY

ABRAHAM A. LOW, M.D.

Founder of Recovery, Inc.

WILLETT PUBLISHING CO.

Glencoe, Illinois 60022

TO MAE

The Mother of My Children

and

A Mother to My Patients

The

National Headquarters

Recovery, Inc.

The Association of Nervous

and Former Mental Patients

802 North Dearborn Street

Chicago, Illinois 60610

TABLE OF CONTENTS

8 CONTENTS

PART III

THE PRINCIPAL METHODS OF SABOTAGE

PART IV

GROUP PSYCHOTHERAPY INTERVIEWS

10   CONTENTS

PREFACE

The present volume is meant to give an account of the psychotherapy methods evolved in the past fifteen years by Recovery, Inc., a non-profit group whose purpose it is to train post-psychotic and psychoneurotic persons in the practice of psychiatric self-help. An extensive report on the association's history, scope of activity and mode of operation was offered in 1943.[1] A concise but fairly comprehensive description was published in 1949.[2]

The contents of the book are in the main reproductions of panel discussions conducted by the ex-patients and group psychotherapy interviews held by the author with his private patients in the years 1944 to 1949. Several essays on "sabotage" have been added, describing the manner in which patients offer resistance to the physician's instructions. The bulk of the material was previously published in the "Recovery Journal" and "Recovery News," issued by Recovery, Inc. and edited by the author. It deals with a system of group psychotherapy evolved by the writer since 1933.

Psychotherapy, individual or group, is invariably based (1) on a philosophy, (2) on techniques. In years past, the field was dominated by three main philosophies and techniques: Freud's psychoanalysis, Adler's individual psychology, and Jung's approach which, because of its vagueness and mysticism, defies precise classification. More recently, the psychoanalytic doctrine has taken the lead and all but crowded out its erstwhile rivals. It established its hegemony in universities and philanthropic foundations and gained unquestioned prominence in the province of psychotherapy. The doctrine appears to be in firm control in the official psychiatric organizations, in the mental hygiene activities of the national government, in the veterans administration, presumably also in the hospitals of the armed forces. Official psychotherapy, in the United States today, is essentially psychoanalysis.

---

[1] Low, Abraham A., The Techniques of Self-Help in Psychiatric After-Care, Chicago, 1943, Recovery, Inc., 3 volumes.

[2] Low, Abraham A., Recovery, Inc., A Project for Rehabilitating Post-Psychotic and Long-Term Psychoneurotic Patients, published in "Rehabilitation of the Handicapped," page 213, New York, 1949, the Ronald Press Company. The latter article has been incorporated, with the publisher's permission, as a revised reprint in the present volume, page 16.

The author rejects the psychoanalytic doctrine both as philosophy and therapeutic technique. In point of philosophy, he cannot share the view that human conduct is the result of unconscious drives, sexual or otherwise. To his way of thinking, adult life is not *driven* by instincts but *guided* by Will. In emphasizing the priority of Will over Drives he is merely echoing the principles and teachings of the late Professor Emil Kraepelin, founder of modern psychiatry, and those of the late Professor Wilhelm Wundt, father of modern psychology. Quite proudly he claims also to echo the voice of common experience and common sense. Whatever may be meant by drives, be they instinctual cravings (the favorite psychoanalytic term), or emotional trends, desires, wishes, yearnings and leanings, they all eventuate in impulses, acting or ready for action. To the author it is inconceivable that adult human life can be ordered without a Will holding down impulses. What precisely is meant by the term Will is amply demonstrated in the text.

In point of psychotherapeutic techniques, psychoanalysis must be accounted a failure on the evidence of its own testimony. The most startling defect is the insignificant number of patients which can be reached by the method. The Chicago Institute for Psychoanalysis, for instance, has been able to report no more than 319 patients treated six months or longer during a ten year period[3]. The Menninger Clinic of Topeka, Kansas, tops this record of poor productivity with a report[4] of 100 patients similarly treated for six months or longer in the course of ten years, 1932-1941. In order to fully appreciate the story told by these astonishing figures one must remember that the two institutions are generously staffed and richly financed. Knight[4], tabulating the results of treatment as published by the psychoanalytic institutes of Berlin, London, Topeka (ten year surveys) and Chicago (five years) was unable to quote more than 660 cases treated for upward of six months in the four clinics during a ten year period (five years in Chicago). Of this total, 363 patients were treated in Berlin, 114 in Chicago, 100 in Topeka, 74 in London. Stating it otherwise, the productivity of the psychoanalytic techniques, as reported from four leading clinics, ranged, in point of the number of patients carried per year, from 7.4

---

[3] Institute for Psychoanalysis, Ten Year Report, 1932-1942, Chicago.

[4] Knight, Robert P., Evaluation of the Results of Psychoanalytic Treatment, American Journal of Psychiatry, volume 98, page 434, November 1941.

(London) to 36.3 (Berlin). Figures of this kind admit of one conclusion only: The psychoanalytic techniques are available for a small fraction only of the multitude of post-psychotic and psychoneurotic patients. The reason for its restricted availability is the egregious amount of time needed for the administration of the treatment, an overall average of hundreds of hours being required for each individual patient. For patients cared for in private practice there is the added handicap that the time-consuming process involves a necessarily exorbitant expense. Whether the emphasis be on the time factor or the cost element, in either case, the method is all but unavailable for the masses of patients.

Aside from its limited availability for numerically significant groups of patients, psychoanalysis is also, again on the evidence of its own testimony, therapeutically ineffective. Knight [4], assaying the therapeutic results obtained in 660 analyses conducted for six months or longer in the institutes of Berlin, London, Chicago and Topeka, tells us that 183 patients (27.7 percent) were considered "apparently cured"; 186 (28.2 percent) were "much improved"; 291 (44.1 percent) were either somewhat improved, or worse, or showed no change. Needless to say, a 27.7 percent yield of "apparently cured" patients, even adding the 28.2 percent of the "much improved" contingent, constitutes a serious indictment for any psychotherapeutic method. Oberndorf [5] is authority for the statement that 40 percent of the "psychotic cases treated by psychoanalysis plus institutional regime at the Menninger Clinic" were discharged as cured. He comments that this is also the percentage of those "discharged as cured from mental hospitals in the United States." It is well known, however, that the forty percent figure for cures of state hospital patients represents the spontaneous recovery rate. Is it permissable, then, to draw the inference that, for psychotic patients at any rate, the results of psychoanalytic treatment are identical with their spontaneous chances for "outgrowing" their psychosis? Taking either the hint offered by Oberndorf or the disappointing figures supplied by the above mentioned statistics, the conclusion seems inescapable that psychoanalysis has failed as a therapeutic technique.

It is not intended here to criticize psychoanalysis with a view to extolling the work of Recovery, Inc. But inasmuch as the

---

[5] Oberndorf, C. P., Consideration of Results with Psychoanalytic Therapy, American Journal of Psychiatry, volume 99, page 374, November 1942.

psychoanalytic method has well nigh monopolized the field of psychotherapy it is incumbent on a diverging approach to measure its record of accomplishment against that of the recognized procedure. A few simple figures culled from the files of the author will demonstrate that the combination of office treatment with the group methods practiced in Recovery, Inc. achieves a range of availability which dwarfs that of psychoanalysis.

Between January 1, 1946 and December 31, 1947, in a representative two year period, the author was able to examine in his office a total of 425 new patients. Deducting from this figure those patients who did not return after the initial examination (140) and those who suffered from somatic or neurological conditions (24), there remained 261 subjects who were available for psychotherapy. Of this final group, 156 were given treatment for six months or longer. In other words, employing the method described in this book, one man was enabled to give active psychiatric care to a considerable multiple of the patients serviced in a comparable period by large staffs of psychoanalytic institutions. Clearly, the Recovery method is vastly superior to psychoanalysis in the matter of availability to the masses of patients seeking psychiatric care.

As concerns the therapeutic effectiveness of the Recovery techniques, as distinguished from mere availability, it is sufficient to point to the basic character of the organization: the members know one another; they meet frequently and regularly in classes and at parties; they get together in family gatherings and consort socially; they form sewing clubs, bowling parties and dancing teams; many of them spend evenings or Sundays together, dining or visiting theatres and amusement places. One can readily surmise what would happen if no more than a negligible 28 percent of the lot would finally reach the status of "apparently cured." The organization would explode in no time. Instead, the association, staffed by one physician, financed without outside assistance, shunning though not completely escaping publicity, has prospered close to fifteen years. This record speaks for itself. It needs no statistics to support its claims.

A CONCISE OUTLINE OF RECOVERY'S
SELF-HELP TECHNIQUES[6]

Recovery, Inc. was founded, November 7, 1937, by thirty ex-patients who regained their health after receiving shock treatments and/or other therapies at the Psychiatric Institute of the University of Illinois medical school, the predecessor of the present Psychiatry Department of the Illinois Neuropsychiatric Institute. The author was at the time the assistant director of the Institute. Between 1937 and 1940 the organization limited its services to the patients admitted to the wards of the Psychiatric Institute. In fall of 1940 it expanded its work to include the psychoneurotic patients of the out-patient department. In September 1941 the group severed its connection with the University of Illinois medical school and established headquarters of its own in the Chicago Loop District where it is now located at 116 South Michigan Avenue. In the years since 1942 the bulk of its membership was recruited from the author's private practice. As is evident from this brief description, Recovery, Inc. has had the opportunity to try out its techniques (1) with an intramural patient population, (2) with an out-patient group, (3) with private patients. The object of the organization, apart from its tendency to save time for the physician and money for the patient, is to help prevent recurrences in mental diseases and to forestall chronicity in psychoneurotic conditions. Its techniques place the emphasis on self-help.

THE "RESIDUAL SYMPTOM" OF THE RECOVERED MENTAL PATIENT

After leaving the hospital the mental patient is supposed to be restored to health. This is true in most instances if by mental health is meant the absence of delusions and hallucinations, of violent impulsiveness and indifference to group standards. But

[6] Revised reprint, with the publisher's permission, of a paper contributed by the author to "Rehabilitation of the Handicapped," a volume issued, 1949, by the Ronald Press Company, New York. The paper bore the title, "Recovery, Inc., A Project for Rehabilitating Post-Psychotic and Long-Term Psychoneurotic Patients."

returning home the patient still suffers from restlessness, tenseness and preoccupation. His inability to relax is aggravated by the sense of being stigmatized. Many returned patients are so suspicious of being watched or mistrusted that even simple inquiries like "how do you feel?" or "how are you today?" are likely to cause irritation. These innocent questions may suggest to the patient that the reality of his recovery is doubted. Feeling stigmatized, the patient becomes self-conscious and introspective. On a given night he might have difficulty falling asleep. This is apt to alarm him. The alarm increases the difficulty of sleeping. Then more alarm, more sleeplessness and more alarm yet. A vicious cycle is thus set going which may keep the patient from properly resting night after night. Other vicious cycles may soon establish themselves. The patient notices a sense of fatigue which in itself may be as insignificant as any sensation of fatigue experienced by the average person. But feeling stigmatized he correlates his tiredness with the possibility of a relapse, and the more he dreads the relapse the more intense becomes his fatigue; the heavier the fatigue the more haunting the fear of the relapse. One patient had a nocturnal itch after returning home, another complained of a twitch in one arm, a third felt a hair on the tongue. Experiences of this kind are distressing enough to conjure up the vision of an impending relapse. The experiences become far more terrifying when the patient observes, for instance, that the arm suddenly begins to shake in automatic motion or when "awful flashes" shoot across the eye. Patients reported an "electric buzz running through the muscles," that "the tongue lay stiff in the mouth," that "my own voice sounded strange," that "the ear felt pushed in," that "I can't seem to hear myself when I speak." Palpitations, numbness, head or chest pressures, dizziness, difficulty of concentration, dimness of vision, air-hunger, headaches, nausea and scores of other disturbances were reported by numerous patients. Observations of this sort may give rise to the vicious cycle which has the familiar character of the symptom increasing the fear and the fear intensifying and perpetuating the symptom. While there are no statistics to substantiate the claim it is fair to assume that many recurrences of mental ailment are the direct result of these "residual symptoms" which, fanned by the fury of the vicious cycle, produce anxieties and panics which finally necessitate the much dreaded recommitment. Recovery, Inc. insists that the patient, prior to leaving the hospital, attend group psychotherapy classes in which he is given adequate instruction how to face the threat of the residual symptom and the pressure of stigmatization. At the time, the members of the family are urged to attend discussion courses in which similar instruction is offered. In this manner the pre-discharge care prepares for the after-care effort.

THE DEFEATISM OF THE CHRONIC PSYCHONEUROTIC PATIENT

Most residual symptoms from which the returned mental patient is likely to suffer are similar to or identical with the common complaints voiced by psychoneurotic patients. Hence, the possibility of treating both groups by the same method. The psychoneurotic patients admitted to Recovery, Inc. belong in the category of chronic, protracted cases mainly. Patients with symptoms of a few months' duration are rarities in the ranks of the group. Most members have a record of from two to twenty years of suffering. These "experienced sufferers" have made the rounds of physicians and clinics and were assured on numerous occasions, explicitly or by implication, that some therapeutic measure will cure them. The assurance never materialized with the result that they no longer believe a cure possible. They know, however, that some or most of the past therapies had a transient, palliative effect. The palpitations were milder after a reassuring talk; the dizziness yielded to a sedative. Hence, they treasure the "pep-talk" or the prescription. In order to secure these elusive aids they must complain; they must convince the physician that they "really" suffer, that their pains are not imaginary, that they can "positively not stand" their fatigue. To get a hearing from the doctor is all the more important because at home their complaints are likely to be met with impatience or ridicule. Complaining, then, becomes a vital part of their daily routine. In the course of years they develop the consummate art of the "expert complainer." What these long-term patients crave is a sympathetic ear which, after years of griping, they can no longer secure from their relatives and friends. They delight in a lengthy discussion of their fears and frustrations. Their ideal is to be explored, analyzed, sounded and probed. Essentially they have decided that their case is beyond repair. What they expect is a hearing, perhaps some temporary relief, but not a final cure. The "chronicity" of this group has little to do with the nature of the symptoms, with diagnosis or etiology; it is self-appointed defeatism.

Since Recovery places the emphasis on the self-help action of the patients, it must ignore investigations and explorations which are not within the province of inexperienced lay persons.

Complexes, childhood memories, dream experiences and subconscious thought play little part in the class interviews conducted by the physician and are entirely eliminated from the self-help effort carried on by the patients. The psychoneurotic individual is considered a person who for some reason developed disturbing symptoms leading to ill-controlled behavior. The symptoms are in the nature of threatening sensations, "intolerable" feelings, "uncontrollable" impulses and obsessive "unbearable" thoughts. The very vocabulary with its frenzied emphasis on the "killing" headache, the dizziness that "drives me frantic," the fatigue that "is beyond human endurance" is ominously expressive of defeatism. The first step in the psychotherapeutic management of these "chronic" patients must be to convince them that the sensation can be endured, the impulse controlled, the obsession checked. Unfortunately, the physician is far from convincing. His attempt to "sell" the idea of mental health arouses the "sales resistance" of the patient. "The physician doesn't dare tell me the truth," muses the patient. "It would be against his ethics to declare me incurable." The resistance is easily overcome in the group interview. The fellow sufferer who explains how he "licked" his frightful palpitations after years of invalidism cannot possibly be suspected of trying to sell something. That "colleague" is convincing. He convinces the novice that "chronic" conditions are not hopeless.

THE PATIENTS MEET ON THREE DAYS EVERY WEEK

On three separate days each week the patients take part in group discussions, either as panel members or listeners. On Wednesday, family gatherings are held in private homes in the various neighborhoods of Chicago. The patients are sub-divided into seven neighborhood groups, each comprising from ten to twenty families. Three such family groups function on the Northside, two on the Southside, one on the Westside of the city; one serves the West suburbs. On the occasion of the family meetings panels of three or four experienced members discuss a chapter of the author's three volumes on self-directed after-care or an article from the now discontinued Recovery Journal or from its successor, the Recovery News. The theme is centered on the topic of symptoms and the proper means of conquering them. The physician is not present at the family gatherings although he reserves the right to attend occasionally to check on the effectiveness of the procedure. Reports are currently conveyed to him by the panel leaders. Tuesday evening is devoted to a group psychotherapy class, conducted by the physician. Saturday afternoon, a public meeting takes place at Recovery headquarters, 116 South Michigan Avenue. It is attended by the patients, their relatives and friends. The first half hour is given over to a panel discussion similar to that held at the Wednesday home gatherings. In the second half the physician delivers an address in which he sums up the conclusions reached by the panel, approving or correcting their statements. The panel members are led by a panel leader.

TREATING THE "SETBACK"

Patients are required to attend classes and meetings for at least six months. The average patient experiences a considerable improvement in the first or second week of participation in the program. But the improvement is, as a rule, as short-lived as was the relief which the patient used to gain from the visits to clinics and doctors' offices. No meetings are held on four days of the week. During these days the novice is apt to suffer a "setback." He is again tortured by "that awful fatigue" or has been unable "to sleep a wink for three nights in succession," or the fear of doing harm to the baby reappears after it was gone for a short while. Every patient is warned to be on guard against the unavoidable setback. He is cautioned to contact a veteran Recovery member immediately after the symptom has reappeared. The assurance offered by the veteran is in accord with the language used by the physician, and the interpretations given to the novice coincide with those used in the physician's classes and in his writings. New members are assigned to veterans whom they may call in distress. The veteran functions in the capacity of the physician's "aide." The contact is generally made by telephone but may be done by a personal visit to the aide's home. If the result is not satisfactory the novice is permitted to call on the leader of his local panel. If this is ineffective he may contact the chairman of the organization who serves as deputy to the physician. Finally he may call the physician. The effectiveness of the scheme is evidenced by the fact that few instances are recorded in which the physician was called by novices.

THE SYMPTOMATIC IDIOM

If the patients are to help and teach one another they must be instructed to use a language which is not confusing. This is particularly important because language, if used glibly, tends to be alarmist and defeatist. By dint of its defeatist insinuations, language frequently engenders tenseness which reinforces and perpetuates symptoms. To avoid the fatalistic implications of the language used by the patient the physician must supply a terminology of his own in matters of health. There are many languages. Features and gestures speak. So do symptoms. Their language is a one word idiom: DANGER. This is called the "symptomatic idiom." Accepting the suggestions of the symptomatic idiom the patient considers the violent palpitations as presaging sudden death. The pressure in the head is viewed as due to a brain tumor. The tenseness is experienced as so "terrific" that the patient fears he is going to "burst." His fatigue does not let up "one single minute," and "how long can the body stand it?" In these instances, the implications of the symptomatic idiom are those of an impending *physical collapse*. If phobias, compulsions and obsessions dominate the symptomatic scene the resulting fear is that of the *mental collapse*. After months and years of sustained suffering the twin fears of physical and mental collapse may recede, giving way to apprehensions about the impossibility of a final cure. This is the fear of the *permanent handicap*. The three basic fears of the physical collapse, mental collapse and permanent handicap are variations of the danger theme suggested by the symptomatic idiom.

THE TEMPERAMENTAL LINGO

Another source of defeatism is temper. The patients are taught that temper has two divisions. The one comes into play when I persuade myself that a person has done me wrong. As a result I become angry. This is called the *angry or aggressive temper*, which appears in various shades and nuances: resentment, impatience, indignation, disgust, hatred, etc. The other variety of temper is brought into action whenever I feel that I am wrong. This gives rise to moral, ethical and esthetic fears or to the fear of being a failure in pragmatic pursuits. I am afraid that I sinned, failed, blundered, in short, that I defaulted on a moral, ethical or esthetic standard or on the standard of average efficiency. This is called the *fearful or retreating temper* which may express itself in many different qualities and intensities: discouragement, preoccupation, embarrassment, worry, sense of shame, feeling of inadequacy, hopelessness, despair, etc. The fearful temper is likely to lead either to a feeling of personal inferiority or to the sentiment of group stigmatization. Whether it be of the angry or fearful description, temper reinforces and intensifies the symptom which, in its turn, increases the temperamental reaction. In this manner, a vicious cycle is established between temper and symptom. The temperamental reaction is kept alive mainly by the unsympathetic and unthinking attitude of the relatives. By means of coarse statements or subtle innuendo they provoke loud explosions or silent agonies on the part of the patient. They tell him to use his will power, implying that he makes no effort to get well. With this, they indict him as a weakling, worse yet, as purposely shamming disease. They urge him to "snap out of it," indicating that the symptoms are so easy to deal with that a mere snap would shake them out of existence. Other insinuations frequently levelled against the psychoneurotic or former mental patient are equally disconcerting. Complaining of fatigue he is told not to be lazy; mentioning his "awful palpitations," he is admonished to be a man. The net result of this concerted environmental assault is that the patient is continually angry at his detractors and, gradually accepting their insinuations, becomes ashamed and fearful of himself.

In telling the patient that wrong was done to him or that he is wrong his temper speaks to him. The language which it uses is called the *temperamental lingo*. Its vocabulary is limited to the terms "right" and "wrong." Unless the patient learns to ignore the threats, warnings and incitements of the temperamental lingo he will be the victim of angry outbursts and fearful anticipations. His tenseness will be maintained and intensified; new symptoms will be precipitated and old ones fortified. Temper is most dangerous when it plays on the symptom itself. By labelling sensations as "intolerable," feelings as "terrible," impulses as "uncontrollable" the lingo discourages the patient from facing, tolerating and controlling the reaction. The very sound of the labels ("intolerable," etc.) is apt to rouse fear and defeatism. All a patient has to do is to call a crying reaction by the name of "crying spell," and no effort will be made to check the burst of tears. The word "spell" suggests uncontrollability. Make the patient substitute "crying habit" for "crying spell," and the impossibility of stemming the flood at least will not be taken for granted. Similarly, if the patient raves about the "splitting" headache, the dizziness that "drives me mad," the pressure that "I can't stand any longer," the fatalism of diction is bound to breed a despondency of mood. In order to prevent the temperamental response the patient must be trained to ignore the whisperings of his temperamental lingo.

THE "RECOVERY LANGUAGE"

The combined effects of symptomatic idiom and temperamental lingo are checkmated if the patient is made to use the physician's language only. The members of the Association call it proudly the "Recovery language." The most important parts of its vocabulary are the words: "sabotage" and "authority." The authority of the physician is sabotaged if the patient presumes to make a diagnostic, therapeutic or prognostic statement. The verbiage of the temperamental lingo ("unbearable," "intolerable," "uncontrollable") constitutes sabotage because of the assumption that the condition is of a serious nature which is a diagnosis; or, that it is difficult to repair, which is a prognosis. It is a crass example of sabotage if the claim is advanced that, "my headache is there the very minute I wake up. I didn't have time to think about it. It came before I even had a chance to become emotional. How can that be nervous?" A statement of this kind throws a serious doubt on the validity of the physician's diagnosis and sabotages his authority. Likewise, it is a case of self-diagnosing and consequently sabotage to view palpitations as a sign of a heart ailment, of head pressure as meaning brain tumor, of sustained fatigue as leading to physical exhaustion. Once the physician has made the diagnosis of a psychoneurotic or postpsychotic condition the patient is no longer permitted to indulge in the pastime of self-diagnosing. If he does he is practicing sabotage. Patients are expected to lose their major symptoms after two months of Recovery membership and class attendance. If after the two month period the handicap persists in its original intensity the indication is that sabotage is still in action. The patient still listens to the suggestions of the symptomatic idiom fearing impending collapse and permanent handicap. Or, he gives ear to the verbal vagaries of the temperamental lingo, feeling helpless in the face of suffering. Clinging to his own mode of thinking he sabotages the physician's effort.

Contrary to expectation, it is comforting to the patient to be called a saboteur. Considering himself as such he knows that he has "not yet" learned to avoid resisting the physician. The "not yet" is reassuring. It suggests that in time he will learn. The patients encourage one another to wait until they get well. They warn one another against impatience. The most effective slogan handed down from veteran to novice is, "Wait till you will learn to give up sabotaging."

THE "SPOTTING TECHNIQUE"

If the patient is to check his sabotaging propensities he must be trained to "spot" the inconsistencies and fallacies of his own language whether it is merely conceived in silent thought or given formulation in vocal speech. To this end, a system of "spotting techniques" was evolved by means of which the members learn to reject the suggestions of the symptomatic idiom and the temperamental lingo whenever a symptom or a temperamental reaction occur. An extensive though necessarily incomplete description of the spotting techniques is furnished in part 3 of this book.

SOCIAL ACTIVITIES

The social calendar of the organization is remarkably crowded. The activities are largely spontaneous, little supervised. Practically all events, be they group psychotherapy classes, public meetings or family gatherings, are somehow linked to sociability. After a group psychotherapy class the patients form small groups heading for the nearest drug store or restaurant where they rehash the theme discussed in class or chat about private affairs. The most stimulating social event is the "kaffeeklatsch" following immediately upon the Saturday afternoon public meeting. After the panel and the physician have finished their discussions the assembly hall is speedily converted into a sort of lounge. The patients, relatives and friends seat themselves around small tables and are treated to coffee and cake. Mothers and fathers then exchange views about the progress of their still suffering or already recovering offspring. The patients join the chat, and the atmosphere is one of mutual encouragement, gratitude and hopefulness. The "kaffeeklatsch" may last an hour or longer. The physician moves from group to group, engaging in brief conversations or listening to the stories and views presented by members and guests. This informal mingling with patients and relatives provides the physician with information which he could hardly obtain otherwise. The men and women speaking to him are spontaneous, divorced from the official and cramping situation of the interview carried on in the ordinary examining room. Mrs. Jones reports an incident which she observed in Mrs. Smith's home on the occasion of the last family gathering. The account is unreflective, reportorial, descriptive. These casual chats with the members are an invaluable means of acquainting the physician with the personal details of the patients' home life.

The family gatherings are similarly patterned. A panel discussion of about thirty minutes is followed by a modest repast furnished by the family in whose home the meeting is held. The physician does not attend the family panels but is currently kept informed by the panel leaders about what transpires about adjustment or maladjustment of the patients and about the quality of home life prevailing in the particular family. The panel leaders meet with the physician once a month to receive special training in the matter of conducting the panels. This is again an occasion when a vast mass of information is conveyed to the physician about the home life of the patients. It need hardly be stressed that the type and quality of information which the physician is thus enabled to collect is vastly superior to that obtained in his examining room while interviewing the questioning parents and relatives.

The members seem to have an almost unquenchable thirst for social contacts. They visit one another in their homes; they go together to shows and concerts, meet for lunches, for short trips, for joint visits to museums or parks or for plain walks. Some groups have regular schedules for bowling, barn dancing, hiking and swimming. The families of one Northside and one Southside group formed sewing circles. Consciously or unconsciously, the trend is to break through the dismal isolation and loneliness which have always been the blight of neurotic or post-psychotic existence. The patients state it explicitly that formerly they merely existed, now they live again. Formerly they were lonely individuals, now they are thoroughly integrated with the rich, pulsating life of a closely knit group.

A happy outlet for this burning desire for sociability is afforded by the informal afternoon gatherings which take place at Recovery headquarters, 116 South Michigan Avenue. A number of veterans, housewives mainly, volunteer each to spend one afternoon a week in the Recovery office, supervising the activities of that afternoon. Patients or relatives working in the Loop district drop in, partake of simple refreshments and spend time chatting or asking advice or seeking reassurance for disturbing symptoms. The physician's office is two blocks distant. New patients are asked to visit the Recovery office immediately after the termination of the initial examination. There they are met by the other patients and given information about the work of the organization. Panics, anxieties and apprehensions are easily soothed by the calming influence of meeting other patients who having suffered similar disturbances are now presenting the picture of good health.

MEMBERSHIP, FINANCES, ADMINISTRATION

Membership, at three dollars per year, is open to any psychoneurotic or former mental patient. At this writing (January 1950) the membership stands at 376. About 75 percent of the total is secured from the author's private clientele. The organization is financed by membership fees, donations, proceeds from the sale of Recovery literature, collections at meetings. The organization is almost but not quite self-sustaining. The yearly deficit is met by the author.

April 1948 the organization moved to its present larger quarters. With a considerably increased rental and the necessity for new furniture and office equipment it was deemed wise to create a guarantee fund. The members responded promptly and generously to an appeal for contributions. The goal was 5,000 dollars, and close to 4,400 were collected.

The affairs of the organization are conducted by a board of three directors, all ex-patients. Mrs. Annette Brocken, ex-patient and assistant principal of a Chicago public school, is president of the organization and chairman of the board of directors. Serving with her are a vice-president, a secretary, a treasurer and six councilors. The author does not hold office, but functions as the medical director. An ex-patient is the editor of the "Recovery News." Another ex-patient holds the position of the executive secretary doing all the routine work including dictation and typing. This is the only salaried employe. The monthly compensation is almost nominal.

RECOVERY LITERATURE

Between 1938 and 1941 the organization published a bimonthly magazine, "Lost and Found." The author was the editor contributing the bulk of articles. The pages of the magazine were devoted mainly to a thorough discussion of the influence of domestic temper on the fortunes of the patients. In 1943 this material was issued in book form in three volumes entitled, "The Techniques of Self-Help in Psychiatric After-Care." The issue is now exhausted after a total sale of close to 1,000 copies.

June 1946 to June 1947 the "Recovery Journal" was published. In consequence of rising cost of printing it was discontinued after the eleventh issue. It was succeeded by a phototyped news sheet, the "Recovery News," which appeared eight times a year. Each issue contains a contribution from the author. Subscription is included in the membership fee and 2.00 dollars per year for non-members. A second edition of the "Self-Help Techniques" is in preparation.

Eight branches of Recovery, Inc. are now functioning outside the Chicago area. Following are their locations and dates of formation: Muscatine, Iowa (1946), Brighton, Michigan (1947), Evansville, Indiana (1950), Louisville, Kentucky (1951), St. Louis, Missouri (1951), Burlington, Iowa (1951), Denver, Colorado (1951), Dixon, Illinois (1951). Other branches are in the process of formation. The Denver branch is superintended by a local psychiatrist, the others are led by ex-patients. The members meet regularly in their homes, read the Recovery literature, cite examples from their own experience and conduct panel discussions which are modelled after the pattern established in Chicago. The branches are visited by officers of the Chicago organizaton in intervals of about six months, and the leaders of the branches, in turn, come to Chicago to attend meetings and to perfect themselves in the techniques of panel leadership.

RESULTS

It was stated that the objectives of the organization are (1) to help reduce the incidence of relapses in mental ailment and to prevent chronicity in psychoneurotic conditions, (2) to save time for the physician and expense for the patient. It would be easy to furnish imposing tables detailing percentages of improvements and failures. Tabulations of this kind, posing as objective statements, are usually nothing but subjective opinions no matter how heavily they are buttressed by charts and graphs. They are particularly objectionable if compiled without the benefit of a well organized long-range follow-up investigation. Since the latter was not available no computation was attempted. Nevertheless, reasonably valid conclusions as to the therapeutic effectiveness of the system can be drawn from the very nature and structure of the organization. The patients and relatives know one another and if relapses or continued chronicity were frequent occurrences the membership would inevitably become discouraged and lose confidence. An unfortunate event which took place in October 1947 illustrates the point with striking force. A well known member of the group relapsed into a depression and one morning ran into the path of a speeding train. It was not clear whether the fatal incident was suicide or accident. Nevertheless, something in the nature of a demoralization swept the organization. Several of the ex-patients developed severe reactions. One of them had to be hospitalized. The fact that this has been the only instance of suicide, if such it was, in a period of close to fifteen years during which many hundreds of manic-depressive patients had joined as active members ought to be considered an eloquent testimony to the therapeutic efficiency of the system. This system would rapidly disintegrate if it failed to accomplish its therapeutic objectives. Statistical evidence does not seem required to demonstrate its success.

Statistical figures, however, are available in support of the organization's second objective, i.e., its endeavor to effect substantial economies in the physician's time and the patient's expense. Due to the fact that the patients are disciplined there is little quibbling and arguing in the physician's office which means that the so-called "resistance" to his explanations and directions is reduced to a minimum. This alone allows an impressive saving in time. Another time-saving factor is the massive instruction given the patients in classes and meetings and the insistence on continual study of the physician's writings. With resistance restricted and the patient coming to the office reasonably well instructed the private interview can be terminated in a surprisingly small space of time. As a general rule, the author manages to see from four to five patients during one hour of his office time. Accordingly, the charges for the brief visit can be held to a moderate figure. In addition, the intensive class training and the equally intensive patient-to-patient contact make it possible to achieve improvements after a relatively short period of treatment. The total charges are thus lowered considerably. All patients are required to visit the physician's office for six consecutive months after the initial examination. They are seen once a week during the first month, once in two weeks in the second month. During the third through the sixth month the office visits are reduced to once every four weeks if symptoms and difficulties are significantly ameliorated, but the two week ratio continues if improvement lags. The average number of visits in 1947 was 11.9 per patient in a representative six month period. The maximum was 23 visits, the minimum was 5, the median was 12.

PART I

PANEL DISCUSSIONS WITH EXTENSIVE QUOTATION OF EXAMPLES OFFERED BY PATIENTS

1

IMAGINATION, TEMPER AND SYMPTOMS

A Panel Discussion Conducted by Patients

Frank (Panel leader): The panel is ready to start and we are taking our material from the lecture entitled "The Wrong-Fearing Temperament." What we are going to discuss is the dilemma which means a difficulty of making decisions. Has anybody an example of having trouble making up his mind?

Tillie: Some time ago I went to Field's and wanted to get a dress for my little daughter Doris. I couldn't make up my mind between two dresses. I looked at both dresses and felt confused. And when I can't make up my mind I get a tightness in my left side and when I get this I feel like letting everything go. But this time I just took one and felt comfortable. Then I went to the socks department and I thought I would get size nine. But I thought they were too big and I was in confusion again. The tightness came back and I got flushed and felt I couldn't breathe. I was on the point of throwing the socks down and leaving the store but Doris said if they didn't have size eight and a half she was going to take size nine. So she made the decision for me. Then the tightness stopped immediately and I felt comfortable. Six months ago once the tightness had started all kinds of other symptoms would have come on and I would have been in a panic all day and maybe for several days. Today my panics last a short while, and they aren't a bit as severe as they used to be.

Maurice: I used to make conflicts and dilemmas out of things the average person wouldn't think to make an issue of, for instance, going to a movie or getting a hair-cut. I would make a start, then I'd think should I really go? Then I might pick up a book and read. After a few minutes I would feel I should go to the barber's. Then I would put it off again and so it would take me hours to make a simple decision. Months ago I remember I went to the library and I would be in a conflict about what books to take out, and for days I looked over books and never took one out. That made me tense and disgusted because I couldn't make up my mind. Today I can decide in a few minutes.

Carol: My two children have been sick the past two weeks. I thought it would be nice if my husband would suggest eating out tonight. A year ago I wouldn't have the nerve to make the suggestion. I would have been sore at my husband if he didn't make the suggestion himself. This time I said, "How about it," and he was agreeable. But even now I don't know whether it was right to ask him. I get so tense when I have to ask for things.

Frank: All this tenseness derives from the fact that we don't want to make up our mind. We are afraid we'll have to blame ourselves. We'd rather pass the buck. But we have to learn to make decisons and to take chances that we may be wrong. You know the doctor tells us we must have the courage to be wrong in the trivialities of every day life.

Carol: I have another example. I have to take my wash to the laundry to have it ironed. Several months ago I used to be tense on the way home because I had to rush back to prepare lunch for the children and I was afraid I wouldn't make it in time. So I used to put off making the trip to the laundry and let it go day after day till we were most out of laundry. Today I just do it and if I feel tense on the way back I say to myself, "What of it?" The tenseness isn't so bad anymore anyhow.

Frank: These are examples of trivial conflicts and the very fact that they are so numerous keeps us in constant tension and the tenseness, of course, produces symptoms. I will give you an example of my own. As you know I am the editor of the Recovery News* and there is an article I am planning on writing but I keep putting it off. Monday night I was home and I thought I would start on the article but didn't feel like doing it. Suddenly it became important for me to read the daily paper. Ordinarily I don't read it more than twice a week. But now it seemed I had to read it immediately. And so I got myself the Tribune, and read it thoroughly. After I was through with it I noticed the Sunday Tribune was still on the table from the day before. I got a hold of that and read it, again very thoroughly. Ordinarily I hardly throw a look at it. This you can call procrastination. But the point is I didn't make up my mind to do something that I didn't feel like doing. I haven't been able to lick this procrastination of mine as thoroughly as I would like to.

---

*The "Recovery News" was a mimeographed sheet which was edited by Frank Rochford in 1945 and early 1946. It was the predecessor of the "Recovery Journal."

But I am gradually getting it under control, and on that Monday evening when I kept putting off writing I finally made up my mind and wrote and finished the article.

Don: I used to buy medicine from a drug store in the neighborhood. The clerk there knows about my condition because I told him. Now I am sorry that I told him because I feel uncomfortable when I have to go there to buy medicine. Of course, it is the stigma. When I need the medicine I put off going to the drug store. On several occasions I was pretty sick with my asthma but rather than talk to the clerk I endured sickness. Finally I needed the medicine badly and my first thought was again to put it off. But then I said to myself, "No sir, you know you will be tense all day if you don't make up your mind to face that clerk." And if I am tense I get all kinds of symptoms, fatigue, sleeplessness and tremors. So I went and got the medicine and after that I felt I had done something worth while. Otherwise I would have suffered all day.

IMAGINATION, TEMPER, SYMPTOMS

Physician's Comment on a Panel Discussion

The central theme of today's panel was fear, more particularly, the fear of making a decision. Tillie feared deciding between two pairs of socks, Maurice feared taking a book from the library, and Carol, Frank and Don quoted similar fears of deciding, choosing, taking a stand and reaching a conclusion. Frank surmised that all the issues and problems, conflicts and dilemmas listed by the panel members were sheer trivialities. But the fact is that Tillie, while grappling with her difficulty, developed panics and confusions and all manner of frightening symptoms. To her the danger of making a wrong decision did not appear at all trivial. It loomed in her mind as a matter of momentous importance. She thought of serious consequences and grave responsibilities; she anticipated failure and disaster. In other words, her imagination was on fire.

If there were no imagination there would be few panics and anxieties. And without panics and anxieties nervous symptoms would die away. No nervous patient would ever fear collapse unless his imagination told him that palpitations, air-hunger and chest pressure spell the danger of imminent death. Nobody would ever shiver at the thought of "another sleepless night" except that imagination paints a lurid picture of the fatal results that a mythical sleeplessness has on health. I may mention the fanciful notions which patients entertain about the dreadful effects of "nervous fatigue," and you will realize that the idea of danger created by your imagination can easily disrupt any of your functions. If this is true it is clear that the nervous patient is served by an imagination which is out of bounds, rampant, unbalanced. If the balance is to be restored the patient will have to acquire a working knowledge of how his imagination functions. Clearly, all I can offer in a brief address is a sketchy account of its mode of operation.

Imagination is either busy or idle. If idle it is bored, if busy it is interested and either stimulated or frustrated. Its business is to notice, observe and interpret events. Once the event is noticed imagination is aroused or stirred. It may then evince rising concern or stirring excitement. The concern will lead to further investigation and deepened interest, finally yielding some important or trivial discovery. The excitement will give rise to feelings, sentiments and emotions. Note here that concern, excitement, interest, feelings are intimately associated with the function of imagination.

What imagination notices, observes and interprets are events, facts and situations occurring outside or inside the body. Those taking place outside the body, in external environment, "strike" the senses of vision, hearing or touch and are "grasped" by them. This is the *"sensory grasp" of outer experience.* The events occurring inside the body, in internal environment, "affect" our deep sensibility and are noticed by intuition. This is the *"intuitive grasp" of inner experience.* We may then say that imagination is busy interpreting the facts of outer and inner experience. In the one sphere it makes use of sense perception, in the other of intuitive understanding.

In interpreting the meaning of events imagination classes them as either indifferent or significant to our welfare. The significant events are felt or thought of, that is, imagined as endangering or securing our welfare. In this manner imagination produces the sense of security or insecurity. If behavior is to be adjusted imagination must interpret events in such a fashion that the sense of security materially overbalances the sense of insecurity. Once this is accomplished an *imaginative balance* establishes itself.

After interpreting an event imagination renders an opinion which is in the nature of a tentative suggestion or a first guess. It suggests, for instance, or guesses that the person approaching you is a friend. The opinion is, then, that the situation is one of

security. Under such simple circumstances, imagination is hardly likely to go astray. The situation is such that it calls for little
or no imaginative appraisal. The sensory grasp is sufficient for
proper identification. After the friend reaches you his features
may strike your eye as being changed. You imagine they express
anxiety. This is another imaginative guess. If you accept it you
may be inclined to offer sympathy or aid. Suppose now that your
guess was wrong. The offer of sympathy was then misplaced and
may be resented. The tentative opinion rendered by imagination misled you to an incorrect conclusion and an equally unwise
decision to act. In order to avoid premature conclusions, decisions and acts of this kind the opinion, suggestion or guess offered
by the imagination must be verified. I may mention briefly that
verification makes use of logic, past experience and of that
singular capacity of the mature human mind to observe elements
which contradict or support an opinion after it has been formed.

It is the tragedy of the nervous patient that after years of
suffering he develops an unbalanced imagination the first guesses
of which tend distressingly and consistently to interpret inner
and outer experiences in terms of insecurity. The greater
tragedy is that the first guesses are accepted sight unseen without an attempt at verification. Unable to resist its suggestions
the patient becomes the victim of the imagination. An incessant
stream of insecurity suggestions is poured forth with rapid-fire
velocity leading to a continuous succession of wrong opinions,
conclusions and decisions. The final result is that the patient,
realizing that his first guesses tend to be either wrong or harmful
comes to fear forming an opinion, reaching a conclusion, making
a decision. In a sense, his fears are based on good logic. In most
instances, imagination has misled and deceived him. On a
hundred or thousand occasions it told him that his sensations
will lead to collapse. The suggestion never materialized. How
can that imagination be trusted? Whenever a symptom made its
appearance, whether palpitations or numbness or dizziness, imagination suggested invariably that this was the last gasp, that
an emergency was on. The patient went into a panic, clamored
for instant help, insisted that the doctor be summoned without
delay. When the relatives, aware of the "nervous" nature of the
spell, hesitated to call the physician, perhaps in the dead of the
night, the patient passed into a violent burst of temper, and the
wish had to be granted. But the moment the physician arrived
his mere presence or calm manner dispelled frequently both

symptom and temper in a trice. The deceitfulness of his imagination was here clearly demonstrated to the patient. It lied to him,
led him to wrong conclusions, to hasty decisions. It produced
temper, caused unnecessary expense, created domestic friction.
Worst of all, it undermined his self-respect and made him look
ridiculous. Trusting an imagination of this kind, it would seem,
is impossible.

There were other experiences that made for distrust. Neighbors mentioned a remedy, or the patient read about it in the daily
paper or heard of it over the radio. No sooner was the drug
called to his attention than his imagination was absurdly fired
with hope and enthusiasm. In the course of years he spent more
money on pills and capsules than his meager finances warranted.
Trusting the suggestions passed on by his ever lively imagination
he consulted numerous physicians, wandered from clinic to
clinic. He made costly trips because a change in climate was
supposed to be beneficial. He went to sanitariums, watering
places. He even had himself "checked at Mayo Brothers." His
record of inept conclusions and ludicrous decisions is impressive,
indeed. That record was inspired by his imagination, whose
erratic and capricious counsel has been the ruin of the patient's
reputation. How can he ever base a decision on its dubious
recommendations?

It happened at times that he was free from symptoms for a few
days, sometimes for a week, rarely a longer period. Then this
imagination spoke the language of security. It suggested that he
was cured, that the symptoms were gone for good. On these
occasions he concluded he was well and decided to "do things."
He resumed his social life, visited friends, played cards with
them, went fishing and automobiling. Occasionally, he ventured
to return to work. The result of these efforts was dismal
disappointment. Without any warning, "out of a blue sky," the
palpitations recurred "worse than ever," right while he was
engaged in a "grand game of poker." Or, he suddenly fainted
while he worked on the bench. There was no escape from these
dreadful symptoms. His imagination, even when it preached
security, invariably led him straight into insecurity. How can he
ever trust it? How can he depend on its first guesses or final
conclusions? And without dependence how can there be deciding or acting? His life is doomed to be a stark tragedy, a bleak
and barren existence, mechanical, tedious, lifeless.

We shall revert to the experience Tillie had in the store. When she was unable to make up her mind whether to buy a smaller size sock her daughter Doris came to her assistance and made the decision for her. "Then the tightness stopped, and immediately I felt comfortable," Tillie said. But if a little child can guide the nervous patient out of confusion and bafflement the solution for his difficulties seems to be close enough at hand. Every patient has either children or mothers or friends. It should be easy or at least feasible to assign to them the task of making decisions and reaching conclusions. Unfortunately, the device does not work. Men and women have pride, and that pride is readily shaken, wounded and challenged. The fact that Doris had to make the decision for her was a severe blow to the mother's self-respect. It served to emphasize her tragic inability to act, to decide, to be self-sufficient. It accentuated the helplessness and wretchedness of her existence. Doris' intervention, it is true, relieved the symptoms of tightness and discomfort. Now Tillie's physical person felt secure for the brief period of a few minutes. But her moral and intellectual personality was made to feel more insecure than before. The next decision to be made was certain to reveal an increased distrust of herself and of her imagination.

To trust imagination means to let it perform its functions of dreaming, hoping, anticipating. If Tillie had given free play to her fancy she would have planned the purchase of Doris' dress days or weeks in advance. She would have pictured in her mind, that is, in her imagination how beautiful the child would look in a dress of a certain style, cut or color. She would have anticipated flattering compliments from neighbors and friends. She would have beamed with joy at the thought of Doris' delight when finally presented with the garb. On an evening walk with her husband she would have strolled along the show windows, viewing patterns, tentatively accepting some, rejecting others. All along her thought would have dwelled fondly and proudly on the details of the situation when, a week or two ahead, she would arrive at home with the garment neatly wrapped in a box. The surprise, the breathless suspense, the ceremonial of unwrapping, the gasp of astonishment ringing from the child's lips, the kiss of gratitude, the eagerness to slip into the dress immediately and eye it in the mirror. All of this and many other dreams, hopes and anticipations would have currently crowded Tillie's brain, continually feeding and occupying her imagination. This is precisely the point I meant to make. The acts of planning, dreaming, hoping and anticipating keep imagination busy and occupied, interested and stimulated. They prevent idleness and boredom. And if imagination is properly kept from being idle or bored there is no or little occasion for restlessness or irritability. And without restlessness and irritability symptoms do not stand much of a chance of being maintained or precipitated. Had Tillie permitted her imagination to be occupied with dreams and hopes her chest would have currently swelled with pride and her heart would have habitually expanded with joy. Instead her chest became the seat of agonizing pressure and her heart was rocked by wild palpitations because her imagination was allowed to busy itself with fears and anxieties mainly or solely. What prevented her from keeping her imagination fruitfully occupied was her *preoccupation* with terrors and panics, with symptoms and distress, in short, with the idea of insecurity. And if an imagination is more or less constantly preoccupied with ideas of insecurity it will be deprived of the opportunity to occupy itself with those dreams, hopes and visions from which ideas of security originate. If this happens the imaginative balance will be disturbed, the thoughts of insecurity will drown out the ideas of security, and anxious preoccupation will cancel out the pleasurable occupations. The result will be a paralyzing fear of deciding, planning, initiating and acting. But without decisions, plans, action and initiative there is no possibility of developing pride, self-reliance and self-sufficiency. It was the sustained preoccupation with ideas of insecurity that prevented Tillie from acquiring even that modicum of self-trust that prompts the trivial decisions of daily existence.

You will understand now that if the nervous patient is to regain his lost imaginative balance his preoccupations with ideas of insecurity will have to give way to occupations with thoughts of security, that is, with hopes, dreams and pleasurable anticipations. You will also understand that hopes, dreams and joyful anticipations are the very warp and woof of decisions, plans and conclusions. And if you ask how you can manage to rout your preoccupations my answer will be of the simplest kind: Stop listening to the threat of the symptomatic idiom and the imbecilities of the temperamental lingo and your imagination will again be able to indulge in its stimulating occupations and you will be in a position to make decisions, draw conclusions, formulate plans without fearing the dreadful consequences suggested to you by temper and symptom. Learn to use the Recovery language of self-confidence and fearlessness and your imagination will be freed of the deadweight of panics and anxieties. Thus delivered it will once again occupy itself with thoughts of security and ideas of self-sufficiency.

2
TEMPER, SYMPTOMS AND INSIGHT
A Panel Discussion Conducted by Patients

Frank (panel leader): We will discuss today the article on "Temper and Insight." It says there that in a temperamental deadlock people are not quarreling over real issues but over whether one person is right and the other wrong. I shall give an example. A number of times on the panel I mentioned that my mother does not set the breakfast table. One item that is particularly irritating to me is the sugar bowl. It seems to me it is always empty. It is certainly not a matter of great moment whether it is filled or not; it only takes a few seconds to fill it. The fact is I have to fill it practically every morning. Before I had my Recovery training this used to irritate me no end. I felt I had the right, as a son, to have the sugar bowl filled but I was denied that right. Ridiculous as it may sound, my mother and I were in a deadlock over this issue of the sugar bowl until I applied the Recovery language and knew that right and wrong are phony issues in domestic life. I now fill the sugar bowl every other day or so and each time it makes me feel good to know that I don't get worked up over trivialities any more. I think I now have insight into the phony nature of temper.

Tillie: Several months ago I had an argument with the lady upstairs. I wanted to make a telephone call and when I took off the receiver she was talking so I thought I'll wait a while. I waited fifteen minutes, and she was still talking. Then I heard her say to the party, "Somebody is trying to get on the phone." I said, "I would like to make a call and I have been waiting fifteen minutes already." She said, "All right, go ahead," and hung up with a bang. Soon after I finished with the call she came downstairs and asked, "What's the matter? Is something burning?" I said, "No, but I have to go shopping and had to make that call." She got very excited so I said, "If you don't quiet down I will not talk to you." That made her mad. She said, "You have no right to tell me to get off the line. I would never think of doing such a thing. I have too much character." I said, "Are you telling me I have no character?" I lost my temper then and I gave it to her all right. After she left I called Gertrude and she said, "You can't afford to lose your temper because of your health." I didn't just like that and I still thought I was right. But I was awfully tense all that day and I had my air-hunger again and that pressure around the chest and the symptoms did not disappear for more than a week. A couple of days ago I met this lady again. The building is ours and I asked her politely to please tell her boy to keep off the grass. Then she said my daughter Doris caused much more damage to the lawn than her son. This time I smiled and refused to get into an argument. I was sore but the after-effect lasted just a short time.

Ada: A few weeks ago my husband suggested we go to the movies and this particular movie was a mile from home. It was a nice Sunday and he thought we should walk. One thing I can't stand is strolling. I want to walk fast and get there because I am tense. So I told him I wouldn't stroll. He said he rushes all week and on Sundays he likes to take a slow walk and refuses to be rushed. This all happened within two blocks and he said, "I am sick and tired of arguing, and we'll get on a street car." We did and I was angry. But when the show started I forgot all about the argument and I didn't work myself up as I should have done if that had happened a year ago. At that time, I wouldn't have talked to him for several days or I would have thrown up to him that he was inconsiderate and selfish and didn't care whether I suffered.

Frank: I think that what Tillie and Ada said illustrated what I brought out about right and wrong being a phony issue. Tillie talked for about five minutes but I didn't hear one sentence that had to do with objective realities. And Ada didn't say a word about the actual facts of walking. She didn't bring out the fact that the distance was too far to walk or that it was necessary to walk faster to get there in time. All of this didn't matter. The issue was whether one person would get his way or the other.

Ann: Several months ago my husband's sister came through Chicago and had to wait sixteen hours for her train east. So we invited her to spend the night with us. My son offered to let his aunt use his room and he would sleep upstairs. I got flustered because I did not know whether I could clean the house in time. It seemed too much of a job for me to get my son's room ready. So I set about cleaning and I was quite pleased with the effort I made. The room looked really like a guest room. To be sure that it remained clean I asked my boy not to go into the room.

But, lo and behold, before long Johnny was in the room, and his dog with him, and the boy was eating pretzels. I lost my temper and gave him a real tongue-lashing. A few minutes later when I was vacuuming the living room rug I suddenly felt fatigued. It seemed I couldn't go on. It was such an effort. I wanted to lie down, but suddenly it dawned on me that the tired feeling had come on so suddenly that it was, of course, the result of my temper. I took up the work again and the fatigue was gone in no time. I think that the insight that the fatigue was a mere feeling helped me get rid of it.

Ada: Something happened this morning where my Recovery training gave me insight into my temper. Our janitor dislikes children, and when he sees them on the sidewalk he pushes them around. I used to argue with him about it but don't do it any more, as a rule. There is an empty lot near our house and the boys and girls play there. This morning my boy and five others were playing there, and the janitor came along and said he would call the police, and my boy came up crying. He was afraid he would go to jail. I was furious. The janitor has nothing to do with the empty yard and it was none of his business to chase the children. I ran into the bedroom and pulled up the window. The janitor was there and I was ready for him. Then I felt my palpitations and tenseness and I decided I was doing wrong to show temper. I spoke to my boy and told him to go out and play and not to mind the janitor. Later on my way to Recovery I saw the janitor on the street and I paid no attention to him and went my way and saved myself the palpitations and discomfort.

TEMPER, SYMPTOMS AND INSIGHT
Physician's Comment on a Panel Discussion

What the patients sitting on the panel presented so dramatically can be summed up in simple language. In former days, they said, we responded with temper to trivial irritations. There was a severe after-effect with mounting tenseness, with symptoms and agonies of suffering. Today we still indulge our tempers, but the occasions are few, the after-effect is short, and symptoms and suffering are transient and mild. Frank, with his flair for terse and compact expression, gave the proper phrasing to the change in reaction when he remarked that he has now "insight into the phony nature of temper." He made another thought-provoking statement when he surmised that "in a temperamental deadlock people are not quarreling over real issues but over whether one person is right and the other wrong." But what precisely determines whether a person is wrong or right and whether an issue is real or unreal?

When Tillie cut in on the neighbor's telephone conversation was she wrong? And when the woman at the other end of the line hung up with a bang was she right? Frankly, neither you nor I nor anybody else can answer these questions intelligently. Tillie could easily marshal the most compelling reasons for proving that the intrusion was justified. She had been waiting a long time, and her call was important while the "lady upstairs" was merely chatting, wasting her own time and imposing on other people who were busy and in a hurry. But the neighbor on the upper floor would have no difficulty arguing back that Tillie's interference was plainly an act of deliberate provocation, uncalled for and inexcusable. Are Tillie's arguments right and real? Are the lady's counter-arguments wrong and unreal? Where is the judge who could render a decision as to who is the villain and who the victim?

Let us take a closer look at the matter. Tillie interrupted the conversation of her neighbor. That neighbor gave every indication that she had not finished conversing. She clearly intended to continue but was forced by Tillie's intervention to cease speaking. Leaving the question of right and wrong to one side for the present, the situation seems to be clear: The will of one person conflicted with the will of another person. Force was pitted against force, power clashed with power. As it happened the one person yielded, the other triumphed. This was a fight, a show of strength or weakness, a contention for the possession or use of an object (telephone wire). Why inject the issue of right and wrong? Why not rather speak the plain, unadorned, honest and sincere language of warfare, competition, constraint and compulsion? In that language, the thing was a tussle, a test of strength, a resort to force.

Tillie waited fifteen minutes before she finally broke in on the conversation. The impulse to use force was certainly operative during these long-drawn-out fifteen minutes. But it was kept in check. The inclination to exercise power was curbed during the period of hesitation. It was only after her patience snapped that Tillie released the impulse. Why did she wait? Why did she beat down her own pressing inclination? The answer is plain: Tillie knew that using force meant to disturb the peace among neighbors. She knew that the real and only issue was peace or power, force or friendship, not the wholly irrelevant question of right and wrong.

Tillie knew she was using force, but she claimed she exercised a right. The use of force was a fact, the claim to exercise a right was an opinion. You may say she thought or assumed or guessed she had a right to use force. But it was *merely* a thought, an assumption *only, nothing but* a guess; and thoughts, assumptions and guesses of this kind are imagined. The right which Tillie claimed was a figment of imagination, the force which she used was a fact of realistic experience. If Tillie's reaction is somehow typical of temperamental outbursts in general, then, we may conclude that *in temper a right is subjectively claimed and force objectively used.*

A claim ought to be verified. An opinion ought to be tested, proved and substantiated. That calls for a judge. Who is to be the judge in matters of temper? And even if there were a judge all he could do would be to hand down an opinion. His opinion may be final; it may compose and terminate the fight. But it would be nothing more than an opinion rendered by a duly constituted court instead of by the contending parties. True enough, the judge's opinion is supposed to be impartial, unbiased, based on evidence, testimony, records and documents. But no matter how heavily documented and how scrupulously unbiased the court decision may be, nevertheless, it is and remains an opinion. After the verdict is pronounced one legal opinion has been substituted for two private opinions. The lawsuit may then be "settled" and "decided." But the question of who was right and who wrong still remains open. The loser may claim with good logic that the judge erred and justice miscarried. He may even contend that the law is wrong. You see here that the issue of right and wrong cannot be determined, not even by law. It can only be "decided" and "settled" by a court order. Right and wrong are always opinions, assumptions, suppositions, conjectures, speculations. That means, they are guesses, subjective, imaginative, unreal.

Opinions interpret facts. It ought to be clear to you by now that both the opinons and interpretations are guesses, hence, imaginations. It ought to be just as clear that facts are realities. Temper contains one opinion and many facts. The opinion is that of right and wrong. The facts are the sensations, feelings, impulses and acts (verbal and muscular) which are experienced or expressed in the temperamental sequence. In Tillie's altercation with the neighbor the facts were dynamic, impetuous, fierce. On the other hand, the opinion of right and wrong was pale, trite, hackneyed. In spite of that Tillie's attention was almost exclusively focused on her temperamental opinion while the facts of her sensations, impulses, feelings and acts went unobserved or unheeded. Yet, her sensations were pressing, her feelings boiling, her impulses overpowering and her acts menacing and stormy. Her heart palpitated, her knees shook, her throat contracted, and her voice trembled; she was well nigh convulsed with rage, hostility and fury. But these facts received no or little mention in her report about the telephone conversation. All she claimed was that she was kept waiting, that her intentions were frustrated and her plans thwarted. She thought of the wrong only that was done her, of the rights that were denied her. She was certainly not concerned about the fact that she used force and that she disturbed the peace. But force and peace are the outstanding facts of life. Force means that feelings, impulses and acts are given ruthless expression without regard for the rights of others. Peace means that these same elements are properly controlled in deference to the sensibilities, interests and claims of others. We may say: Tillie's thoughts were narrowly focused on one restricted opinion: that she was right and the neighbor was wrong. But of the facts of the situation she was not at all aware. Her insight was warped. It centered on a personal opinion but ignored the objective facts.

You remember that after the telephone call was finished the outraged neighbor appeared in Tillie's apartment. This was the occasion for another temperamental bout in the course of which, Tillie says, "I lost my temper and gave it to her all right." She then called Gertrude who told her, "You can't afford to lose your temper because of your health." This was an admonition to consider the realities of symptoms, sensations and feelings as matters of first importance and to ignore the "phony" theories of right and wrong. Tillie's reaction was defiant: "I didn't just like that," she said, "and I still thought I was right." The phrase, "I still thought . . ." is revealing. It reveals that Tillie refused to accept the insight offered by Gertrude. She obviously realized that Gertrude's counsel was sound and realistic but decided that she wanted temper and not health. The reason for the blunt refusal was that she "didn't just like that." You see here why our patients, prior to being trained in Recovery techniques, struggle against acquiring insight. They don't like it. They don't like insight because it deprives them of the excitement, drama and vitality of soul stirring and heart warming fights. Fights provide the stir of action that is so sorely missing in the fears, confusion and helplessness that characterize the lives of our patients. Fights give them the sense of living that has fled from the boredom of their daily existence. They offer the opportunity to display vigor, strength, decision, eagerness, determination, all of them elements which are painfully lacking in a drab routine of hopelessness and paralysis of will. Our patients want agitation and stimulation, not equilibrium and peace. They want exhilarating theories, not balancing realities. They crave the use of force, not the adjustment of sensations, feelings and impulses. If you tell them that their unbridled tempers will upset health and disturb peace their verbal or mental reply is: "I shall rather disturb peace and lose health than give up temper." It is the crowning glory of Recovery that it was able to reverse this formula and to make patients adopt the principle that temper must be eliminated because it is the sworn enemy of peace and health. This radical change in attitude was beautifully demonstrated by Tillie in an encounter which she had with the same neighbor several months later when, challenged to a fight, she "smiled and refused to get into an argument." She "was sore but the after-effect lasted just a short time." Behavior was finally guided by the realities of peace and health, not by sentimental cravings for excitement and intellectual considerations for fictitious theories.

3

TEMPER, SOVEREIGNTY AND FELLOWSHIP

A Panel Discussion Conducted by Patients

Annette (Panel leader): The subject for today's panel is taken from the article entitled "Temper as Craving for Symbolic Victories." Has anyone an example?

Frank R.: I can give an example that shows two sides of the story, that is, the difference in the results whether temper is or is not controlled. The other night I walked home with Harriette and met my mother on the street. She had a letter to mail. I offered to let Harriette mail it so I could carry the bundles. But mother asked me to mail it. As usual, she had to have her own way. I lost my temper and grabbed Harriette and said, "Let's go," leaving mother to mail the letter. After that I was pretty angry for a short while but it was all over soon. In former years I would have tried to justify myself; I would have been furious about the domineering ways of my mother, but this time I didn't do anything of the kind. The incident was closed as far as I was concerned. Later on when mother came home I spoke to her and she did not answer. A year ago or so I would have got angry again but that evening I simply kept quiet. At supper mother hardly ate anything and after the meal was over she cried. Of course, I didn't like that but since as you all know there is a deadlock between us I couldn't do anything about it. As I said before there is a difference in results between now and before. Before I had my Recovery training the deadlock led to endless quarrels because neither of us would give in. Now I keep quiet and while the deadlock persists there is no argument. More than that, in former days I would have been angry and stayed angry for a long time and incidentally I wouldn't have felt like eating, either, but on this particular night I ate as usual.

Annette: In other words, both you and your mother would have staged a contest as to who would starve most and say least. Well, you say that this time you faced the fact that the manner in which you acted might have been wrong and temperamental. You refused to prove that you were right. That is of course the best way for cutting short arguments.

Tillie: I was in the subway last Saturday and sat down pretty close to the corner and after I was seated a woman entered the coach and wanted to squeeze in right between me and the corner. She persisted and made me move. I was provoked but I moved although there was plenty of room in the coach. I felt my temper going up and I would have liked to tell the person a thing or two. But then I began to get tense and I knew that I had to stop working myself up. So I thought, after all, this is a public conveyance and anybody can sit where he wants to. So when I thought of that my tenseness left and I stopped working myself up.

Annette: What was it that made you stop your temperamental reacton?

Tillie: I noticed the tightness in my side. When I get that I feel choked. Then I can't stay in a closed room. That Saturday in the subway if the tightness and choked feeling had kept up a few more minutes I would have wanted to get off the train. So I stopped working myself up, and the sensations left.

Sophie: Before I had my Recovery training, when I called my children from the outside to come and eat they usually didn't respond to the first or second call. Then I would get this tightening in my throat or a pressure in my head and my temper would rise and the symptoms would get more severe. After I got into Recovery I learned I had to control my temper in order to check this irritation. Now I call the children a half dozen times and I can call in the same level of voice and my temper doesn't rise any more. In the past when I used to work myself up I always feared that something would burst in my head for sure.

Annette: I will quote an example of my own. An elderly aunt of mine, we shall call her Aunt Jane, was the type of person who enjoyed temper tangles. She had never lived with anyone, but during the depression we had to take her into our home. When she came I decided I'd make an effort to get along with her. I felt I could do that because she confessed to be fond of me. But what I actually did was to try to convince her that she was wrong and that of course ended up in pretty terrific temperamental outbursts on both our sides. One time, after a rather heated argument, I awoke in the middle of the night with a very odd sensation in my abdomen. I felt as though something awful had happened and I was going to burst. I was frightened but did not know at that time that these were nervous symptoms. But the sensations followed so regularly on temperamental spats I couldn't help realizing that they were closely associated with my temper. Several years later after I had undergone a good deal of Recovery training I had occasion to get in contact with Aunt Jane again. A friend of mine let me use her car and I invited Aunt Jane to join us on an automobile ride. This time I had a good opportunity to notice how I had changed while my aunt had not. Whenever I found myself wanting to prove her wrong and myself right I knew at that very moment that all I was out to accomplish was a symbolic victory. I stopped short instantly and instead of getting provoked myself or getting her worked up I merely answered her remarks with "maybe" or "is that so?" The argument didn't even get started. On leaving the car my aunt was obviously irritated and said, "I am just worn out. I never spent such a boring day in my life." And if that remark didn't provoke me into a sharper answer I realized that I must have learned the technique of giving up the battling for trivial symbolic victories.

Carol: About this temper. I think it is grand that we have been drilled to get rid of it. In my case it is when I am with Pete, my husband, and I start to blow off steam. Pete, who knows Recovery, then says, "Temper!" and that puts me on the right track again. A year ago or so I would be provoked with him when he would say, "Temper!" and I would snap back, "What of it if I have a temper." After that I would usually let off a honey of temper. But now I know he helps me check it. And when I feel my temper rising I cut the feeling down and it doesn't have a chance at all.

Annette: In conclusion I would like to say that the panel members meant to bring out that we all got into temperamental situations. In former days before we had our Recovery training we would have exploded or fretted with a long-drawn-out after-effect. During the explosion we would have had the momentary satisfaction of letting off steam. That would give us a momentary sense of relief. Besides that we would have had the pleasure of feeling ourselves in the right and the other person in the wrong. It is these two pleasures—letting off steam and feeling in the right—that our physician calls the "dual premium placed on temper." The trouble is that this "dual premium" is short-lived, lasting only a few moments. But then it is followed by an after-effect which may last hours or even days. In that period of the after-effect we suffer many distressing symptoms. I know that I for one learned that the few moments of pleasure enjoyed during the immediate effects are not worth the hours and days of suffering I endured during the after-effect.

TEMPER, SOVEREIGNTY AND FELLOWSHIP
Physician's Comment on a Panel Discussion

A letter was to be mailed and, as a result, an ugly street scene

developed and a family group took their evening meal in the
dead silence of a sullen mood. Tears were shed and feelings were
crushed. And all the commotion, confusion and agony were
caused by—a letter to be mailed. But a letter is a sheet of paper
and as such utterly incapable of rousing tempers and offending
feelings. No issue was involved. The contents of the letter were
not challenged; the propriety, wisdom, advisability of its being
mailed were not questioned. It was simply a fight about nothing,
a struggle for a scrap of paper, a fight without an issue, a fight for
the sake of fighting. How is it that men and women of mature
age engage in fights "for nothing?" Obviously, mature years do
not necessarily mean mature thinking or adult acting.

A fight is centered around an object and rooted in a motive. In
the case of Frank and his mother the object was the letter. What
was the motive? A motive is a force that makes muscles move.
Suppose the letter which the lady wanted to mail was addressed
to a friend. Then the thought of the friend, the desire to
communicate with her, the intention to please her supplied the
motive that made Frank's mother walk into the street and move
toward the mail box. If Frank and his wife Harriette had not
entered upon the scene the letter would have been mailed
without ado and we would have no difficulty understanding the
object of the walk, its motive and its successful execution. We
would say that an act of behavior was manipulated correctly, or
that its purpose aimed correctly at its proper goal. After Frank
and Harriette made their appearance the muscles of the letter
carrying lady suddenly deviated from the goal of the mailbox, the
purpose of mailing was forgotten or neglected and aiming was
directed toward something that had essentially nothing to do
with the original purpose. A new purpose intervened, changed
the goal and redirected the aiming.

The original purpose was to communicate with another person, to give pleasure, to show consideration. The motive here
was service. And service serves the end of peace; it creates good
will and promotes the welfare of the group. This motive of
service and group welfare was suddenly shelved after the arrival
of Frank. A fight ensued, and its motive was hostility, competition, domination. What prompted that change in attitude?
What is it that makes a person abruptly shift from a disposition
to serve to a disposition to dominate?

Whenever you are alone in the privacy of your own home you
are master of your dispositions. You may do as you please and

may release whatever disposition you wish to express provided
you keep within the bounds of law, morals and ethics. If your
present disposition is to undress you may disrobe at will. If you
wish to rest you may lie down on the couch; if you desire to sing,
to whistle, to eat or read, to keep the eyes open or closed there is
nobody to check you, no standard to impose restrictions on your
whim or caprice. Under conditions of privacy you are in unquestioned control of your decisions and enjoy the exclusive and
uncontested right to act as you choose. Being the master of your
destiny and a law unto yourself you are sovereign. That sovereignty of yours is severely curtailed the moment you step out into
the street. Now you are subject to rules which restrict your
rights and put a check to your dispositions. You cannot, for
instance, place a couch in the middle of the street and take your
afternoon rest there. Even should the street be empty you would
not be permitted to use it as your private dwelling place.
Outside your home your conduct is required to conform to
regulations, customs and traditions even if no legal, moral or
ethical issues are involved. The reason is that out in the street
you may meet other people and once you are among people you
are the member of a group, and in a group you are rule-bound
and lose your sovereignty, at least, part of it. In a group the
members are fellows with equal rights demanding that their
rights be respected by the fellow members. This is called
fellowship and is opposed to sovereignty. Fellowship means
service, self-restraint and respect for the rights of others. Sovereignty means or may mean the reverse: domination, unrestricted
power and disregard for the needs, desires or rights of others.
Fellowship is the principle of group action, sovereignty that of
individualism. To the extent that a sovereign recognizes other
persons as his fellows he loses the prerogatives of sovereignty.
To the extent that a group of fellows grants to any of its members
the status of sovereignty it weakens the principle of fellowship.

Groups are either loose assemblages,for instance, a crowd in
the street, or a close knit organization like the family. The
closer a group is organized the more is it pervaded by the spirit of
fellowship. There is hardly a trace of fellowship in the street
crowd; there should be a maximum of it in the family. All kinds
of groups could be ranged between the street crowd and the
family with varying degrees of fellowship governing their mutual relations. On this scale, a group of friends ought to be held
together by a far greater measure of fellowship than, let me say, a

group of co-workers in a shop, and the group of co-workers should score a higher rating in fellowship than a group of voters attending a political meeting. The point that I wish to make is that the family ought to rank highest in point of fellowship among all closely organized groups. In a family fellowship ought to be at its maximum, sovereignty at its lowest possible minimum. That this is not so is clearly evidenced by the almost universal prevalence of domestic temper.

When Frank met his mother he offered to mail the letter. Behind this offer was a desire or determination to be helpful or courteous or considerate. The act expressed the motive of service, that is, the spirit of fellowship. Frank has frequently stated in panel discussions that he and his mother do not get along well together. They live in a more or less continuous temperamental deadlock, in an atmosphere of strife, spite and bitterness. You may conclude, therefore, that Frank's offer was a polite gesture rather than a genuine eagerness to be of help. But in group life an insincere gesture of generosity and fellowship is far more valuable than an outspoken expression of enmity and a brutal assertion of one's sovereignty. No doubt, the rebuff offered by Frank's mother was sincere. It was based on sincere bitterness and sincere hostility. Sincerity of this kind is anything but an asset. A group is interested in peace and order. And peace and order are destroyed or disrupted by the temperamental expressions of anger, vindictiveness and bitterness. A temperamental outburst is sincere, of course. So are murder and burglary. They are based on genuine and sincere desires to kill and rob. That the mother was sincere in her rude reaction to Frank's offer of fellowship was no credit to her. That reaction was dictated by the mother's will to have her own way, by her insistence on domination and her determination to assert her sovereign rights. As such it served the ends of unrestricted idividualism, not those of rule-bound group life. It was based on the principle of sovereignty, not of fellowship.

This is not an attempt to exonerate our friend Frank. He practiced his share of rudeness and sovereignty when in a temperamental act of brusqueness he "grabbed Harriette and said, let's go." Both mother and son are currently disposed to display excesses of domestic temper exercising their disposition to assert their sovereign rights and ignoring the needs for fellowship, mutuality and toleration. What interests us here is the close relation that exists between the workings of an aggressive temper, on the one hand, and the spirit of sovereignty and fellowship, on the other. The members of the panel spoke of symbols and symbolic victories. One of the most pernicious symbols is that of sovereignty. Frank's mother imagined, perhaps unknown to herself, that she represented or symbolized sovereignty in her dealings with the members of her family. Her will to assert her sovereignty provoked the resistance of her son with the result that family life was turned into a battlefield of temperamental dispositions in which both mother and son craved the glory of symbolic victories and both effectively frustrated one another's ludicrous ambitions. In the end, a cruel, implacable deadlock developed in which feelings and sensibilities were ruthlessly slaughtered and fellowship was made a shambles. The realistic objects of the incessant fights were invariably such trivialities as a letter to be mailed or a sugar bowl to be filled. The symbolic goal was the craving to assert sovereign rights. The inevitable results were tears, crushed feelings and refusals to eat or otherwise to share and to practice fellowship.

The deadlock between Frank and his mother is undoubtedly extreme. It is characterized by an extreme insistence on the exercise of unrestricted sovereignty and an equally extreme refusal to practice fellowship. Deadlocks of more moderate intensity were mentioned by the other members of the panel. Annette was in deadlock with her sour-dispositioned aunt, Sophie with her boisterous youngsters, Carol with her soft-spoken and well-intentioned husband. All of them were in one way or another embroiled in the tug-of-war of domestic temper, all of them had in previous years indulged in the cruel game of craving symbolic victories in the battle for their sovereign rights, and all of them had an unenvious record of tears shed, feelings crushed and meals taken in the dead silence of sullen moods. But all of them told you in unmistakable language that for them the concept of sovereignty has been finally exposed as an empty, silly and childish symbol and fellowship has become a living, mature and concrete reality. Even Frank, the helpless party to a relentless and apparently incurable deadlock, was able to state that before he had his Recovery training "the deadlock led to endless quarrels because neither of us would give in. Now I keep quiet and while the deadlock persists there is no argument." In his home, fellowship is not reestablished, but the peace destroying symbolism of sovereignty has been routed and with it Frank's symptoms of fatigue and sleeplessness. And if it is true that Recovery training is capable of laying the ghost of sovereignty, then, we may be pardoned for claiming that our system of self-help is the sovereign means for promoting fellowship.

4

MUSCLES AND MENTAL HEALTH

A Panel Discussion conducted by Patients

Frank (panel leader): I will start off with an example. When I first came to Recovery I had so many symptoms I did not know where to start first. My symptoms were all pretty strong and I did not know which was the weakest. My main symptom was nervous fatigue. Today I know it is not muscular fatigue but merely a sense of being tired. At that time I had difficulty sleeping. It took me anywhere from an hour to three hours to get to sleep, and after I got to sleep I would wake up every hour or so, and this went on practically every night. I also had practically no appetite and had to force myself to eat. I also had blurring of vision, numbness in the arms and legs and pressure in the head. A noise in the ears bothered me a lot. On top of it I had difficulty making up my mind, and the simplest decision gave me trouble. Finally I had to give up my job and did not work for four years before I joined Recovery. Even after I came to Recovery it looked like a pretty hopeless job. Then I remember our doctor once saying in class that it is the minor symptoms that must be worked on first. But I couldn't tell a minor symptom when I saw one. Today I know that it is not so much the weakest symptom that must be handled but the simplest method that must be used. And the simplest method is control of muscles. Ever since I used my muscles to walk on, fatigue or no fatigue, I am no longer troubled with that awful tiredness. And since I have been using my muscles not to toss in bed I have no trouble sleeping.

Harriette: Every now and then when I am talking with new patients they are surprised when I tell them that I was pretty sick for over fifteen years and am now well. They say maybe you were not as sick as I am. Of course everyone thinks they were the sickest person in the world but I think I was very sick all the time before I came to Recovery. I can remember in high school I got my famous headaches and nausea and fatigue and dizzy spells and weak spells and palpitations and my ears ached and my eyes blurred and my throat choked. And I would go to a doctor and he would prescribe a tonic or say I needed a rest and then maybe

I'd be feeling better for a short while and then another series of symptoms would come along. Each time the new series would come they would be intensified until about six years ago they got so bad I decided to quit work. For the next two years I went around to doctors and clinics and had all sorts of X-Rays taken and all kinds of medicine prescribed. But the trouble kept getting worse. So after I had gone all round to every place and even went to consult a doctor in Montana I talked again to the family physician and he recommended I should go to Chicago and consult our doctor who, my family physician said, treated his patients with a new method. He meant the classes and Recovery. Well, three weeks after I came to Chicago I was working part time. After four months I worked full time and have been working ever since, that is, over four years. I can say I feel better than I ever felt in my life and no amount of money could ever pay for what I learned in Recovery.

Frank: Can you say that you attacked your symptoms at their weakest point?

Harriette: I don't know that. But the doctor told me to use my muscles. So I forced myself to eat when I felt nauseated and forced myself to walk when I felt exhausted. It wasn't easy but what helped me was that I accepted the authoritative knowledge of our doctor. I know our doctor would not ask me to do these things if they could do harm.

Christine: My main trouble was a terrific feeling of depression and fatigue which I thought was the hardest thing to overcome. When I got up in the morning I thought I could hardly move and needed rest. But soon I learned that muscles could be commanded to move but that didn't work the first few times. I had to practice a number of mornings and what helped me most was the example of other patients when they were interviewed in classes. I thought what they can do I should be able to do, too. And so I said to myself in the morning you certainly can make your hands and feet work. What helped me was, like with Harriette, that I accepted the doctor's authoritative knowledge that my fatigue was in the mind and not in the muscles. My mildest symptom, I think, was that I had to force myself to eat. When I felt my throat was dry and I couldn't swallow a bite I remembered that muscles can be commanded to work and kept on eating. so I think I probably worked on the mildest symptom by the method which to me was the easiest to use.

In the further course of the panel Phil recounted how he suffered from a lack of self-confidence after leaving the hospital, how he was afraid he made too many mistakes. "If I would get a wrong number on the telephone or forget to pick up a pencil I thought I was going back to the Psychopathic Hospital." As a consequence he kept out of the way of people and experienced great hesitancy doing simple jobs. Finally he learned he could always "command the muscles no matter how weak the mind is." He then reported a recent experience. He was driving his car and on stopping threw the door shut leaving the ignition key inside. When some time later he reached into his pocket he missed the key and knew he had left it in the car. He felt embarrassed. He knew he would have to phone his brother to ask for the reserve key. But then he would have to "admit I made a mistake and would have to look foolish." In former days he would have thought of calling a towing service to have the car pulled in or would have considered some other foolish move, trying by every desperate means to cover up his inadequacy. This time he simply forced himself to use his muscles, called his brother, got the reserve key and didn't feel embarrassed at all.

MUSCLES AND MENTAL HEALTH
Physician's Comment on a Panel Discussion

When Harriette told recent members of Recovery that she recovered her health after fifteen years of futile search for a remedy she met with skepticism. Had she told the doubters that her main means of recapturing health was the use of her muscles their skepticism would have turned into outright cynicism. That the mind governs muscles is a truism accepted even by the most sophisticated mentality. But that muscles can be made to mold and influence mental activity sounds incredible to the skeptic and laughable to the cynic. Fortunately, our patients do not belong to the group of "advanced thinkers," and to their plain common sense and unpolished way of viewing things the humble muscle commands as much dignity as the pretentious brain cell. They know that if in a nervous ailment central management breaks down the peripheral rank and file may be ready or can be trained to "take over." And so, when in the lives of Harriette, Frank, Christine, Phil and many hundreds of Recovery members the machinery of central management was thrown out of gear, the muscles were trained to hold the line until management could be reorganized and revitalized. After the muscles had demonstrated their ability to keep the concern going the self-confidence of the brain was restored and the body regained its capacity for concerted action and balanced adjustment. To the skeptic such "pinch-hitting" of the muscles for the brain may sound incredible, and to the cynic it may appear laughable. But skepticism and cynicism are off-shoots of intellectualism, and Recovery stands for realism, plain common sense and an unspoiled way of viewing life.

At the time when Harriette joined Recovery she suffered from a condition in which her brain had almost ceased giving directions to the muscles. If any guidance was supplied it was in the form of fearful anticipations, gloomy misgivings and dismal threats. The brain had retreated from active management of the body. It cowered away in abject defeatism, shivered at the thought of giving orders and trembled at the prospect of having to take the initiative and to shoulder responsibility. There were tasks to be finished, decisions to be made and actions to be planned but the brain, paralyzed by fear, terrified the muscles into helpless inactivity and the inner organs into chaotic functioning. Harriette was tortured by "headaches and nausea and fatigue and dizzy spells, by weak spells and palpitations." Her ears ached and her eyes blurred and her throat choked, and for solid years her brain warned her not to walk when she felt dizzy, not to work when she was fatigued, not to eat when she experienced her nausea. The sense of hopelessness in the brain created an attitude of helplessness in the muscles. Action was held in abeyance, life was suspended.

After fifteen years of unrelieved agony Harriette learned in Recovery that if the brain defaulted on its managerial duties the muscles can be made to "take over" and to "pinch-hit" for the cringing cerebral manager. At first she had her doubts. The method seemed too simple. When her nervous fatigue made her feel exhausted and her brain threatened that the next step meant unfailing collapse how was she to force her muscles to venture into that next step that might lead to destruction? But then she heard a patient recite in a class interview how she had routed her fears by "commanding the muscles" to do what they dreaded to do. That patient had developed the habit of growing panicky at the mere sight of a knife, fearing to do harm to the baby. During the interview I urged the patient to practice touching knives and assured her that the mere act of contacting or handling the "dangerous" object was certain to convince the jittery brain that there was no reason for jitters. The resoluteness of the muscles would conquer the defeatism of the brain. The patient accepted my suggestion, practiced touching knives and purged the brain of its fears. "I would have never believed," the patient exclaimed, "that such a simple method could cure my fears. But it did." Other patients reported similar experiences. One of them was afraid of crossing the street. Stepping out of the house meant to set going a chain of frightening symptoms, palpitations, sweats, dizziness, muscular weakness and dimness of vision. The brain sounded the customary alarm, warning of a dire emergency. After due instruction the patient learned to brave the empty threat of the sensations and the defeatist babble of the brain. He compelled his muscles to walk on, and convinced his cowardly cerebral manager that no danger existed and that the warning signals flashed by the brain cells were false alarms not to be taken seriously. After Harriette witnessed several class demonstrations of this kind she decided to give the method a fair trial with the result that she worked part time after three weeks of practicing muscle control and engaged in full-time activity after another four months. The brain had been convinced by the muscles that all that was required to shake off nervous fears was to make the muscles do what the brain feared to do.

That the brain receives the greater part of its knowledge from the muscles ought to be plain to anyone who is not blinded by the glamor of fanciful theories. Knowledge means experience, and the bulk of our experience stems from our actions, and our actions are carried out by our muscles mainly. I do not wish to deny that a great deal of experience is gathered from vision and hearing, touch, smell and taste. But the type of knowledge secured from these sources is chiefly informative. Practical knowledge, the knowledge of how to behave, of what to do at a certain time in a given situation comes to you from acting and practicing, that is, from the activity of your muscles. With regard to that variety of knowledge and experience that tells you what to do and what not to do there can be hardly any doubt that the *muscles are pre-eminently the teachers and educators of the brain*. It is true that after the brain has received from the muscles its education about things practical it stores, analyzes and codifies the items of knowledge which it has acquired. It sorts them according to their importance and value, their harmfulness and innocence, their promise of success and threat of failure. It formulates rules and standards and elaborates an imposing system of logic and wisdom for the sound guidance of conduct. But the fundamental teaching and educating are done by the muscles. That a flame causes a burning pain the child learns after the muscles have touched the burning object. Once the pain and burn have been experienced through muscular action the brain forms the rule that the finger must be kept at a safe distance from flames. The relationship is clear: Muscles teach the brain, and the brain, enriched by knowledge, guides the muscles.

Before Harriette fell victim to a nervous ailment her brain had acquired a generous store of useful knowledge from the countless muscular acts of behavior which she had practiced in a busy childhood and active adolescence. From these endless series of muscular reactions her brain derived a set of rules, principles and policies which regulated her daily activities. One rule was that headaches, nausea, dizziness, palpitations and symptoms of a similar kind are average happenings not calling for emergency reactions. Another rule was that if doubts arose as to whether any of the symptoms were of an average or emergency character a physician possessed of authoritative knowledge should be consulted. A third rule, we may assume, was that the dictum of the freely chosen physician was to be accepted as sound guide for thinking about and acting on the inner experience. These rules had served Harriette well. They told her what to worry about and what to ignore, and they settled her opinions, beliefs and convictions about health. But after she developed her nervous incapacity she forgot the previously well established rules, indulged in self-diagnosing and produced sustained fears, panics and vicious cycles. Eating, sleeping, walking, conversing were now considered as acts fraught with danger. The brain was crammed with ideas of threatening collapse and impending disaster. All her opinions, beliefs and convictions gained from previous muscular behavior were drenched in a flood of defeatism. Fear ideas and emergency impulses poured forth from an intimidated brain down to the leaderless muscles, and action turned into inactivity, initiative into paralysis of will, self-confidence into helplessness and hopelessness. When after fifteen years of an agonizing existence Harriette decided to consult me, my problem was to convince her brain that eating could be done in spite of the threat of nausea, that nocturnal restlessness and brain storms were no bar to normal sleep performance, that brisk walking was perfectly compatible with "nervous exhaustion" and that a lump in the throat was no impediment to well articulated speech or to resolute swallowing. It was at that time that "commanding the muscles" was prescribed as the proper remedy. As was mentioned Harriette was at first skeptical. But when in classes and at Recovery meetings her skepticism melted she commanded her muscles to lie quietly in bed when she was tense and restless, to walk on when she felt exhausted, to eat when the mere sight of food produced nausea, and to speak forcefully when the throat felt choked. And after the muscles swung into action, disregarding the "symptomatic idiom" of the organs, Harriette's brain was instantly convinced that exhausted muscles can do a fine piece of walking, that a weary body can lie motionless in bed until sleep supervenes, that a stomach harried by the prospect of nausea can be made to take in food without sending it back, and that a throat, drained of its moisture and contracted to a pin-point, could be induced to voice a well-modulated speech. With continued practice of systematic muscle training the brain finally was rid of its defeatism and invigorated by a newly gained conviction, mustered the courage to resume leadership and to reinstate the ancient set of rules, policies and principles for healthy conduct. Harriette's muscles had re-educated her brain.

Had Harriette retained her skepticism she would have refrained from practicing muscle control, and defeatism would have nullified or retarded her cure. Unfortunately, too many patients persist in their skepticism, scorning the use of a method which appears "too simple" to promise results. One such patient recently tried to challenge my statements about the role of muscles in shaping conduct with the question, "But, doctor, I don't suffer from palpitations or dizziness or fatigue. My trouble is an obsession. How can muscles cure an obsession?" The obsession from which the lady suffered was one of jealousy. The patient knew that her husband was a model of matrimonial loyalty, but could not shake off the thought that he was unfaithful. She was told: "I grant that yours is what is called an obsession. But if you ponder the meaning of the word you will realize that what obsesses your brain is an idea. You know from experience that ideas come and go. How is it you cannot get rid of your idea? How is it that it 'obsesses' you and occupies your attention all the time? The reason is that the actions of your muscles feed this idea and reinforce it incessantly preventing it from leaving the brain as ideas ordinarily do. Command your muscles not to act on the obsession, and it will die of inanition.

What you do is to keep the thought of jealousy alive by means of your muscular action. You rummage in the pockets of your husband's clothes to find evidence of his philandering. When you arrive home you search rooms, garret and basement to discover tell-tale objects left by an unwelcome visitor. You spy on your husband's activities, telephone his office numbers of times to check on his whereabouts, scrutinize his mail and notebooks and keep a close watch on every one of his movements. When he arrives in the evening, you subject him to a relentless bombardment of quizzes, questions and suspicions. All of this is done by your muscles. Every search, every act of watching, every sequence of questioning intensifies your tenseness and keeps your attention forcefully riveted on the obsessive idea. That idea would die a natural death within a short time, as ideas commonly do, if you permitted it to expire. But the action of your muscles keeps it alive, prolonging your suffering and refusing to let your brain find its normal equilibrium. The surest way to make the obsession depart from your brain is to command your muscles not to ask questions, not to telephone your husband's office, not to launch into endless searches of rooms, pockets, drawers and notebooks. In your case, the muscles, if properly restrained, would not only re-educate the brain, they would also give it the much-needed breathing spell and would relieve it of the well nigh intolerable tenseness under which it is placed through the action of your muscles."

I could quote numerous other examples illustrating the many uses to which the method of muscle control lends itself in its task of either convincing the brain that defiance of symptoms is possible and harmless, or relieving it of pressures caused by morbid preoccupation with disturbing ideas and impulses. But my time is up and I shall close with the assurance that what Harriette did can be done by every nervous patient and that the simplicity of the method which she used ought to be no occasion for skeptical shrugs and cynical sneers. Precisely because the method is simple, it is prompt, effective and—convincing.

5

REALISM, ROMANTICISM, INTELLECTUALISM

A Panel Discussion Conducted by Patients

Annette (panel leader): The subject for today's panel is taken from the article "The Myth of Nervous Fatigue." When I became ill I was always exhausted. When I came home after a day's work I felt as though I had to crawl into bed. Many an evening I thought I was too tired to eat and so I did not eat. I just crawled into bed and stayed there. The doctor prescribed a program of rest and I followed it faithfully. Returning from work at about 4 o'clock in the afternoon I went to bed and sometimes I slept and sometimes I did not. I got up for supper and went right back to bed again. The first few days I got a little relief, but very little. Very soon I felt just as tired lying in bed and resting. Of course, I thought the fatigue was physical. I thought I was gradually losing my vitality and resistance. But I went on with the program, spending more and more time in bed and doing fewer and fewer things. But I felt more exhausted than ever. Physicians had told me my condition was that of a nervous exhaustion and I formed the idea that the nerves in my body were exhausted and shriveled and incapable of performing their job. When I came to the Illinois Research Hospital I was told in classes that my trouble was not fatigue but self-disgust and discouragement. I didn't like that very well because I knew how my muscles felt and it didn't just sound right that disgust and discouragement should make them feel exhausted. But as I continued to attend classes I became convinced that our physician was right and I learned to be more objective about my symptoms. After I returned home from the hospital I wanted to move a large piece of furniture and did not want to wait until my husband came home. So I did the job and moved it and then I decided to move the other pieces and when my husband came home, instead of being in a state of exhaustion I felt fine. After that experience I was convinced that, as our doctor says, nervous fatigue is in the mind and not in the muscles. Any other example?

Gertrude: I have one. The other day I got up early, about a quarter to six and started my ironing. About eleven thirty I felt tired and thought I couldn't go on another minute. I became quite dizzy and had the idea, "I've got to lie down because if not I'll faint." I thought I was exhausted from being up so early. But in a second I realized that what was really the matter was that I did not want to finish the ironing. I had a few shirts to do which I don't enjoy doing. So I said to myself this is a nervous fatigue and lying down will not help any and also will not get the ironing done and I kept right on. It did not take more than five minutes and the fatigue was gone, so I realized it was a mental fatigue.

Annette: Did you have experience with this sense of fatigue in previous years?

Gertrude: I had it practically all the time when I was first sick. Even on days after I had a good night's sleep I used to be so fatigued I would lie down and rest. But then I felt just as fatigued no matter how long I rested. I could never figure out the reason till I got my Recovery training and learned that this nervous fatigue was nothing to worry about. Now I am interested in things and don't get bored so easily, and so I don't feel fatigued any more.

Christine: When I was ill my strongest symptom was I would get up in the morning feeling so fatigued I had all I could do to wash my face and put my clothes on. When I came to Recovery I learned that was discouragement and self-disgust but I still sabotaged at times and whenever I did not feel well I said I needed rest. Every doctor had told me I needed a rest cure. The other day I felt miserable and tense and tired and I thought I just couldn't get dressed. But I made up my mind to go to the Recovery office to have a cup of coffee with the other girls:* But I felt so draggy I didn't think I could make it. But I went and when I left I felt fine and all fatigue was gone.

Annette: Walking to the Recovery office involved a walk of about six blocks. Do you think you would have attempted a six-block walk, let me say a year ago, when you faced this intense feeling of fatigue?

Christine: No, my legs used to get weak and shaky and they felt like they were going out from under me and I really thought

---

*Every afternoon between two and five, two members of Recovery volunteer their time to supervise activities at the Recovery headquarters. Members drop in and spend the afternoon in the company of other patients. Coffee and cake are served on this occasion.

I couldn't walk. I was afraid I would collapse if I forced myself to walk. But last week, after my daughter's wedding, I felt plenty fatigued after all the activity and excitement. But I carried on. I said to myself, "If it is nothing but the sense of discouragement it doesn't matter. And if it is muscle fatigue it will disappear."

Marcelle: When I first got out of the hospital I felt terribly fatigued in the morning. I had to get my husband's breakfast but went right back to bed the moment he left. I would stay there till eleven or twelve o'clock and when I got up I felt just as tired as if I had not rested at all. After I got my Recovery training I knew that this was a feeling of discouragement, and our doctor had told me I should take brisk walks, fatigued or not fatigued. And I did that and felt fine. At times I still sabotage and stay in bed in the morning but that is getting less and less.

Frank R.: Before I had my training in Recovery I was always tired. I always wanted to go to bed. But I couldn't sleep. I dreaded lying in bed struggling to sleep. So I put off going to bed till one or two o'clock. Finally I would doze off but I would be awake at five o'clock. When I joined Recovery and heard about nervous fatigue being just discouragement I was very skeptical about that. I had had that fatigue so many years that I was convinced it was real muscle fatigue. But I listened to our doctor and practiced ignoring the fatigue. Today I go to bed early and have no trouble sleeping and feeling refreshed in the morning.

Rose E.: I used to hate to get up and make my husband's breakfast. But I did it anyhow. But the minute he left I would just fly back to bed again. I would lie there for an hour or two and feel worse than before. Then I joined Recovery and learned that the tiredness is nothing but a sensation and I can now ignore it and do my work even if I sometimes feel tired. I have practiced that and found it to be so. I found it is just nervous fatigue and it leaves.

REALISM, ROMANTICISM, INTELLECTUALISM

Physician's Comment on a Panel Discussion

Annette felt tired and thought the "fatigue was physical." She then formed the idea that her nerves were "exhausted and shriveled and incapable of performing their job." After she was told in classes that nervous fatigue has its source in the patient's sense of discouragement and self-disgust she "didn't like that very well because I knew how my muscles felt." With this she formulated the familiar philosophy of nervous patients which can be condensed in two sentences: I *feel* tired; hence, I *am* tired, and I *think* my muscles are exhausted; hence, *they are*. On the basis of this philosophy, patients are convinced that what they feel is real and what they think is right. And it is the supposed reality of what they feel and the presumed rightness of what they think which keeps patients from ironing and dressing and preparing the breakfast. Protesting solemnly that their nerves are "incapable of performing their jobs" they do a perfect job at coddling their feelings and pampering their thoughts. Pronouncing their coddled feelings real and their pampered thoughts right they prepare the groundwork for manufacturing a self-made incapacity.

I want you to know that this is a philosophy, confused and absurd, it is true, but a philosophy, nevertheless. My patients claim they suffer from frightening sensations, overpowering impulses, torturing thoughts and devitalized feelings. But I tell them that this is a half-truth at best; that what they actually suffer from is—their philosophy. And if their philosophy is based on the assumption that in their spells and tantrums their feelings are real and their thoughts are right, well, that is precisely the philosophy of temper. In the ordinary burst of temper, whether it be presymptomatic or postsymptomatic,* you *feel* the insult or injury was a "real" outrage, and *think* you are "right" in considering it a deliberate hurt.

If I speak of a philosophy I do not refer to a complex system of thought as described in textbooks. What I have in mind is what has been called the philosophy of life. Let me add immediately that I know three philosophies of this kind only: realism, romanticism and intellectualism. If in the pursuit of your daily activities you coddle your feelings you will act as a romantic; if you pamper your thoughts your conduct will be that of an intellectual. Your behavior will then be governed by feelings whose telltale story has been hastily believed, or by thoughts whose immature suggestions were uncritically accepted. In either case, your action will be guided by the subjective promptings of your inner experiences instead of by the objective requirements of outer reality. If you were a realist you would give first consideration to the actual facts of the prevailing situation and

---

*About presymptomatic and postsymptomatic see Part 3, page 252.

would not hesitate to suppress your thoughts or shelve your feelings if you found they conflicted with the realities of the situation. I shall illustrate the point presently.

You enter a bakery shop intent on buying a cake. The requirements of the situation are such that you must stand in line and wait. No doubt, you will not relish the prospect. You will be provoked, and will experience irritation, discomfort and impatience. These are the *subjective feelings* with which you respond to the realistic facts of the situation. We shall call it the *feeling response*. Before long your thought processes swing into action. You surmise that the saleslady could certainly move a trifle faster. And the customer who is just being served could indeed speed up her selection without insisting on being shown all varieties of cookies in the show case. How inconsiderate people are! And what kind of government is this anyhow! A year after V-J Day and still this nuisance of wartime restrictions,scarcities and rationing! This is your *thought response*, as intuitive, impulsive and spontaneous as was your feeling response. I doubt whether any human being endowed with normal sensibilities will avoid the feeling of irritation and the thought of frustration in a situation of this kind. Be he realist, romantic or intellectual, he will respond with aroused feelings to an imposition and with critical thoughts to the persons who prolong or aggravate the frustration. He would not be "human" if he responded otherwise. In point of *inner responses* men are alike. They differ only in their readiness to convert their inner responses into *open reactions*. The realist is inclined to control his feeling and thought responses; the romantic and intellectual tend to express them. It is all a matter of your philosophy (of life), and if your philosophy is realistic you will exercise control; if it is romantic your feelings may be expressed the moment they are aroused; if it is intellectual your thoughts will tend to be voiced the very instant they are born.

A philosophy tells you which goals to choose and how to aim at them. You who are readers of our Recovery literature know that goals are of two kinds: group and individualistic. The realist aims at group goals mainly. His ambition is to adjust his conduct to the requirements of group life. In the instance of the visit to the bakery shop he considered himself a member of the group of shoppers. He knew that by expressing his feelings of irritation or his thoughts of resentment he was bound to arouse the enmity of some members of that group. And antagonizing the group meant maladjustment. If his goal was to create good will in the group he had to curb his individualistic inclinations to express his inner responses. He exercised control and remained adjusted. To the romantic and intellectual person the good will of the group means little. Group standards are odious restrictions to their craving for individualistic expression. In the episode at the bakery shop the romantic would not have hesitated to voice his indignation with a candid and perhaps studied indifference to the sensibilities of others. He prides himself on being frank and above-board. "What is wrong about expressing a feeling?" asks the romantic enthusiast for frank expression and forthwith, without scruple or hesitation, he rolls off a list of his likes and dislikes regardless of whether they are offensive, tactless and out of place. He will tell you, without mincing words, that your furniture is not properly arranged, that if he had planned a house like yours the rooms or entrances or exits would have been differently placed. If it is a woman romantic she will intimate plainly that she has no taste for your jewelry and that her way of cooking a roast is different and "if you want to get a real coat let me take you to my tailor." It is all an expression of feelings and if in the process the feelings of others are hurt, well, it is about time they got used to language that "comes straight from the shoulder." Presently, this unrestrained talker will steer the conversation into the channels of sickness, hospitalization, oper- ations. She will revel in gruesome recollections of the "excruci- ating pains" she suffered without being able to convince her husband or physician that the pain was "real." What agonies she went through. She felt pain and tugging and pulling in the lower abdomen. "It was there, I felt it all the time. But they thought it was my imagination. Finally I got my physician to take me to the hospital, and on the operating table they found adhesions all over." Her feelings had told her she had a tumor or something of the sort, and it was "really" there.

I could go on indefinitely describing the amusing though by no means harmless mouthings of these romantic souls. I could portray their lust for complaining, their zeal for being consid- ered a martyr. But it would merely illustrate the fact that their philosophy is one of reckless expression of feelings. These feelings are coddled and treasured and magnified and thrust at every innocent listener who consents to be an audience.

I shall now give you a brief account of the intellectual mentali- ty, the counterpart of the romantic soul. His stock in trade is the insistence, repeated tirelessly and ruthlessly, that he is right, that you better take his advice, that he could have told you how to avoid trouble if you had only cared to listen to him. Thinking that he is right he promptly assumes that the others are wrong. Hence, he delights in correcting the statements and opinions of those about him. He is critical, aggressive, meddlesome. He not only knows things but knows them better than others. His views are advanced and modern, theirs are stand-pattish and outmoded. His supreme delight is to change things, to reform laws and institutions, to do away with the old and to create something new; hence, he is impatient with tradition, custom and standards. He knows how to arrange things, how to plan them, how to predict and prevent. Enjoying a self-appointed monopoly in correct thinking he is eager to mend and "reform" the defective thought processes of others. These others are backward, benighted, reactionary. He is forward-looking, enlightened, progressive. The essence of his attitude is that he knows and is right and that the others are ignorant and wrong. And if they are wrong it is his duty to tell them. There is no reticence about this intellectual. He talks and argues and fights for his opinions. His pet ideal is "free speech," not only in the political scene where it may have a legitimate place, but also in social and domestic contacts where it merely serves the purpose of shocking settled convictions and established views. Waiting in line at the bakery shop the intellectual would or might let loose a stirring tirade of criticism against "that bunch of stuffed shirts" and their "red tape." He might inveigh against the greed of the "vested interests" and the oppression of the common people. Voicing their thoughts and opinions, particulary if they are shocking to the "lethargy" of the "standpatters," is a consuming passion with these right-thinking and enlightened intellectuals.

I do not wish to be misunderstood to imply that my patients are generally addicted to a romantic or intellectual philosophy of life. Presumably, some of them are, but so are some members of every group. At any rate, I am little concerned about the political, economic or social views of my patients. What interests me is their philosophy with regard to symptoms and temper. The fact is that my patients, prior to receiving training in Recovery, have been stubbornly romantic about their symptoms and emphatically intellectual about their temper. They coddled their defeatist feelings of "really" being exhausted and of "really" not having slept a wink for months, and pampered their thought of having the "right" to wail and complain and make extravagant demands on relatives and friends. What the panel members demonstrated convincingly is that persistent and systematic training in the realistic principles of Recovery is the superb means of ridding our patients of the pretentious pseudo-philosophies of decadent romanticism and arrogant intellectualism in their dealings with their common inner experiences.

6

EXCEPTIONALITY AND AVERAGENESS; SENTIMENTALISM AND REALISM

A Panel Discussion Conducted by Patients

Annette (panel leader): The subject of today's panel discussion is taken from the interview entitled "Average Existence and Exceptionality." The doctor speaks there of desirable and undesirable exceptionality. Has anybody got an example?

Ann: I had a silly fear similar to the one described in the article. My sister told me something that had happened to a neighbor. He had been hurt in an accident. I got the idea I was responsible for that accident. But I knew immediately it was a delusion and was ready to wait till it would disappear. You know, I mentioned it on previous panels, that I get delusions of this kind but I have learned to handle them. But this time all of a sudden I laughed hysterically. That frightened me. After I hung up I had the fear that my sister would know my behavior was maladjusted. I called Rosalie, and she told me how she handled a similar story of an accident. I again got this idea that I was responsible. Rosalie said, "You know what you are doing? You are misinterpreting an event. You know that nobody in this world would think he is responsible for an accident he heard of. And if you think you are responsible you think you are not like other people. You think of yourself as exceptional." That helped me. And last Saturday when I had that feeling again that I was responsible for what somebody did I had no fear in connection with it and it just disappeared.

Annette: Ann has learned in Recovery that even delusions can be controlled if you know how to eliminate the idea of danger. Such delusions are ideas. And our physician has told us repeatedly that ideas come and go if you do not add the thought of danger. Ann has proved that is correct.

Ann: Of course, I don't handle them right yet. Just thinking of these fears and bringing them out on the panel gives me tremors. I have some right now but I can control them.

Annette: Several weeks ago I had a trying day and I was quite tired and somewhat irritable. I had stayed up late and when I went to bed my feet were very cold. I mentioned it to my husband but he did not reply. I resented that. A little while later

I got a cramp in my foot but I didn't tell my husband perhaps from fear that he might not be any more sympathetic than he was to my first complaint. I became tense and felt that I thought of danger but did not know exactly what kind of danger was in my mind. Later the cramp went away, and it was then that I recalled that a very close friend of mine had died that week and that there had been a blood clot in the leg. Today it is clear to me that the blood clot suggested to me that my cramp was dangerous. As I now know through my Recovery training, the patient likes to complain of something spectacular and exceptional. When I had the cramp I should have thought of an innocent pain or muscle fatigue. But as our physician says, the nervous patient will not settle for anything less than a rare, incurable or hopeless ailment. I think that after that experience I understand now why we think of the spectacular and exceptional.

Gertrude: One of the ideas I had was the thought of death. In Recovery I learned that we cannot be exceptions and if the average man and woman can think of death we can, too. But in the beginning I was afraid of the thought. Now I can think of death as the average person does. I live only a short distance from three cemeteries, but most of the time I am not even aware of their being there.

Carol: If I am among people I feel I want to be tops, but I feel I am not genuine. Our physician has told me that means I hope to be exceptional but fear that I am not even average. On the train I think the people are watching me. I know now that this is what our doctor calls the sense of undesirable exceptionality. I also want to be an exceptional mother but I don't handle it right. I feel I have to watch Susie, my little daughter, every minute of the day. But the other day when a neighbor girl came over and asked whether Susie could have lunch with her I got objective about it and let her go.

Annette: What happened when you went against your desire to keep an eye on Susie?

Carol: At first I had all kinds of wild thoughts of danger. But then I said, "All right, I am going to say 'no' to my sensations and feelings and be like my neighbor." I was tense but I dropped the sense of exceptionality and was no longer afraid of being average.

Sophie: The other day I went to the basement to do my washing. The children were home from school. I said, I am going downstairs, and don't you make noise. As soon as I went the noise started. I became furious. I shouted up to them to stop that noise. But they made such a racket they didn't hear me. I felt so frustrated I felt like crying. I dropped the linen and I couldn't move for a few minutes. It seemed to me I was paralyzed. But then I stopped and looked into myself and said, "What are you doing?" I was setting an exceptional standard for my children not to make noise. When I recognized I had that standard the tenseness left me and I went on with my work.

Frank: I can give an example. It is not so dramatic. It happens frequently that I have something to do, and I just don't want to do it and I don't know why. I just can't get started. I am now working on the Recovery News and it is necessary to type up the stencil. It is a simple job but it takes me a week or more to warm up to it. I think it is because I don't think it is good enough. I guess my standard is too high and I still think in terms of exceptionality. When I realized that, I just made up my mind that I would type up the stencil and I did it in no time. If I hadn't done the work I would have condemned myself and got more tense. After I finished it I felt quite proud of myself and there was no vicious cycle as there usually is when I procrastinate.

EXCEPTIONALITY AND AVERAGENESS; SENTIMENTALISM AND REALISM
Physician's Comment on a Panel Discussion

When Ann, in distraction, turned for help to Rosalie she was warned not to consider herself different from other people. If she did she thought of herself as exceptional and not as being like other people. I shall ask: Do you really believe that anyone with a spark of vitality and ambition will content himself with being "like other people?" To have no other qualities than the ones found "in other people" means to be colorless, ordinary, dull, perhaps common and commonplace. Who would relish the reputation of being unimaginative, impersonal, nondescript? People wish and crave to have distinction, singularity, personality and character. They shudder at the thought of being just a cipher, one of many, nothing but average. What men and women actually hope, boast and pretend to be is—exceptional. And if my patients think of themselves as being not just average they do what everybody does. Why do I then urge them to shed their sense of exceptionality?

Exceptionality is a hope, a dream, an illusion, that means, an imagination. Averageness is the reverse; it is a subtle fear, a sober fact, a disillusioned self-appraisal, that means a plain, uninspiring reality. People hope to be exceptional and fear to be nothing but average. If you choose to live in a world of hopes, dreams and illusions you are a sentimentalist; if you prefer the realm of factual existence and everyday life you are a realist. But you are not permitted to make a choice or to state your preference. You are what you are: sentimental and realistic, imaginative and matter-of-fact at the same time. What counts is the proportion, balance, and ratio. Does your realism outweigh your sentimentalism? Or does the balance tilt in the opposite direction?

I am fond of believing that my patients represent a wholesome and desirable cross-section of the general population. If that is true their personalities are as well or ill balanced between sentimentalism and realism as those of their relatives, neighbors and friends. They feel just as exceptional and are just as average as the social set to which they belong. When they deal with their children, their wives, mothers and fathers they indulge in a pardonable sense of exceptionality taking pride in the supposedly superior qualities of their family, clan, race. But I doubt whether my patients carry this sentimental bias into the regions of business, social activities and home management. There they are exactly as realistic and average-minded as the situation requires. The sentimental trend exhibited in one sphere of life is neatly balanced by a corresponding realistic attitude governing their activities in other spheres. There is solid balance, sound proportion, sane ratio.

If I ask my patients to be realistic instead of sentimental; if I insist that they renounce their romantic sense of exceptionality in favor of sober self-accounting in terms of averageness I refer to the attitude they are supposed to take with regard to their symptoms. There they must not indulge in sentimental dreams of exceptionality; there they must plant themselves solidly on the ground of realistic averageness. If the average person experiences pressure in the head he does not permit himself to be rushed into a hysterical panic. He suffers but remains calm. True, my patients suffer from conditions that are not average in intensity and duration. Nevertheless, I ask them to retain their balance even in the face of extreme agonies. Ann demonstrated with singular clarity how this can be done. She had a delusion and manipulated it as an average experience. How could she manage to think she was "like other people" at the very moment her brain was the seat of a delusion? Do people have delusions "on an average?" What Ann did *was* exceptional. It was the exact reverse of what could be expected "on an average." She turned realist and was calm and poised in a situation that was frightening, exceptional and extraordinary. With this she carried the principle of averageness to the very limits of plausibility and possibility. Such feats are possible in Recovery, and in Recovery they are no feats. There they are average occurrences, the result of patient and systematic training. What Ann demonstrated was that under our system of training sentimentalism can be so thoroughly overbalanced by realism that even under exceptional circumstances the sense of averageness can be made to assert itself successfully.

Delusions are, of course, outside the domain of realism. And there can be no objection to ranging them among the sentimentalities of thoughts or wishes. If a patient claims to be Napoleon, if another thinks he is being observed and watched and spied on as if he were an important personage you may call the one a delusion of grandeur and the other a delusion of persecution. But in essence it is romanticism and sentimentalism. Annette and Gertrude mentioned no delusions. They reported their experiences with the fear of a blood clot, the dread of dying. Is the fear of a blood clot sentimental? Average people certainly worry about death and vascular accidents. And if Carol worried about her daughter Susie and Sophie became furious about the noise made by her children and Frank couldn't get himself to warm up to a simple job what is the warrant for calling these reactions sentimental or exceptional?

Take the case of Annette. Her feet felt cold and developed a cramp. This was an experience of discomfort and pain. The experience as such had all the earmarks of averageness. What could be more average and commonplace than cold feet and crampy muscles? There is no distinction, no glamor, no excitement in coldness and crampiness. The incident is so trivial that it cannot excite interest. It could certainly not be used as the subject for a telling story. But the moment Annette conceived the suspicion that the cold feet and crampy muscles might be the result of a blood clot, well, there was the plot for an exciting story that could stir the imagination. With a mere chilly skin and cramping muscle her experiences were drab, trivial, uninteresting, uneventful. But with a clot, there was danger, excitement, drama. A blood clot is not everyday life; it is a dire emergency, a tragedy, perhaps a good story. To reach the dizzy heights of emergency and tragedy Annette had to infuse the elements of temper and emotionality into an event that was otherwise plain, simple and devoid of thrill.

Take now the case of Carol. She was worried about the health of her daughter Susie. On the face of it no sentimentalism seems to be involved in a mother's concern about the health of her child. A concern of this kind is realistic and average. Even if Carol felt she had to watch the daughter "every minute of the day" the sentiment was still within the scope of average anxiety although decidedly overdone. But when Carol carried her apprehensiveness to the extent of refusing Susie to be watched by neighbors whom she knew to be responsible people she displayed an unrealistic distrust in the reliability of the average person and indulged in what she calls herself a sense of "undesirable exceptionality." She set herself up as the only person to whom Susie's welfare could be entrusted. She alone had the requisite sense of responsibility. The others could not be relied on. Moreover, she conceived of Susie as a child that needed special watching, extraordinary care, exceptional supervision. With this she injected into everyday life concepts and sentiments of exaggerated duties and responsibilities that have no place there. Suppose Susie, while attending a luncheon in a nearby home hurt her leg or felt a "tummy ache" or got involved in a fracas with the other children; the hostess could certainly be credited with ample sense of duty and responsibility to take proper care of the situation. You see, Annette and Gertrude exaggerated the importance of their own bodily feelings and sensations and became *emotional*. Carol gave herself over to a vastly exaggerated sentiment of duty and responsibility and became *sentimental*. You will now understand what the terms emotionalism and sentimentalism imply. Emotionalism means that plain and innocent sensations, impulses or feelings aroused by events of average intensity are conceived as so alarming that nothing short of an extraordinary fear reaction seems to suit the situation. Sentimentalism means that equally plain and average experiences are viewed as so exalted and valuable that nothing short of an excessive sense of duty and responsibility can meet the requirements of the momentous event.

Average life consists of trivialities mainly. Average home life, for instance, calls for buttons to be sewed, dishes to be washed, children to be watched, pain and discomfort to be endured. All of this is routine, offering little stimulation or excitement and providing a great deal of irritation, a good measure of drudgery and some amount of suffering. Occasionally there is a birth or wedding, sickness or death. Then the routine is interrupted by an exceptional event but is resumed in all its deadly monotony as soon as the event has passed. The irritation incidental to this sort of routine life is patiently borne by persons who are not too irritable. But nervous patients are unfortunately blessed with an excess of irritability. As a result, the average irritations of routine existence are well nigh "unbearable" to them. They hate the routine chores. Routine, to them, is an infliction. It inflicts disturbing sensations, confusions, doubts and anxieties. To the average housewife the breaking of a glass is a plain occurrence not to be fussed over. It causes a mild irritation that is easily disposed of by the consideration that the loss is trivial and replacement easy. But to the nervous housewife the breakage may suggest that she is inadequate, that all effort is futile, that the inefficiency, incoordination and lack of attention revealed by the dropping of the glass are beyond hope. She may now become provoked at herself and work herself up to a pitch of excitement and emotionalism. Or, she may bring into play the sentiment of self-pity and condemn herself as a neglectful person, oblivious to duty and responsibility. The sentimentalism of self-blame may finally produce a panic. Then sentimentalism and emotionalism join hands to create exceptional fury in response to an event of average triviality.

The excessive irritability of my patients predisposes them to a grotesque hatred of routine. With the average housewife, sewing buttons and darning socks do not figure as exalted tasks or sources of great excitement. They are chores, devoid of thrill and inspiration. But the darning is done for the husband, the sewing for the son. Being meant for the ones she loves the activity acquires a significant meaning in the eyes of the housewife. Every stitch and every patch has the meaning of doing something necessary, useful and valuable. Life is still a chore and unpleasant routine, but the routine is now meaningful, important, perhaps even vital. The inherent meaning of the work creates enjoyment. The enjoyment provides stimulation, gives a sense of living, a feeling of accomplishment. Added to the feeling of joy and satisfaction is the realization that the mending and patching constitute a duty performed and responsibility discharged. In this manner, the feeling of joy is supplemented by the sentiment of dutiful and responsible activity. Life of this kind is one of sustained feeling and sentiment. It is vibrant, stimulating, perfused with zest and interest.

We may draw the same picture of the average man working in a shop or at an office desk. The work itself may be a boring and dull routine, repetitious and tiring. But if done with an eye to its usefulness and meaningfulness in terms of maintaining the family the otherwise uninteresting job assumes the aspect of importance, dignity, duty and responsibility. The shop or office routine as such may give no stimulation, but the thought of the ones for whom they are performed produces the feeling of joy and the sentiments of responsibility, dependability and consistency.

You will realize now that for routine to become palatable and acceptable it must be capable of supplying a moderate amount of feelings and sentiments. The feelings are mainly those of joy, satisfaction and stimulation. The sentiments are those of duty and responsibility and their attendant sense of dependability, consistency, dignity and self-importance. Viewed against this background the nervous patient is in a pitiable condition. When the housewife, incapacitated by a nervous ailment, sets out on her sewing performance her fatigue interferes with the nimbleness of her movements. The muscles feel heavy, the fingers cramp, the lids droop wearily. Being determined to finish the job she may continue the dreary occupation. But the work is done mechanically; every stitch requires the utmost in effort; the needle lies limp between the fingers, the garment flops to the floor. She picks it up, resumes the sewing, but she has to use every ounce of her flagging energy to perform the simplest movement of the hand. Finally she gives up in despair. There is no use trying to do something for husband and child. This life of daily routine is an endless torture, squeezed dry of every drop of joy, drained of every semblance of importance, usefulness or value. There is no possibility of experiencing feelings or sentiments in this atmosphere of utter futility and helplessness.

Unable to infuse feelings and sentiments into the routine of daily activity the nervous patient endeavors to eliminate routine from life altogether. The formula is simple: There must be nothing trivial, meaningless, unimportant in the sphere of daily existence. Everything must be drenched in a flood of feelings and sentiments. Plain conversations, questions and answers must not be tolerated. They must be converted into a stirring argument or an intense fight or a pathetic complaint. The fight makes room for feelings of indignation, the complaint provides the setting for sentiments of self-pity or self-blame. All of it is absurdly exaggerated and morbidly intensified. But the illusion is created that feelings and sentiments are again governing the daily activities. That the feelings have degenerated into wild emotionalism and the sentiments into vapid and shallow sentimentalism does not count. Life is again pulsating, vital, important. True, its vitality and importance have been derived from an underhanded trick that falsifies feelings and sentiments into something that only remotely resembles them. But the fact is that the life-pulse, no matter how shaky, has been restored and vitality, no matter how empty, has been recaptured. Trick or no trick, life is or seems worth living again.

7

HELPLESSNESS IS NOT HOPELESSNESS

A Panel Discussion Conducted by Patients

Annette (panel leader): Today we want to discuss a problem which most of us faced during our sickness or in the process of getting well. It is a problem closely akin to sabotage. Sabotage has many different forms, and one of them bears on a condition when we experience a general letdown, a feeling as though we had no interests, no feelings, no spontaneity. Everything we do during this condition requires a tremendous effort. This makes us unhappy and despondent. Any examples?

Regina: You described my trouble; only I think the symptoms were much worse than you described them. I had that awful feeling of fatigue as if I couldn't even get out of bed. I didn't want to. I couldn't eat or sleep, and the household tasks I did before were such an ordeal. I couldn't even fill the sugar bowl. I almost got into a panic when I thought of it. I had a fatigue that seemed unbearable. I had to drag myself all the time. After I came to Recovery our physician said you are not tired. If I went downtown I would walk around for ten minutes and think I had to sit down. But the doctor told me that wasn't fatigue; it was just a feeling of fatigue. Now I walk for hours and it doesn't bother me. I don't even have the feeling of fatigue any more.

Annette: When you had to go through the movements of getting the sugar and filling the bowl, did that look like an impossible task to you?

Regina: It certainly did. If I even looked at the sugar bowl it made me nervous and tense. Every time I looked at it I wondered is that much sugar gone again? Will I have to fill it again?

Annette: When you had to go through this tremendous struggle, what conclusions did you draw about your illness?

Regina: I felt hopeless and was sure there just wasn't any cure. I blamed myself for letting myself go like this, and the more I blamed myself the worse I got. I know now that I set up a vicious cycle.

Annette: After you got into Recovery how did you handle that?

Regina: The doctor told me to walk and do things regardless of the fatigue. And I learned that I slept even if I didn't know I did, and all of that helped me. But in the beginning it was hard. For a few days I accepted the doctor's assurance. But then I sabotaged and thought that was good for others and not for me. I thought nobody felt like I did. But then I heard other patients describe the same difficulties in the interviews and panels. That gave me great relief. And I read the books and went to meetings and finally I got well.

Frances: When I was sick I had two small children and I got so I didn't want to take care of them. The house was a mess and the children were neglected and I would run out of the house and go to my sister's and I had the feeling I wanted to go back right away but didn't know how. I tried many times to do something but I just couldn't. Frequently I would just lie down and wouldn't get up. I remember how awfully hard it was for me to wash dishes. I would stand by the sink and felt I was going to topple over and everything was going blank. When I was with people I felt a sort of wave of darkness coming over me and I felt like fainting. Finally I avoided people and wouldn't see them. That was three years ago. But two weeks ago an uncle came from California and about thirty members of the family met at my sister's and I remembered the feeling of self-consciousness I used to have with even two people. And here I was with thirty people and I enjoyed myself and played cards with them all night and won eighteen dollars and, I tell you, it was very comfortable.

Annette: It seems to have been profitable, too.

Frances: Three years ago they could have given me a million dollars and I couldn't enjoy it.

Annette: How did your illness affect your feelings toward your children and your husband and other members of the family?

Frances: I can hardly understand it now. But at that time I had no feelings for my children or for my husband or for anybody else. I had no interests and nothing gave me enjoyment. Today it's different, and my husband often remarks about how enthusiastic I can be.

Annette: I wish to mention an experience I had many times when I was ill at the hospital. Getting out of bed, as you described, was such an effort, and going to eat my meals seemed as though I couldn't get the food down. My husband brought me jig saw puzzles which I used to enjoy. I started to work one, picked up a piece, looked at it and thought this is too much for me. It seemed every time I picked up a piece I had to make twice the effort to move it from place to place. When my husband visited me the nurses would say, "Oh my, you have a nice husband," and one attendant said, "My, you must get well for such a nice husband," and I realized that was correct but I had no feeling about it. During the first few months I was indifferent to whether he came to see me or not. I certainly did not look forward to visiting days. But gradually my feelings returned but in a peculiar way. One day I still did not feel any particular enthusiasm about having visitors but on another day should my husband not arrive at the expected time I got sore because he was late. I then realized that my indifference was lifting. After returning home my interests were not very active immediately. I did the simple tasks because I knew they had to be done. If I kept the place clean it was not because I enjoyed it but because it was my duty. I assure you that today when I clean my apartment I get a sense of pleasure seeing it clean. I get spontaneous feelings now. I didn't get them for a long time after leaving the hospital and did things "from duty and necessity" as our physician says. Had it not been for my Recovery training I am afraid I would have gotten into a vicious cycle watching myself and thinking I am not improving; noticing the sluggish feelings and worrying about them; seeing things neglected and blaming myself for it. The more I would have worried the worse, I expect, would the condition have been; the worse the condition the more worry. In those days the most distressing thought was that I would never again have the capacity to feel, that I would never again be enthusiastic about things. Today I know this was a prognosis and sabotage.

Frank B.: A few months ago everything looked hopeless to me. I had intense fatigue and would spend about three days a week in bed or take afternoon naps of about four hours. I wasn't working and the worst thing was I still had the idea I was railroaded into the state hospital eight years ago when I first got sick. I was afraid to go to see a doctor because he might say I was nervous and I thought I wasn't and he would put me in the hospital again. But finally I went to see a doctor and he said it was nervous fatigue and I should rest. But the more I rested the more tired I felt. I watched my diet and that didn't help either. I got worse and worse. I thought that when my nerves are fatigued I'd better quit swimming which I enjoy very much, I also stopped going out socially and everything was an ordeal. But since I joined Recovery I go swimming a few times a week and go out socially and I am seriously considering going to work. A few weeks ago if the doctor had told me I would be doing these things again I would not have believed it.

Annette: Did you find you got over these difficulties immediately after joining Recovery?

Frank B.: No, I had to be satisfied with small gains. Going out socially was still a big problem. But after I learned to be sociable with the members of Recovery I gradually enjoyed myself with outside groups. In Recovery I learned to throw off the stigma. That wasn't easy because I had been picked up by the police and brought to the hospital by them. Now I feel that's the past and I think of the future. Of course, I am still sabotaging every once in a while. But I am just a rookie yet.

HELPLESSNESS IS NOT HOPELESSNESS
Physician's Comment on a Panel Discussion

Regina had difficulty eating, walking, sleeping. Everything she did required effort, even the act of filling the sugar bowl. Annette had similar complaints and summed them up correctly as a "lack of spontaneity." When then Frances and Frank added their reminiscences of past ordeals they merely contributed a new chapter to the old story. The story is that of having dragged along for months or years without initiative, zest or interest, i.e., without spontaneity and having regained *spontaneity* through the self-help techniques practiced in Recovery.

To be spontaneous means to have no difficulty making up one's mind, to carry out one's plans and decisions, to feel like doing something and get it done, and all of this means *vitality*. The patients described a condition in which they lacked vitality when they were ill and regained vitality after they recovered. Previously they felt lifeless and spiritless: now they live with spirited alertness. I grant that a person who does not feel the pulse of life, a person who has no affection, no anticipation, no sense of accomplishment, I grant that such a person is helpless. What more dramatic picture of helplessness can be drawn that the scenes in which Regina could not bear the thought of having to fill the sugar bowl or Annette could not command sufficient vitality to move a little piece of cardboard (jig-saw puzzle) from one place to another? At the time they were certainly devoid even of a shred of vitality. Theirs was a mechanical existence, not a dynamic life.

When Annette lacked the strength to move a little scrap of paper she had a right to feel weak, helpless and unhappy. She had also the right to feel distressed when she noticed that her feelings were low or gone. But when she became despondent and thought she "would never again have the capacity to feel" and "would never again be enthusiastic about things" she permitted herself to predict future developments, and this she had no authority to do. As she said herself, "Today I know this was a prognosis and sabotage."

A patient is competent to describe his present condition, his pains, pressures and palpitations, his lack of strength and vitality, his fears, panics and compulsions. If he wishes to place the label of "helplessness" on any of these experiences I shall not quarrel with him. I have not seen a patient who was not helpless, totally or partially. Patients are helpless to stop their pressures, they are helpless when they find themselves seized with air-hunger or night terror. And if any patient claims to be helpless I shall not challenge the correctness of his statement. But when a patient declares himself hopeless I shall warn him that he has presumed to make a prognosis and has trespassed into my territory. The physician alone is capable of deciding whether a condition is hopeless or hopeful. The patient who assumes the diagnostic or prognostic function of the physician sabotages his authority. The patient can declare himself helpless but he has no right to pronounce himself hopeless. Description is the domain of the patient, prediction is the province of the physician.

I well remember the time when Regina and Frances sat in my office reciting their tales of woe. There was a great deal of description, but most of it was prediction. They predicted that they could not get well; that they were doomed to lead a lifeless existence; that the hope I held out for them could never materialize. If I mentioned that she slept better and this was indication of a beginning improvement, Frances hastened to correct me, "But doctor, last night was terrible again. How long can I stand that?" If I ventured to suggest that my patients had to wait but got well in the end, the retort was, "But doctor, they are not as run down as I am." All my reassuring statements were promptly swallowed up in a rebuttal sentence that invariably had the phrasing, "But doctor . . ." Both Frances and Regina were confirmed "but-knockers." I had merely to voice a positive thought and it was immediately knocked out by a negative answer. I presented them with a hopeful prognosis, and they swept it aside with a dire prediction of hopelessness.

I shall ask you to visualize the situation in my office when a depressed patient sits opposite me. We discuss a condition but we never meet. Whatever I may say is instantly disputed or discarded by my opponent. But the patient is no opponent. He is a wretched creature begging for help. He insists on help, he clamors for it, protests he "would do anything to get it." If he is not my opponent why does he oppose me so vehemently? If he is ready to "do anything to get help" why does he not do that "little something" I ask for: to drop his pessimistic and accept my optimistic view? Views are thoughts and can be dropped, other views can be adopted in their place. If that can be done why does the patient refuse to do it?

I have given much thought and study to this absurdity of clinging to a harmful view when acceptance of a helpful view was certain to give relief. I have seen women who go through depression each month before or during or after their menstrual periods. They are depressed and helpless but do not indulge in doom prophecies. The reason is clear; their depressions are of short duration, and a rich past experience has taught them to be optimistic about relief to be expected. My nervous patients come to me after months and years of suffering. Their pessimistic views have gained depth and strength. Their pessimism has become a habit, hardened and crystallized by continued practice. Such habits pervade the organism, color every move and thought of the person and are not easily dislodged.

You can observe such habits of thought everywhere and at all times. These days particularly it is not difficult to spot prophets of doom right at your elbow, at home, in the neighborhood, in the shop. You have heard all kinds of gruesome predictions in the past few years. Things in general were painted as utterly hopeless. The county is going to pot; inflation is certain to come, or it is here already to stay; democracy cannot survive. These gloom peddlers "knew" that our country could not possibly win the war; that industry would never catch up with the demands of the armed forces; that the end of the war would see an incurable rise in unemployment. The fact that their predictions fell flat did not discourage the soothsayers. Although promptly disavowed by actual developments they nevertheless continued to roll off new gloom stories from their never-resting assembly lines. All these people had imbibed the view of pessimism; the view hardened and crystallized into a stubborn habit of thought, until finally the habit acquired such momentum that evidence to the contrary was powerless to shake it.

Everybody is pessimistic and optimistic at the same time. In the ordinary mature person the two views are so balanced that optimism outstrips pessimism.   This is true of every habit. Everybody is both generous and miserly, cautious and bold, loving and hating, forgiving and vengeful, appreciative and critical. It is in the very nature of human habits that they range themselves in pairs the one member of which is antagonistic to the other. Pessimism and optimism are nothing but such a pair of mutually antagonistic features. Everybody is pessimistic and optimistic at the same time. Once a person has matured the antagonistic habits have attained their balance. Then we have two varieties of persons, the ones mature and realistic in whom generosity, caution, love, forgiveness, appreciation and optimism overbalance miserliness, boldness, hate, vengefulness, criticism and pessimism; the others infantilistic and emotional in whom the negative features prevail. Before Frances and Regina came to consult me they lived a life of balance in which the positive trends outweighed their negative antagonists. After they drifted into their depressions the negative features took the lead and dominated their habit structures. They became extreme in their reactions and lost their balance.

The calamity is that when two traits join to form a pair of habits (pessimism—optimism, miserliness—generosity) the more undesirable trend (pessimism, miserliness) is pushy and aggressive and always ready to assert itself. It is easy to throw off a good habit. All you need is consistent poor example. A life-long habit of honesty can be destroyed in short order by bad company or cajolery. Your well established habit of caution can be easily weakened or shattered by the ridicule of the "smart set." This is difficult with poor habits. If you are addicted to nail biting you know how desirable it is to drop it; you know that it is harmful to your standing in your group; you are eager and determined to abandon it, and yet how difficult it is to discard it. I am not going to tell you the reason for this distressing tenaciousness, with which bad habits cling to their useless existence. I merely mean to point out the fact that the more ugly or disturbing is a habit the stronger is its hold on the individual. Pessimism is an ugly and upsetting habit of this kind. It disturbs balance and renders behavior ugly and melancholy to behold or endure. Were it necessary to fortify my argument with another example it could easily be borrowed from the field of drinking. It is easy to induce a sober person to become an alcoholic. But try to steer a drinker back to sobriety and you will realize the strength of poor habits and the weakness of good habits.

All my patients have acquired bad habits. The good habits which used to balance them have been swept aside. Previously when the patient had a pain or pressure he bore it with patience. Now he demands instant relief. The habit of endurance has given way to that of self-indulgence. In the same manner, habits of courage yielded to fearful anticipations; trust in one's body functions was replaced by an abysmal distrust of the organs. In the course of months and years the undesirable habits acquired strength and cunning and tenacity. If the patient attempts to fight them off he finds himself confronted with a ruthless, stubborn and obstinate force. He puts up some resistance but soon realizes that his good intentions are no match to the resourcefulness of his opponent. He feels helpless, despairs of ever being able to regain his balance and conceives the idea of hopelessness. If that happens, then, the balance between the antagonistic habit traits of optimism and pessimism is destroyed and the patient is reduced to an existence of mechanical action. Regina and Frances, Annette and Frank demonstrated how the balance can be restored and how life can be made to regain its vigor and vitality. All they did was to refrain from sabotaging the physician's authority. He alone knows which ailments are hopeless and which are hopeful. To cure a nervous illness means to rid the patient of his pernicious tendency to sabotage the physician's effort. Once this is done the patient has learned that Helplessness does not mean Hopelessness.

8

EXTERNAL AND INTERNAL ENVIRONMENT

A Panel Discussion Conducted by Patients

Annette (panel leader): The subject of today's discussion is entitled, "Constitution, Environment and Temper." When I was sick I did not know what was constitution and temper. About temper I thought I knew something but I did not. What I knew was the explosive temper, flying off the handle, perhaps throwing things, at least throwing words excitedly and viciously. In Recovery I learned that temper takes in everything that is an individualistic trend and opposes a group standard. For the patient, temper means particularly everything that goes against the standard set by his physician. Two factors disturbed me a great deal when I was sick. They were: what kind of a constitution I had and what kind of environment I lived in and would return to after I left the hospital. In Recovery I learned that if I had a weak constitution that did not mean I had to keep it that way. I learned how to strengthen my constitution. I was surprised to find that the way to strengthen my nervous constitution was to avoid tenseness and to handle it properly when it developed. One Sunday my husband called for me at the hospital and we went to the Recovery meeting that was held at the hospital in those days. After the meeting we went to the zoo. The street car was crowded and someone jostled me and I became irritated and at the same time fearful. I did not have enough Recovery training yet to know that this was a trivial incident over which I shouldn't work myself up. I felt hurt and stepped on. I interpreted the simple incident as meaning I was the type of person who would never be able to take care of herself in a crowd. I felt I did not know how to stand up for myself. Today I know that I let myself drift into a vicious cycle between temper and tenseness but I did not have enough training then to know just how to stop it. By the time I arrived at the zoo I was extremely tense. I thought, how can I ever start out again in this world if I am going to be upset like this over every trivial instance? I am much too sensitive, perhaps because I have a nervous constitution. But if my constitution was weak what could I do about it? Before long I felt a blurring of vision and a tightness in the abdomen and worried about eating the dinner and was most uncomfortable.

About a year later I was standing one evening with my husband in front of a show window, and a woman shouldered her way between us. My reaction was not to give an inch, to stand my ground and not permit anybody to push me around. But no sooner had I become aware of the impulse to stand on my rights when I began to laugh. I instantly knew this was a trivial incident, and I was determined not to stand on my rights and to make myself uncomfortable and to produce tenseness and symptoms. As far as I am able to determine that meant one thing to me, that during my Recovery training I had learned to ignore that matter that I called my constitutional sensitiveness, to be indifferent to my rising temper and to let my feelings rise and fall. I knew that both constitution and temper are nothing unchangeable.

Phil: I told the folks here before that I had some sort of nervous trouble when I was about twelve years old. I was already in the eighth grade and was supposed to graduate but for some silly reason I did not want to go to high school and tried to flunk. But I was not successful though I made a good effort to flunk and graduated. All through high school I had trouble with teachers and argued with father and mother and when I was at college I developed the habit of telling people where to get off. My father had made a very good fraternity but I was not wanted by them because I was too cocky. So I made up my mind I was going to show these fellows a thing or two and demonstrate to them that I could lick them any time. To make the story short, I studied hard to show them off; I got on the magazine staff and did a good job at writing. I joined the dramatic club and did well there. I was always busy flitting from one activity to the other. I was hardly ever in my room during the day. My roommate said, "You don't want a roommate, Phil, you just want somebody to help pay the rent." But finally it caught up with me. When the examination came I was all exhausted. I would lie in bed for hours unable to sleep. That was the time I did not know yet that sleep has little to do with health. So I fretted over my insomnia and that made matters worse. In the end I broke and had to come back to Chicago. I can see now clearly that my nervous constitution was not equal to the strain and my sassy behavior was all a matter of temper.

Annette: After your breakdown did you stop trying to top everybody?

Phil: That kept on. I did not learn from that experience till I came to Recovery. Then I learned to be average and humble and get along with people. I think it is getting into my blood to be average and plain.

Annette: You have learned in Recovery that the sense of importance is perhaps stimulating but does not make for balance. And to preserve your health you need balance. And the sense of averageness gives you balance.

Phil: I have a pretty reasonable balance now. I am not tense any more. I gave up making a human dynamo of myself.

Anna: My case is mostly one of temper. Until lately I had quite a bit of trouble sleeping. I used to wake up in the middle of the night, felt tense and had all kinds of disturbing thoughts and sensations. The minute I woke up I felt an electric current going through my body, and I got disgusted with myself and got sore at the doctor and everybody else. Then while lying there my mind would argue with the doctor and I would say how long did I have to suffer like that, and I would diagnose my own case and ask how does the doctor know I will get well, and I would go on arguing that way back and forth.

Sometimes I would lie in bed till daybreak and work myself up to a vicious cycle. But lately I thought I better start practicing what I learned in Recovery. So now when I wake up in the middle of the night I just lie there and don't work myself up and I relax and wait till I fall asleep. Sometimes it takes quite a while but it is not as bad as it was when I used to work myself up. At times I fall asleep in half an hour or sooner, and in the morning I feel all right. I know now that working myself up makes the condition worse.

Annette: When you woke up and it felt like an electric current, how did you handle that?

Anna: Before I practiced Recovery I would get sore at myself and the longer I would argue with myself the longer it would take before I could sleep. Now I no longer work myself up and I don't diagnose my own case and I know the doctor said I will sleep if I don't worry about sleep, and if I lie in bed for hours I will sleep part of the hours. I know now that it is true.

George: When I was little I would get myself worked up so much that I would take my fists and hit myself on the head. All through public school and high school and college I made life miserable for myself and my parents. I practiced the angry and fearful temper. Last December, shortly after I came to Chicago to join Recovery, I experienced a good example of what I think is fearful temper. I must mention I could never hold a job before getting the Recovery training. In December I was working for a Loan Company, and again I felt like quitting because I didn't like the work. I stayed home and thought I should call the boss but I didn't. Frankly, I don't think he missed me much. But the next day I asked Frank to call the office and tell the boss I was too sick to work. But Frank talked me out of this. He said that is sabotage. And then it came to me that the doctor said if you fear to do something you do not fear the thing but your sensations; you fear being embarrassed or self-conscious. And the cure is to do what you fear to do and to brave the sensation. So I phoned the office and the boss just asked me to come back soon. That only proved that the doctor was right and that I was afraid of my own embarrassment. After that I felt embarrassed on several occasions but faced it and did not try to ease out of it.

The other day I went through an experience of angry temper. I was waiting for a train on the Elevated platform and I wanted to go to Evanston and a train was just coming in. A motorman was standing on the platform and I asked him whether it was an Evanston train. The fellow looked mean and did not answer and didn't even look at me. I asked him again and he didn't answer. Finally I said, "I am talking to you," and he said, "I don't have to tell you anything, buddy," and I got angry and said, "You are nothing but a doggone conductor." But there was lots of noise, and I guess he didn't hear it. The good thing was my temper didn't carry over, and in about two minutes I was laughing at myself and I had no after-effect. Two or three years ago I would have been proud that I had the nerve to tell him off but this time I felt a little ashamed.

Annette: It seems a bit silly, but we do not prescribe perfect behavior. In Recovery we say we must learn a lot about temper but we will not perform one hundred percent. If you have a temper outburst, be sure if you immediately recognize that the explosion is silly and childish then the possibility that you will be ready for another temper outburst at the slightest provocation is reduced greatly and therefore you are not going around tense all the time like I used to be, ready to be on the defense and to stand on your rights in senseless trifles. If you can laugh at yourself immediately after the outburst then you are relaxed. Any other example? If not I will bring the panel to a close.

EXTERNAL AND INTERNAL ENVIRONMENT

Physician's Comment on a Panel Discussion

Annette was jostled by a street car rider and as a result felt irritated and tense for hours and ultimately developed blurred vision, tightness in the abdomen, disturbance of appetite and general discomfort. She recounted this example when dealing with the topics of constitution, environment and temper. Undoubtedly, the jostling man was her environment. But what he jostled was Annette's muscles. It was nothing but a jostle, a jar, perhaps a jolt. How is it possible that a mild encroachment of this sort produced serious derangements of vision, appetite, abdominal function and general well-being? Was Annette's constitution so weak that a trivial push from the outside could cause a violent upheaval of her inner organs? It does not seem at all likely that mild pressure against her muscles should occasion such a severe inner reaction.

The jostling street car rider was environment to Annette. But by the same token, Annette was environment to the jostling man. His muscles pushed her muscles. And it will be useful for you to know that men and women are environment to one another and that the one acts on the other by means of muscles. Even if they speak or merely look the speaking and looking are done by the muscles of the mouth and the eyes. But if environmental effects proceed from muscle to muscle how is it they reach down to the inner organs and even to the depths where the thoughts, moods, impulses and sensations of the personality are embedded? For Annette did not merely respond with organic distress (vision, digestion and tenseness); she was also irritated, fearful, "felt hurt and stepped on," doubted whether she "could ever start out again in this world." Her muscles were merely jostled, but her inner organs were profoundly upset, and her personality was thrown out of equilibrium. How was it possible for a trivial environmental event to release such wide-spread effects?

You who have gone through the process of Recovery training know that the careless street car rider did not merely jolt Annette's muscles; he also jolted her temper. And temper is the bridge over which environmental irritations can reach across the muscles to the inner organs and to the depth of the personality. Along this road it penetrates to the domain which we call internal environment.

Roughly speaking, everything that exists or lives outside your muscles is external environment, everything that is inside your muscles is internal environment. Your home and its furniture, your father and mother, your friends and neighbors, your employers and employees together with a host of innumerable things, conditions and persons make up your outer environment. But inside you there is the inner environment, far more potent and vital, more readily disturbed and shaken than anything outside you. This inner environment is made up of your internal organs, on the one hand, and your personality functions, on the other. The latter are your feelings and moods, thoughts and decisions, sensations and impulses. Let your outer environment be disturbed by war, bereavement, fire or financial loss, and the chances are that you will bear the shock and emerge from it unscathed. But let your impulses be deranged, your sensations get out of control, your feelings become the seat of fear, envy and jealousy, your thoughts the prey of torturing obsessions, and the resulting commotion is likely to unsettle your nervous constitution.

Annette experienced another jostling episode a year later when a woman pushed her in front of a show window. She felt irritated again, but this time for a moment only. The next moment she laughed, and the irritation passed. There was no effect on the inner organs, no jolting of her personality functions. You will instantly realize the difference. In the first instance, in the street car, the environmental irritation was reacted to with temper; in the second instance, before the show window, the response was directed and mitigated by a sense of humor. The sense of humor, born of indifference to irritations even if they are severe, prevented the emergence of temper which takes annoyances seriously even if they are trivial.

We may conclude that the trivial irritations of external environment—they comprise the bulk of irritations in general—can be approached either with temper or with a sense of humor. If the approach is temperamental the inner organs and the personality functions of the internal environment will be thrown into commotion; if the approach is humorous the internal environment will be spared the anguish of frustration and the agony of disordered functions. The jostling or jolting will be felt by the muscles only; it will be prevented from spreading through the muscles to the inner confines of the personality there to work havoc with emotions and sensibilities. But in order to prevent this spread you must learn how to control your temper and to develop a sense of humor. In Recovery you have learned that temper is your worst enemy, humor your best friend.

The experiences of Phil, Anna and George fit into the same pattern. Before they underwent Recovery training their approach to environment was temperamental. It caused them no end of distress, unsettled their inner functions and unbalanced their personalities. Phil was or felt rejected by the men and women in his external environment. He took the rejection seriously and decided to demonstrate to his adversaries that he "could lick them any time." He became "cocky" and "was going to show these fellows a thing or two." This was temper. Instead of humorously ignoring external environment he fretted over the rebuff and girded for a fight. The result was a disorder of inner functions and derangement of personality. His temper landed him in the hospital. Today he has acquired a sense of humor, and the rebuffs suffered at the hands of external environment hardly cause a ripple in his inner life.

Anna had difficulty of sleeping, and was troubled with all kinds of disturbing thoughts and sensations. The electric current running through her body was a severe disturbance, indeed. She became disgusted with herself and "sore at the doctor and everybody else." The temperamental approach to environmental irritations reached here a climax. It engulfed the entire sweep of environmental existence. She was disgusted with and sore at her own person, her own personality and "everybody" outside her. How was it possible for Anna to reduce this torrential force of her temper to the level of calm detachment? In the face of electric currents shooting through her body, in the presence of threatening thoughts and violent sensations how did she manage to drop her temperamental fears and angers and replace them with a sense of humor? For the present, I merely wish to state that she did and that it can be done. As Anna says, "I know now that is true."

The account which George gave of his temperamental exploits brings back to my mind the day, about six months ago, when I received a letter from him inquiring whether training in Recovery was likely to cure his condition. Since this involved moving from the West coast to Chicago I hesitated to encourage the move in view of his history of temperamental maladjustment since childhood. But here he is, and his temper is under control although at times it still slips from under control as in his altercation with the "doggone conductor." Well, it is an instance of uncontrolled temper if such a remark is made, but it is an inspiring exhibit of a good sense of humor if the author of such unrestrained behavior can subsequently report the incident and laugh about it.   Moreover, George experienced merely the immediate effect of his outburst but mastered the after-effect when he laughed soon after the explosion. He laughed at himself and refused to take seriously the importance of his own dear self. With this he practiced the Recovery system of self-discipline which insists that temper is the outcome of an inner arrogance which sets itself up as judge as to who is right and who is wrong. This arrogance is due to the sense of one's own importance and cannot be overcome unless the sense of humor is cultivated to the point where humility, plainness and averageness take the place of arrogance, exceptionality and self-importance.

Annette, Phil, Anna and George demonstrated that internal environment can be protected successfully against the dangers of emotional agitation if the patient learns to control his temper. This is an important enough accomplishment. But the abiding value of a demonstration of this kind is that it emphasizes a principle that has general application. We live in the age of technique and boast that we have conquered time and space and matter and nature. Perhaps it is true that we have accomplished all of this. But of what good are conquests if they play solely in the field of external environment, leaving internal environment prostrate and helpless to be ravaged by the onslaughts of unbridled tempers? Of what good is your automobile if all it has brought you is the possibility of experiencing your palpitation at a speed of fifty miles an hour? Are you interested in external speed or in inner peace? You hear it stated these days on every street corner and in every newspaper column that moral progress has not kept pace with technological advance. Well, it is truer to say that the emphasis on technological progress made us forget the importance of progressing in the domain of morale. Recovery has reversed the proportion, and the reversed position was given beautiful expression by the members of the panel. To us at any rate, control of our internal environment is infinitely more important than all the possible triumphs we may be able to score over external environment.

9

FEELINGS ARE NOT FACTS

A Panel Discussion Conducted by Patients

Annette (panel leader): I remember a distressing sensation which gave me no end of alarm. It was a severe cramping or pain in the side of my abdomen. It was so severe that when it hit me I felt I could not walk. I had the same sensation on numerous occasions and was always afraid it would return. I know now that anticipating its return made matters worse. I was alarmed when I had the sensation and was perhaps more alarmed when I didn't have it but anticipated its return. After six years of almost constant suffering I finally went to the hospital but the doctor couldn't find anything wrong with me physically and sent me to the Illinois Research Hospital. It was then that I came under our physician's care and joined Recovery. It was only then that I realized that it was not the sensation that caused all the discomfort but the panicky feeling that something terrible was about to happen.

At the time I felt like something would burst in my side. I was sure I wouldn't be able to stand it, that I would go to pieces. When the doctor told me, "Your sensation is distressing but not dangerous," it took me quite a while before I understood what he meant. I had to take his word for it but I continued to feel something awful was going to happen. Today the sensation comes back occasionally. I have a slight twinge in my side even right now. In former days I would have been concerned. Today I know and know for sure that the sensation is merely distressing and not at all dangerous. I no longer anticipate trouble. Any other example?

Margaret: Recently I had company from out of town. I hadn't seen them for two years so I asked them to dinner. The cooking and the preparations were too much for me, and I got quite excited. I had again that pressure in my chest, and the palpitations were just awful. And I got a terrible pain in my head and my eyes smarted, and every time I turned my head it cracked. A year ago I would have become panicky and my husband would have called the family physician, and I would have fussed and stewed for days. This time I knew they were symptoms and they were distressing but not dangerous.

Annette: Did you go ahead with what you had to do?

Margaret: I felt like giving up but I didn't. I knew there was no danger.

Mary: Yesterday I was invited to spend the afternoon with a friend. I took my little nephew along and had no trouble at all making the trip. I didn't feel nauseated as I used to feel on street car rides. By seven o'clock I got ready to leave the party. As soon as I reached the street my legs started to give in and my heart pounded and my stomach flew around and I looked at my nephew and didn't know what to do. My first thought was to rush back to my friend's house and ask somebody to bring me home. But I knew these were symptoms and the sensations were not dangerous and I just stood there waiting till the symptoms would disappear. But I couldn't even wait because my nephew looked up at me and asked, "Aunt Mary, aren't we ever going home?" I was still very uncomfortable. But I took the next street car and we got home without trouble.

Annette: This is a beautiful example how you can be very uncomfortable and can manage to stand the discomfort if you keep in mind the physician's authoritative knowledge that you are not in danger. Any other example?

Caroline: I had a very gratifying experience this morning after my husband and I got up. He said, "What's the matter, don't you feel good today?" I asked, "Why?" He said, "You are very quiet today." Usually I am very talkative in the morning and, for that matter, all day. I have always a desire to talk about my symptoms and I guess I drive people nuts. This constant talk about my symptoms is sabotage. I know that but I haven't been able to check it so far. This morning I decided to stop talking and complaining and kept quiet. So I said, "I have a pain in my head but I know it will go away." We then talked of something else and I couldn't help but realize how different it was than a year ago. A year ago I would have said I have a terrible pain and I would have been sure I had a brain tumor and the doctor just won't tell me and I don't know what to do and if Recovery and our physician can't help, who can? But this morning I stopped that.

Before I came to Recovery when I had this particular pain in my head I would give in and go back to bed and my husband would bring me a hot water bottle and it seemed that made the pain worse and then he would bring me an icebag and in the meantime I would work myself up and he would suggest I take an aspirin but that did not help. After I came to Recovery regularly and talked to the other members of the group I learned to handle this symptom. This morning my husband offered to go to the store for me as he always does when I complain of my headache. Usually I become dramatic and say that my pain is so severe that I can't even think what I want from the store. This time I merely said, "Give me a few minutes and I will write the list."

Annette: Here we see Recovery training at its best. Not because Carline did so much better this time and is improving, but because Caroline has learned to make fun of herself and her symptoms. She has gained insight and knows now that she dramatizes her symptoms. She knows she plays a game and plays for attention. She has learned not to take herself and her symptoms seriously. This is a great advance. Any other examples?

Gertrude: As most of you know, my husband has been discharged from the service. Before he went in I was quite sick and one of my difficulties was getting his breakfast. I would have a terrible feeling of helplessness when I would make it and I would say I can't do it. I would then get a feeling of tightness in my throat and feel like crying. On these mornings I used to have a feeling of unreality. I would feel alone and things looked changed and distant and I felt I was changing. When my husband was discharged and came home I made up my mind I was going to do my job and he gets up at five-thirty. I anticipated this feeling of helplessness but even so I got up and I just felt fine. I discovered I was just looking for things but they didn't happen. Really I was only anticipating a danger but there wasn't any if I didn't anticipate it.

Annette: I had similar experiences with the feeling of unreality and with anticipating. You know our physician tells us that anticipation is nothing harmful but it must be calm and not fearful. You may anticipate a palpitation. But don't think of it as dangerous. I remember one day I had to take some responsibility about a social function being given by Recovery and I was the social chairman and had to arrange for a picnic grove. I didn't like being on the job but I knew it was good for me. About a day before the picnic was scheduled I became very uneasy. I thought I had to appear at my best at the picnic and what will happen if I get some extremely distressing sensations? I may get this dizzy feeling and a sense of unreality. With me this is a feeling as though I couldn't really feel things. I would handle them and

although I knew I touched them I had the feeling I didn't touch
them. I realized I had a fearful anticipation and knew I was not
supposed to anticipate in fear. But I had difficulty shaking off
that fearful anticipation so I called another member of Recovery. I said I know I shouldn't anticipate danger and maybe I was
merely tense as anybody might be preparing a picnic. This
member then said, "You think you are merely tense but I can tell
by your tone of voice you are quite anxious about that symptom
and the fact it may return." Then she said, "Why, you can
handle that. You have handled it before." Then she told me
how she used to be fearful and she learned not to anticipate
danger. I realized then how the older members of Recovery did
things and I was not experienced yet and didn't know yet how to
handle that anticipating. But with months of practice I soon
learned how to anticipate calmly. What helped me most to
overcome this anticipating was the thought that I was average
and not supposed to do an exceptional job. You know the doctor
always tells you the average people you meet are not critical. If
you make a mistake they will know that people on an average do
make mistakes. They will not condemn you. We must always
keep in mind how we judge other people. If they commit a
blunder we think nothing of it. We do not think they are
imbeciles. We simply notice the fact that somebody made a
mistake and know that people do make mistakes. As the doctor
says, "People are tolerant with others but they may be intolerant
with their own mistakes." We nervous and former mental
patients must learn to become tolerant toward our own mistakes. We must not want to be exceptional. It is time now to
bring the panel to a close.

FEELINGS ARE NOT FACTS

Physician's Comment on a Panel Discussion

As I listened to the panel and heard one patient after another
repeat that sensations are distressing but not dangerous, it occurred to me that nothing could symbolize more beautifully the
close union that exists in Recovery between patient and physician than this fundamental Recovery principle that sensations
are merely distressing but not dangerous. The patient alone
knows how distressing is his sensation; the physician alone
knows how harmless and devoid of danger it is. The patient

knows his feelings, the physician know the diagnosis.

Annette suffered cramps, Margaret had chest pressure and palpitations, Mary, Caroline and Gertrude were stricken with headaches, vomiting, tightness in the throat and feelings of unreality. Each had their own assortment of symptoms, and it would be absurd to assume that Annette felt Margaret's palpitations or Margaret experienced Annette's cramps. You see, sensations and feelings are intensely personal and subjective and are known to him only who happens to experience them. You may say that a feeling is known to the person only who feels it. To the outsider it is unknown unless he is told about it. His knowledge of other people's feelings is hearsay knowledge. With regard to the patient's feelings the physician is an outsider who cannot attain anything but hearsay knowledge of what the sufferer experiences. Without being told he would not know that the patient has palpitations unless he counted the pulse. He could certainly not know how intense, threatening or tormenting they are.

Contrast now this highly personal and subjective quality which we call feeling with its celebrated counterpart—thought. If Margaret had the thought that the sun was shining or spring was in the air she would have no difficulty communicating her idea to Annette. If Annette agreed to and accepted Margaret's idea the two would share it, and there could be no doubt that both knew exactly what they meant by sunshine and spring and air. But suppose the two spoke of cramps. To the one the word may convey the experience of a wild panic, to the other that of a mild twinge. You see the difference: thoughts can be exchanged, accepted or rejected like an objective commodity. Feelings are strictly personal and singular, incapable of being exchanged or shared.

The basic distinction between feelings and thoughts is the physician's dilemma and the patient's calamity. It is the main reason why patient and physician have so much difficulty understanding one another. The physician speaks the language of thought, and the patient replies in the language of feeling. How can they meet? Take, for instance, the matter of sleep and sleeplessness. I know that patients who complain of insomnia get their due share of sleep. But after the patient awakens he feels for certain he has "not slept a wink." My thought about sleeplessness is founded on expert studies and thorough knowledge and can be communicated to any patient. But will he accept it? Will he consent to share it with me? I tell him he

slept, but being fagged out and listless he is told by his feelings
that he has not slept. Will he listen to the language of the
physician or to that of his feelings? You know the answer given
in Recovery. If the patient is inclined to cooperate he will be
guided by the physician's thought. If he is ready to sabotage he
will consult his feelings. Whether he does the one or the other
means all the difference between health and suffering.

Another example of the clash between the patient's feelings
and the physician's thoughts: My thoughts about "nervous
fatigue" and "nervous exhaustion" are known to you. The
patient merely feels fatigued but is not. His "fatigue" is a
psychological feeling and not a physiological condition. Being
discouraged and "having nothing to live for" or to "look forward
to" he arises in the morning with the dreadful anticipation of
one of those drab and depressing days in which he will have to
perform a deadly routine without zest or inspiration. The
monotony and lifelessness of that day stares him in the face.
Being discouraged and "sick and tired of it all" he cannot relax;
his muscles feel heavy and limp. The physician knows it is
discouragement and self-disgust but the feelings of the patient
speak forcibly and persuasively of a real, physiological fatigue.
Who will the patient listen to? To his physician or to his
feelings? The answer is the same as with sleep: the patient is
inclined to accept the verdict of his feelings and to sabotage the
physician's authority.

I want you to know that your feelings are not facts. They
merely pretend to reveal facts. Your feelings deceive you. They
tell you of danger when there is no hazard, of wakefulness when
sleep was adequate, of exhaustion when the body is merely
weary and the mind discouraged. In speaking of your symptoms
your feelings lie to you. If you trust them you are certain to be
betrayed into panics and vicious cycles.

I said that your feelings lie to you, that they deceive and betray
you. How can that be? How can feelings be true or false? If you
are sad what has that to do with truth, deception or treachery?
Feelings are either experienced or they are not. They are
present or absent but never true or false. Thoughts alone possess
the quality of truth and falseness. And if the patient's feelings
tell lies they do so because an incorrect and deceptive thought is
attached to them. The deception is accomplished by the
thought, not by the feeling. The panel members expressed this
relation between thought and feeling with convincing plainness.

One after another they stated that before joining Recovery they *thought* of their panics as dangerous, but now they *think* of them as merely distressing. You see, a panic is a feeling of extreme distress which annexes either the thought of danger or that of harmlessness. The panics experienced by patients are not pure feelings, they are overlaid and modified and taken captive by a thought. If the annexed thought is that of danger a vicious cycle will develop and the panic will be prolonged. If the thought is that of security the panic will be stopped abruptly. It all depends on whether the patient will accept the physician's thought of security or his own thought of danger. If this be so, then, it is no longer a question whether the physician's thought ought to prevail or the patient's feelings. It is no longer the problem of thought versus feeling but of one thought versus the other. The patient is not asked to change his feelings or to discard them or to disavow them. He is merely asked to substitute the physician's thought for his own. You will now understand the meaning of my introductory statement that the Recovery slogan "Sensations are distressing but not dangerous" symbolizes the close union between patient and physician. If it is assumed that the physician approaches the patient with an objective thought and the patient reciprocates with a subjective feeling the two could never meet. Feelings cannot be exchanged or shared. If the patient were nothing but distressed or sad or despondent, the physician's thought could hardly reach him. Communication and mutual understanding would be blocked effectively. But if the feeling experienced by the patient is reduced to a "quarter-feeling" of despair, associated with a "three-quarter-thought" of danger, then, the physician's thought of security can easily meet the patient's thought of danger. It can modify or eliminate it. In Recovery this has been done with singular success. As the panel members quoted themselves: In former years they entertained their own thoughts that the panic was dangerous. Now they accept the physician's thought that it is merely distressing.

10

OBJECTIVITY AS MEANS OF TERMINATING PANICS

A Panel Discussion Conducted by Patients

Annette (panel leader): The subject for today's panel is "The Vicious Cycle of Panic." We all had to deal with panics and may have to deal with them occasionally even after we have improved. I remember the first panic I experienced. Shortly before I went to the hospital I awoke at night with a numbness in my arm. I looked in the mirror and it seemed to me I saw a slight swelling in the side of my nose. Looking on the swelling in the nose I became more painfully aware of the numbness in the arm. Suddenly I was gripped with fear. I rushed into the bedroom where my aunt was sleeping and said, I feel my arms are paralyzed. The moment I said this the numbness seemed to spread all over my face. My aunt offered to call a doctor. That scared me more. I felt as though I couldn't get my breath, as if each breath was the last. While my aunt called the doctor I began to tremble. The numbness disappeared now but the trembling continued. Then the tremor went and the numbness returned. Then the numbness passed and the tremor came back. By that time the doctor arrived and after examining me carefully said he could not find anything wrong. He prescribed a sedative and rest. The next morning I was tired but I dragged myself to go to work. After that I dreaded the thought of numbness. I was always in fear of it. I developed the vicious cycle. If I only thought of the numbness it was there. And each time I thought I was going to die. Then I went to the hospital and came in contact with Recovery and attended the physician's classes. There I learned that sensations are distressing but not dangerous. It took me a long time to understand that fully. I remember once I had a slight numbness and kept repeating, a sensation is not dangerous; it is not dangerous. I repeated that again and again but finally I got sore and decided it didn't help. Then I thought what else can I do? I started out again chanting it isn't dangerous, it isn't dangerous and I did not work myself up to a vicious cycle. One night I awoke with a sensation that I felt in every muscle of my body, something like you feel when the elevator drops slightly. I got tense and weak and felt like waking my husband to ask him for a glass of water. But I remembered my Recovery training and knew that if I gave way to the impulse to awaken him that meant I was helpless and needed help. And that meant that I was on the way to establish a vicious cycle. I knew if I was to control the vicious cycle I must not act on the impulse. It was difficult to restrain myself. So I lay quietly, but then I got mad because there my husband slept peacefully while I was so uncomfortable. I was provoked at the idea that I had to curb my desire to call for help. But I didn't give in. Suddenly I remembered the doctor had told us the best way to calm down is to do something absolutely unemotional, something that has definitely nothing to do with excitement and temper, something that is utterly objective. So I said to myself, "I am going now to view this sensation objectively and without fear. I shall look at my sensation as I would look at an object." I asked, "Where is that sensation? Where do I feel it most? In my arms, or in my stomach or legs? Just exactly what kind of sensation is it? Could I describe it? I had by now become objective, indeed. And then something extraordinary happened. When I set out to look at the sensation and to describe it it was gone the very moment I started to look at it, and I fell asleep. In the morning I felt refreshed and proud of my accomplishment. Has anyone else got an example?

Gertrude: One of my most distressing symptoms when I was sick were palpitations. One night, shortly after I joined Recovery the palpitations were just terrifying. I remembered that all the doctors I had visited had told me my heart was in good condition. Our Recovery phyisician had given me the same assurance. But when I had the palpitations I felt that was my last minute, and I was going to collapse. The more I became alarmed the faster did the heart beat, and the faster it beat the greater was my alarm. I know now I worked myself up into a glorious panic. The palpitations seemed intolerable. I got tremors and my hands perspired. I felt weak and shaky and was positive something dreadful was going to happen. Like Annette, I thought of waking my husband and when I saw him lying there I was tense and irritated because I thought there he is sound asleep and I almost dying from agony. I jumped out of bed and jumped quite heavily hoping the noise would wake him. But he continued to sleep. I slipped back into bed, giving loud sobs and breathing heavily, but he slept on. Finally it occurred to me that that was all sabotage. I remembered the doctor asked us to do nothing about sensations, that they were distressing but not dangerous. So I tried to lie in bed quietly. But then it seemed I did not sleep all night. Now I recalled what the doctor told us about sleep, not to toss and to know that sleep has little to do with health and if you lie in bed for hours you sleep part of these hours even if you feel you haven't slept at all. Finally I fell asleep. On the following nights it got better and better. I felt more secure because gradually I accepted the doctor's authoritative knowledge that sensations are distressing but not dangerous.

Annette: The point is that you kept practicing night after night till it produced results. This continuous practicing is not easy but it can be made easier if you talk to others in Recovery and find they have gone through the same experiences and got their sensations under control. Any other example?

Ada: When I first broke I was terribly afraid I lost my mind. Later when I joined Recovery the doctor assured me it was a case of nerves but I couldn't believe it. One Saturday afternoon I was to come to the panel discussion, and my sister made some remark about my condition and I misinterpreted it as doubting my mentality. I thought they all knew I was mentally ill but they are not going to tell me. The more fearful I got the more tense I was, and the more tense the more fearful. One of my symptoms was vomiting. It had improved but now I vomited again. That scared me more and I called Rosalie. I told her I was positive something was wrong with my mind. But she said, "Did the doctor say so?" I said, "No." Then she said, "That's your own diagnosis, and you know we must not diagnose." That reassured me, and I went to the panel and got more assurance. Several months later I met my mother-in-law and she asked me how I was. I said I felt fine and she said, "One thing I can tell you; that sickness you have doesn't run in my family." At this I developed a temper and it took me some time to check the vicious cycle. A month ago I saw my sister-in-law, the daughter of the mother-in-law, that made that remark about "in our family." She told me she had seen her doctor because she had pains and felt run down and irritable. He told her he couldn't find anything wrong with her and it was a case of nerves. "The idea of that doctor," she said, "To call my condition a case of nerves." It so happened that I saw her mother about the same time. I inquired about her daughter, and she let loose against that doctor who had the crust to say that her daughter was a "case of nerves." "My daughter," she said, "is very sick and has extreme pain and can hardly drag herself to work, and that doctor, mind you, calls that nerves." I remarked that I had a case of nerves and got well and suggested that her daughter come to see my nerve doctor. "That is all right for you," she said, "but not for my daughter." This time I smiled and there was no temper and no panic.

Annette: What Ada wanted to explain is that in the first encounter with her mother-in-law she had a flare of temper which developed a strong immediate effect. To this she added an after-effect that lasted for hours and maybe days because it was aggravated by a vicious cycle. When she met the mother-in-law the second time the temperamental flare was slight, the immediate effect was mild, and the after-effect did not come off. As a consequence the whole flare blew over quickly, and no vicious cycle developed. Ada was able to do that because of her Recovery training. If these terms of the "temperamental flare," "immediate effect" and "after-effect" are not clear to some of our listeners I shall advise you to read volume 3 of the "System of Self-Help." Any other example?

Sophie: I don't know what would have happened to me if Recovery had not come my way. One day an idea got stuck in my brain, the idea of losing my mind. With that I developed a pain in my head, and the stronger the idea became the stronger got the pain, and I worked myself up into a vicious cycle. Finally I landed in the hospital where I got three months of shock treatment. When I came home I had a battle on my hands. I wasn't well at all and still had the pain and the fear of losing my mind, and then I got all kinds of other symptoms. My husband was impatient, and I don't blame him, either. I complained all the time, and of course he couldn't stand it. Then I met Gertie, and she told me about Recovery. But my husband had by this time got sick of it all, and he wouldn't listen. He said he was all through, and he wouldn't let me go to see another doctor. But from what Gertie told me I knew Recovery was my real chance. At first I didn't believe what I hear at the meetings. But when I noticed others getting well I decided to stick to Recovery whether my husband wanted it or not. And now I can truthfully say I never felt better in my life.

Annette: What is your husband's attitude now?

Sophie: He knows I am well, and he rather likes to come to

meetings himself. His family is now won back, too. They used to say there was no hope for me, and for him to put me away somewhere. Now they don't say that anymore.

Annette: Is there any other example?

Ted: It appears that the vicious cycles I get into are relatively mild ones. I have no panics or excessive fears. But to me they appear extremely distressing and they last a long time. I form an idea of danger, that I am helpless and a sissy, that is, that I am a weak fellow that won't show gumption. I think I have been in this sort of mild vicious cycle for many, many years.

Annette: How does it affect you?

Ted: In the presence of other people I have the sensation of fatigue and a heaviness in my muscles like I would rather sit still and in one position for a long time instead of moving and looking around me. Since I have joined Recovery I have learned to reject the idea I am a sissy. I am now a member of a young people's group at church, and before I joined Recovery I couldn't do that.

Annette: It is late now, and we will bring this excellent panel discussion to a close.

OBJECTIVITY AS MEANS FOR TERMINATING PANICS

Physician's Comment on a Panel Discussion

I shall limit myself to discussing the remark about objectivity made by Annette in the latter part of her example when she said she remembered the physician had told her "the best way to calm down is to do something absolutely unemotional, something that has definitely nothing to do with excitement and temper, something that is utterly objective." She then proceeded to look at the sensation as she might look at an object. "I asked," she continued, "where is that sensation? Where do I feel it most? In my arms, or in my stomach or legs? Just exactly what kind of a sensation is it? Could I describe it?" But when she thus transported herself into a mood of objectivity the sensation "was gone the very moment I started to look at it, and I fell asleep." With the simplicity characteristic of Annette she added that when she awoke in the morning she felt proud of her accomplishment.

Annette had indeed reason for feeling proud. What she had accomplished was to demonstrate the fundamental principle of

Recovery that symptoms can be conquered by means of simple and innocent procedures initiated by the patient, i.e., through self-help. The particular principle of self-help mentioned by Annette was formulated several years ago when one day our friend Frank Rochford recounted a simple and innocent experience he had while thinking about and observing his fatigue sensation. Frank's account was approximately as follows: "You tell us we have to have patience. We have to wait patiently till the sensation disappears. Well, the other day I felt fatigued again. I knew I had to wait, so I pulled out my watch to see how long I would have to wait. While I was looking at the watch counting the minutes and seconds I suddenly noticed that I no longer felt this fatigue. Next time I tried that stunt with the watch again but I couldn't count the time because before I could look at the hands of the dial the tired feeling was gone."

Frank conquered an intractable sensation through objectivity, and Annette stopped a blazing panic with the same simple means. And I told you repeatedly that the wildest temper outburst can be checked instantly if you take the objective attitude that you are not the judge as to who is right or wrong. I could extend indefinitely the list of occasions in which disturbances can be disposed of without much ado by adopting an objective view. You have pressure in the head and shudder at the thought of a tumor. Then you substitute my objective diagnosis for your fanciful imaginings, and the pressure is relieved.

What, then, is objectivity? And what is the reason for its magical effect on nervous symptoms? I shall ask you to view this conference table where I am just now delivering my address. I shall describe it as being about one yard and two inches in height, having a brown color, four legs, two drawers, adding a few other items of a similar nature. This mode of description deals with height, color, number of legs and drawers, and I could mention as further descriptive details the position of the table relative to walls and windows, the number of chairs it will accommodate, and the hardness or softness of its wood. If this is all I say then everyone of you could easily verify my statments simply by using a tape measure or by touching and looking at the table, i.e., by the use of your senses. You will now agree that one criterion of objectivity is the possibility of verifying a statement, either by measurement or by sense perception.

Suppose now that while speaking of this conference table I display feeling. I dwell tenderly on the moments of great inspiration which I experience when I behold this eager audience of patients rapturously listening to my remarks. I may go on in the same emotional vein, extolling the singular value of Recovery activities of which this table is a symbol, or the great deeds of human salvation which have been performed right here from this table. If I continue in this exalted style you will realize that what I say has nothing to do with measurements and sense perception. It is an account, flowery and exaggerated, of my personal and *subjective feelings,* not a description, plain and unadorned, of the unemotional and *objective qualities* of the table. My first report (of color, height, distance, hardness and softness) was objective because, employing measurement and sense perception, I steered clear of emotion. My second report was subjective because, eliminating measure and sense, I emphasized feeling. Objectivity, then, means (1) employment of measurement and sense perception, (2) elimination of feeling and emotion.

I have answered my first question which asked: What is objectivity? I shall now try to give the answer to my second question: What is the reason for its magical effect on nervous symptoms? One thing ought to be clear to you by now. If the patient is to be objective he must rid himself of emotion. But why should he do that? What is wrong with having emotions? What is wrong even with having fears, angers, indignations? Eliminate fear and you lose the valuable qualities of caution, foresight and premeditation. Throw out your anger, and you will deprive your personality of its capacity to be aroused to action by personal insults and group crises. Without emotion you are chilly, unresponsive, uninspired and uninspiring. Emotions are values, and I do not think of inveighing against them, except in regard to nervous patients and nervous symptoms. Emotions have their rightful place in the family, in religion, civic life, business and politics. Moreover, emotions are of two kinds. On the one hand, there are love, devotion and affection, enthusiasm and sympathy, the sense of fellowship and the spirit of self-effacement. These are the *emotions of stimulation.* They stimulate the organs of the body into more vigorous breathing, digesting and heart action. They operate to raise and harmonize the functions of the organism. On the other hand, there are fear and consternation, anger and indignation, envy, jealousy and disgust. These are the *emotions of frustration.* They lower the functions of the body and throw them out of equilibrium. The emotions of stimulation create *stimulating tenseness;* the emotions of frustration create *frustrating tenseness.* I do not have to tell you that you cannot go far enough in cultivating stimulating emotions and their attending stimulating tenseness. You cannot go wrong if you do your utmost to dwell on them, to enhance and coddle them to your heart's delight. Should you be "gripped" by any of these stimulating emotions just permit yourself to become warm and responsive, emotional and subjective. But if you are seized, as is the case in panic, with the frustrating emotions of fear, anger and despair, with jealousy and envy, with indignation and disgust then you must bend all your energies to becoming and remaining cool, chilly, unemotional and objective.

Annette demonstrated how this can be done. She was in the throes of a panic and passed through the whole gamut of frustrating emotions. Fear, anger, indignation, self-disgust and despair rocked her body down to every cell and fiber. An overwhelming amount of frustrating tenseness was produced pressing on the nervous system and creating symptoms which caused more fear and therefore more tenseness till the vicious cycle swept her organism to a climax of agony. This vicious cycle was maintained only as long as she allowed herself to be emotional, i.e., subjective. The moment she began to ask the objective questions, "Where is that sensation? Where do I feel it most? Could I describe it?" she changed subjectivity into objectivity, became unemotional and calmed down almost instantly. What she did was essentially to apply measurements and sense observation to processes of inner experience and to eliminate emotionality from the field of bodily functions. The remedy was simple and innocent and represented the most consummate technique of psychiatric self-help.

You remember I meant to say a word or two about the magical effect of objectivity on nervous symptoms. But if I called Annette's performance "simple and innocent" how is it possible to consider it magical? Magic may be innocent, but is it simple? Well, if you conceive of a task as utterly complex and impossible of accomplishment then you will think it miraculous and magical if a simple move "does the trick" of accomplishing it. You see, patients have a way of viewing their panics as uncontrollable, i.e., they consider control of emotionalism as a task "impossible of accomplishment." Annette demonstrated that objectivity wipes out emotionalism. Once she established an objective, unemotional attitude "it was no trick" to quash the panic in an instant. But that emotionalism can be removed instantly once you have become unemotional ought to be considered perfectly natural and not at all magical.

Annette forgot to mention one item that may sound casual but is of great significance. She forgot to state that she practiced the method of objectivity on numerous occasions prior to the panic which she described during the panel discussion. She had frequently tried to be objective but failed. Success came to her after many unsuccessful trials. Credit is due to her not so much for the final triumph but rather for her refusal to be discouraged by so many previous failures. What she did was to practice faithfully and untiringly the method of trial and failure till finally she acquired an amazing skill of handling the method of trial and success. Many of our patients have made an effort to apply the self-help method of objectivity but met with initial failure and gave up. Annette persisted after many failures and finally scored a signal success.

PART II

PANEL DISCUSSIONS WITH ABBREVIATED
QUOTATION OF EXAMPLES OFFERED BY
PATIENTS

1

THE WILL SAYS YES OR NO

Claire, on the Saturday panel, recounted how several weeks ago her husband told her he had to leave town for a number of days. She knew it was a business trip which could not be postponed. Nevertheless, she was thrown into a panic at the prospect of being left alone. She felt a heat wave sweeping over her body, her throat choked, the heart raced and the entire body felt limp. She was tense and dizzy and weak. She said nothing and could hardly have said anything because she was terror stricken. But her husband noticed the disturbed feelings and upbraided her for being selfish and inconsiderate. In the course of the panel discussion she stated that her husband "obviously didn't care how I felt." Later she added that she was able to stop her feelings by applying her Recovery training. She spotted the panic as an instance of temper and self-pity, hence, as sabotage. The spotting produced instant relaxation. "I was surprised," she said, "that I was able to control my feelings as quickly as I did. I think I am learning how to handle my feelings."

Claire became terrified at the thought of her husband leaving town. The terror meant to her that her *feelings* were disturbed. The disturbed *feelings* were noticed by the husband who upbraided her presumably for failing to control her *feelings*. That suggested to Claire that her *feelings* were not properly appreciated. Recovering her composure she was surprised to find that control of *feelings* was easy. In the end she concluded that her Recovery training had served her well in the matter of handling her *feelings*. After listening to this report of an incident in which feelings fairly leaped over one another I must confess that the dexterity with which Claire manipulated feelings is surprising, indeed. And I shall ask: did Claire deal with feelings? Or did she play on something which she merely called by that name?

What happened to Claire was that she suffered a scare. Previous to the scare she was reasonably calm. Being calm her condition was that of relaxation. Her *thoughts* were relaxed.

They were focused on the little household cares of cooking and shopping, or they reviewed the trivial happenings of the preceding day or dwelt on the funny dream she had the night before. There was no stewing over issues, no worry about problems, no conflict of ideas, no confusion of plans. The *feelings* were in the same state of relaxation, and she experienced neither fear nor anger, nor excessive joy nor inmoderate grief. The relaxed thoughts produced a serene spirit, the relaxed feelings gave rise to a mood of comfort. Whenever a person is serene and comfortable his inner organs tend placidly and peacefully to their functions of circulation, respiration, digestion and elimination. Hence, no violent sensations, no choking, air-hunger or nausea. We may say that when Claire was serene and comfortable her *sensations* were just as relaxed as were her thoughts and feelings. With no disturbance rocking the body there was no occasion for the *impulses* to become turbulent and impetuous so that the total of her experience (thoughts, feelings, sensations and impulses) was that of calm, rest and composure. We conclude that prior to being struck with terror Claire's *total experience* was that of security producing a state of relaxation.

I want you to understand what is meant by the word "total experience." Our body has only two ways of experiencing a situation. No matter what is the nature of the situation, it is approached either with a sense of security or one of insecurity. If your attitude happens to be that of security your entire body will partake of that experience. Your thoughts, feelings, sensations and impulses, your inner organs, outer muscles and skin, even your tiniest fibers and most minute particles of tissues will share in the total experience of security which now governs your body. Experiencing security they will all be largely devoid of strain, tenseness, commotion and excitement. Barring certain organic diseases, no human experience is possible, even thinkable, in which thoughts express security and impulses are restless and erratic. Nor is it feasible that at one and the same time feelings should be relaxed and sensations disturbed and muscles taut. The just prevailing sense of security may be mild or exalted; the experience of insecurity may be moderate or severe. But whatever may be its degree or intensity the entire body is affected. It is a total experience.

A total has parts and the total experience has its part experiences. I have mentioned them already. They are thoughts, feelings, sensations, impulses. These are the *dominant parts of the total experience*. If any of them become disturbed the disturbance will spread to the other members of the team. If any of them is pacified the entire team will regain calm and peace and the disturbance will be stopped. This calming and stopping of disturbances is what is generally referred to as "control" (of disturbances). You will now understand that if you wish to control the total experience of insecurity you must use a method which will control, that is, stop and calm any one of the dominant parts of that experience. Control one dominant part, for instance, the confused thoughts, and the rest of the team (feelings, sensations and impulses) will follow suit. The dominant part which Claire chose for control was her feeling of terror and despair. She claims that after this feeling was calmed and stopped the sensations, thoughts and impulses quieted down and she relaxed. But I shall ask: how can feelings be stopped, calmed or controlled? Which method did Claire use for controlling them? Feelings are spontaneous; they rise and fall and run their course, and no deliberate effort will ever put a halt to their spontaneous progression. Obviously, Claire did not control her feelings but some other dominant part of her total experience of insecurity.

That feelings and sensations cannot be stopped, calmed or controlled by deliberate effort ought to be familiar to you because I have emphasized the fact on numerous occasions. I told you repeatedly that thoughts and impulses alone are subject to control. Evidently, when Claire "applied her Recovery training" she applied it to her thoughts and impulses, not to her feelings or sensations. I shall repeat: two inner experiences only are subject to control: thoughts and impulses. I shall add that one factor only is capable of controlling them: the Will. The inference is that when Claire put a check to her total experience of insecurity the feat was accomplished through the intervention of her Will. It was her Will which exercised control over her thoughts, perhaps also over her impulses, perhaps over both. Emphatically, it did not and could not control feelings and sensations.

You remember I mentioned frequently that the Will has one function only: it rejects or accepts ideas and stops or releases impulses. In either case, it says either "yes" or "no" to the idea or the impulse. Suppose an idea lodges itself in the brain suggesting danger. It is then for the Will to judge and decide whether or not danger exists. If the will accepts (says "yes" to) the idea of danger, then, the thought of danger will mobilize feelings of insecurity and will release in their wake rebellious sensations and vehement impulses. The total experience will then be that of insecurity. Conversely, if the Will decrees that no danger threatens the thought of insecurity will be discounted and feelings, sensations and impulses will retain their customary equilibrium. You will understand now that ideas rising in the mind offer suggestions to which the Will replies with "yes" or "no." This has been called the denying and affirming function of the Will. The same function may be exercised by the Will in response to impulses releasing them with a "yes" and restraining them with a "no." How is it that this process of denying and affirming can be used for thoughts and impulses only and not for feelings and sensations? You will grasp that readily if you will consider what precisely the words "yes" and "no" mean when employed in connection with an inner experience. When the Will disposes of the thought of danger by rendering the verdict "no" the denial can be expressed as saying, "No, there is no truth to this suggestion of danger. Perhaps, there is not even a probability or possibility of it." Similarly, when an impulse presses for action and the Will interposes its veto it says in essence,"No, this impulse is undesirable, and its action will prove unwise and harmful." No such ratings in terms of truth and falseness, desirability and harmfulness, wisdom or folly are possible in the instance of feelings and sensations. If a person is seized with grief or stimulated by joy it would be senseless for the Will to claim that the joy is false or the grief impossible. Feelings are either experienced or not experienced. Their existence, wisdom and probability cannot be denied or affirmed. The same holds for sensations. If the head aches it would be absurd for the Will to object that, "No, this is no headache. It is unwise, untrue or improbable." Clearly, if the Will is to intervene in order to control the total experience of insecurity its "no" cannot be directed to feelings and sensations. Instead, it must address itself to thoughts and impulses.

We can now sum up our analysis of Claire's reaction. When her husband announced his planned trip the idea of danger leaped into Claire's brain. The thought of danger mobilized feelings of insecurity, threw sensations into violent uproar and released a host of turbulent impulses (to cry out in despair or shout in anger, to argue, protest, run). When this happened Claire's Will was inactive and the thought of insecurity was accepted. The result was that the body was thrown into the total experience of insecurity. Suddenly she remembered her Recovery training and presumably recalled the Recovery motto that sensations are distressing but not dangerous. Now the thought of "no danger" dominated her brain and she decided to ignore or deny the existence of danger. Her Will had been alerted and said "no." The "no" calmed her thought processes and the calm communicated itself to sensations, feelings and impulses. The total experience was now one of security. When Claire noticed that her body had relaxed so miraculously she felt the need for explaining the miracle and in doing so she employed the clumsy and incorrect language of the man in the street. According to this language feelings are subject to control. Had she used the Recovery language she would have surmised that her total experience of insecurity had been remedied by the intervention of the Will which said "no" to the idea of danger with the result that one dominant part of the experience was brought under control and spread the effect to the other parts. Claire had done the right thing but, trying to explain it, called it by the wrong name.

2

WILL, BELIEFS AND MUSCLES

The Saturday panel discussed the subject of "Real Sensations and Fantastic Interpretations." Phil, as one of the discussants, mentioned how in previous days when he was not yet "sold on Recovery" his pressures, dizzy spells and confusions made him neglect his work till finally hospitalization was the only way out of trouble. "These symptoms," he said, "have not disappeared altogether. They still bother me every once in a while. But now when I have them I remember what Dr. Low has told us frequently: 'You can throw off any nervous symptom at any time for a few seconds or minutes if you spot them as distressing but not dangerous. The symptom will come back in the next minute or so. But you can get rid of it again for a short while, and then again and again and before long you will be rid of the trouble for hours or for days. The symptom will return and keep returning but in the end you will bring it under control by plugging away at it.' " Phil then continued, "That was hard for me to believe. It just didn't seem to make sense that an awful head pressure would disappear if I made an effort to spot it. But I can tell you that when I have these symptoms now all I have to do is to practice Dr. Low's rule and before long they are gone."

When Phil set out to practice my rule why was it hard for him to believe it would work? Why did he feel it made no sense? Nervous symptoms are the result of tenseness and if you "spot them as distressing but not dangerous" you dismiss the idea of danger; and without the thought of danger in your brain you feel safe; and if you feel safe you relax; and if you relax you lose your tenseness; and with tenseness gone the symptom disappears. What can be more simple, what more easy to believe and more thoroughly in accord with sense? And if this is so, why did my rule appear senseless and unbelievable to Phil?

Clearly, Phil thought of nervous symptoms as afflictions which require complex and elaborate means for conquering them. He obviously shared the current view that in order to deal effectively with a nervous complaint the patient must be subjected to a searching investigation for the purpose of unravelling hidden mysteries of thought and tracking down the crafty maneuvers of mischief brewing emotions. If this were true my rule would be naive, unsophisticated, unbelievable and decidedly unsuited to the purpose. But it may be that what is really naive and unbelievable is the modern trend to view thought as mysterious and emotion as mischievous. And I shall advise you to reject this contemporary superstition that your thoughts are forever scheming against your welfare and your feelings continually plotting against your health. I shall grant that in our present-day setting leadership is lacking and confusion rampant. And with the amount of confusion governing this world of ours it is easy to get thoughts muddled and feelings confounded. But Recovery refuses to be modern, and the leadership which it supplies aims precisely at teaching you how to conquer confused ideas and perturbed emotions through simplicity of thinking and humility of feeling.

I instructed Phil to stop thinking of danger and to command his muscles to relax. His head pressure suggested to him that he was losing his mind. I told him he will not lose it. Two ideas were presented to him. Of these he chose one. There was nothing to prevent him from choosing the other. Get it into your heads that a human being has the power to choose what to believe and what not to believe. This power to choose is called the Will. The main beliefs between which the Will must choose are that in a given condition you are either secure or insecure. If you accept the thought that your head pressure is the result of a brain tumor you have formed the belief of insecurity. If instead you choose to think of a mere nervous headache you have rejected the belief of insecurity and put in its place that of security. Why did Phil think he was unable to swap thoughts? He had been swapping them all his life. For upward of thirty years he had practiced the game of accepting ideas, rejecting them, exchanging the one for another, dropping them and picking them up just as he wished, wanted and chose. The swap was usually effected with facility and rapidity; sometimes it required hard work and long pull. But whether easy or difficult the wanting was practiced and the choice made. What made Phil believe that all of a sudden he had lost the capacity for wanting and choosing? And as to commanding your muscles to do your bidding? This is done every second of your daily activity. You want to sit down and do it. You wish to stand and rise from your seat. You decide to make a trip, to enter business, to marry, to save a life or sacrifice your own and you carry out your decision either instantly or after hesitation and deliberation. Nothing is needed for the successful execution of these acts and plans but Will and choice. And thoughts and muscles are made to obey the dictates of Will and choice. Why did Phil assume he could not choose "at will" to direct his thoughts and to command his muscles?

Beliefs are frequently stubborn and obstinate. They may become fixed offering resistance to the summons of the Will. This is particularly the case if the belief has persisted for years. You know how difficult it is for me to shake your beliefs that you are doomed, that your heart will give out, that your fatigue will lead to exhaustion. Muscles are just as likely to develop obstinacy. They tend to acquire set patterns of behavior preferring certain well grooved acts and avoiding others. Just think of the habits of procrastination, of twitches and spasms, of restlessness and sluggishness, and you will realize that muscles are not always pliant tools in the hands of the Will. In order to pry loose the resisting beliefs and rebellious muscles attempt after attempt must be made to dislodge them from their comfortable berth and to force them to give up resistance. The resistance may be so strong that the attempts to break it must be repeated in innumerable trials before success is achieved. This requires the Will to use a great deal of power in continued strenuous practice. Hence, the terms "will power" and "will practice." By exercising its power the Will masters its task and learns how to rearrange beliefs and redirect muscles. Having gone through the *learning process* the Will gains experience and becomes an *expert Will*.

In our days of modern progress this learning process with its inherent will practice has been largely abandoned. Children are seldom taught to exercise will power for the mastery of reading and writing. Things are made easy for them. The schools supply all manner of "aids" to help them avoid exertion. The same holds true for work done in the fields of commerce and industry. A person entrusted with a commercial or industrial job is not likely to be subjected to the grinding procedure (learning process) of apprenticeship. Instead, he is "broken in" by the expedient of accelerated courses in which a number of manipulations are demonstrated to him. This method of giving hurried demonstrations (to the senses) and facile explanations (to the intellect) instead of thorough training (to the Will) has permeated most spheres of our daily existence. A few flimsy explanatory phrases and the housewife "learns" how to use a machine for sewing, cooking, washing, cleaning. A few perfunctory demonstrations "teach" the buyer of an automobile how to run it. In all of this, modern men and women imbibe the lasting impression that technique has eliminated the necessity for learning, patient application and practice of will. Most devastating to the learning process and to the exercise of will power has been the contemporary trend to spoonfeed information. In radio forums, newspaper columns, popular magazines and sundry other vehicles of public "education" brief discussions are offered by obscure persons of doubtful authority in which weighty issues are hurriedly "explored" and speedily solved by versatile analysts, columnists and essayists. The learning process is scrapped and replaced by a growing habit of passive listening and easy acceptance.

Without the benefit of a Will trained to choose beliefs and direct muscles the men and women of our generation have lost faith in the correctness of their decisions and the relevancy of their plans. They drift along in the shifting currents of a rushing existence with little knowledge of how to approach issues or tackle problems. Having neglected or evaded the discipline of the learning process they lack the "know-how" of pursuing tasks, of aiming at goals and accomplishing purposes. Faced with difficult situations they feel helpless. As a result, the modern tendency has been to shy away from responsible pursuits and to entrust their proper execution to "experts." These go by the name of "specialists" who are supposed to possess the requisite "know-how" for solving problems. The specialist is expected to formulate plans for the rearing of children, to make decisions for marriage and divorce, to determine the degree of vocational fitness, to advise in matters of dieting, budgeting, housekeeping, love making, reading selections and what not. With the spread of specialism, self-help and self-management have ceased to play a significant part in the present-day domestic, marital and social scene. The habit of rushing to the expert for advice has resulted in a vicious cycle of helplessness: the more the expert's aid is solicited the more helpless is the applicant bound to feel; the greater the helplessness the more urgent the need for further consultations; the more frequent the consultations the more poignant the sense of helplessness. In the end, an individual emerges who has a stunted Will, a meager "know-how", and a famished sense of resourcefulness, in short, Modern Man, the pathetic creature of an extraneous Will, without plans or directions of his own and in abject dependence on forces outside his inner self.

I am not a reformer and have no intention to crusade against the modern mania for undisciplined "self-expression" in a life of senseless speed and meaningless change. My duty is to treat patients, not to cure the ills of the age. But my patients are unfortunately exposed to the detrimental influence of the spirit of the age. That spirit is inimical to the process of learning, to patient striving and persistent willing. If I am to teach my patients to dismiss their settled beliefs of insecurity; if I am to direct them to give orders to their muscles and have them properly executed; if I am to train them to practice self-help and not to depend on the questionable expertness of outsiders; if I am to accomplish all of this I must first divest their minds of the modern fallacy that being shown a method means learning it, that witnessing the demonstration of a skill means acquiring it. With machines this may be feasible; with life tasks it is impossible. My patients will have to realize what former generations always knew: that a life task can be mastered only through a gruelling, exacting learning process in which all the resources of the Will must combine to achieve final fulfillment. Health is a task of this kind. It can be secured only if the patient's Will initiates a system of ceaseless trials and trials and trials until in the end the task is accomplished. If this is done even the most stubborn belief will yield to the influence of the learning process, and the most sluggish muscle will obey the dictates of the Will.

3

THE WILL TO BEAR DISCOMFORT

In a recent panel discussion Phil stated: "All my life I have had difficulty with my handwriting. When I had to write anything or sign a paper I became tense and the strain made it impossible for me to write clearly. I always thought I just couldn't help it. I get nervous and can't write, that's all.....In Recovery I have learned that everybody can command his muscles to move. And now when my hand tenses up while I am writing I know I can make the muscles of my hand to move calmly instead of racing ahead with the scribbling and then the tenseness will pass...."

Phil, in his pre-Recovery days, had the conviction he could not write and the certainty he could not help it. His credo was "I can't do it, that's all." After joining Recovery he discovered that convictions and certainties can be discarded and credos can be changed. When he changed his belief and dropped his conviction which method did he employ?

Phil's fingers were never paralyzed. Hence, he was able to write. But for some reason he developed a sense of embarrassment and self-consciousness about the act of writing. The self-consciousness produced tenseness which caused the fingers to go into a mild spasm whenever they were made to wield the pen. The spasm may have given rise to some sort of a cramping sensation. That created discomfort. In order to avoid discomfort he avoided writing. He feared to write because he dreaded the discomfort it entailed. But the more he feared it the more annoying grew the discomfort; the greater the discomfort the more intense the fear. In the end, the vicious cycle, relentlessly fanning both fear and discomfort into extremes of agonies, made Phil believe that smooth, effective and painless writing was impossible.

What seemed impossible to Phil was not the act of writing but rather the necessity to face, tolerate and endure the discomfort connected with it. This is an important conclusion because it describes the pattern which applies to *every* nervous fear. Some of my patients go to bed with the fear of not sleeping. They think they fear sleeplessness because it ruins health. But what actually frightens them is the torture, that is, the discomfort of lying awake in the dreadful stillness of the night. Or, a patient becomes panicky on entering a street car. He thinks his fear is that of threatening collapse. But what actually scares him is the prospect of being tormented during the ride by palpitations, choking sensations, dizziness and sweats. Again, it is the anticipation of discomfort and nothing else that causes the apprehension. I could easily quote hundreds of situations in which nervous patients are convinced that what they fear are certain acts or certain occurrences while, in point of fact, the only fear they experience is that of a discomfort which they conceive of as "unendurable" or "intolerable" or "unbearable." To put it bluntly: nervous fear is the fear of discomfort.

Phil disposed of his fear of writing by commanding the muscles to carry out the requisite movements. In Recovery, he said, he learned that everybody can do that. But a command is not a method. I shall ask: How did Phil learn to make his muscles obey his command? Long before he knew of Recovery, long before Recovery existed he had issued commands to his muscles to write but they balked. On a thousand occasions he had made his fingers pick up the pen and run it across the paper but the order miscarried. The fingers shook and the pen tottered. The product of his painful effort was an illegible scribble, not a clear script. Why did his muscles defy his command in pre-Recovery days and heeded it promptly after he passed through Recovery training? Which is the Recovery method of making muscles obey directions?

In his pre-Recovery days Phil issued orders to his muscles to perform the act of writing. Had he done nothing else there can be no doubt that the writing would have been accomplished. But while giving directions to his fingers his mind was obsessed with the thought that writing was an "unendurable" torture and that he could not go through with the task. Your muscles will not move, of course, if you suggest to them the fear that the movement will lead to disaster. The very thought of disaster ("unendurable" torture) will block motion. Fear even if mild makes muscles tremble and the trepidation thwarts proper execution. If you want your muscles to carry out your commands you must not scare them into anxiety and hesitation. To strike the muscles with fear and then to ask them to act with precision is absurd. My patients are guilty of this absurdity. Gripped with a grotesque fear of discomfort they first tell the muscles that the contemplated action is impossible or fraught with danger and then command them to act. The muscles, with a better logic, release a tremor and bungle the job. Whenever that happened to Phil in his pre-Recovery days he felt hopeless and concluded "I cannot write. That's all." But that is not all by any means. The "I cannot" ought to read more correctly "I care not." Phil could write very well but did not care to bear the discomfort of a painful and difficult writing with fingers scared into fumbling and trembling. In Recovery he was trained to face, tolerate and endure discomfort and once he learned to be uncomfortable without wincing he gained confidence and passed on to his muscles the assurance that writing was possible though uncomfortable. The muscles, then, swung into action without tremor or delay. The method which was here at work was plainly and simply THE WILL TO BEAR DISCOMFORT. It is the only and authentic Recovery method of making recalcitrant muscles obey directions.

If the nervous patient is to rid himself of his disturbing symptoms he will have to cultivate the Will to bear discomfort. Time was when bearing discomfort was considered part of life, a part accepted by everybody and practiced everywhere. Children were reared with an eye to making them stand up under hardship. Heavy labor, sustained exertion, privations and drudgery were regarded as incidental to the sweat and toil of daily existence and were borne with patience, resignation and humility. But in our days comfort is hailed as something in the nature of a supreme achievement. It is cherished, worshiped, idolized. When we catalogue the accomplishments of our age the first item we are likely to point to with mounting pride is the fact that our modern technique has eliminated drudgery from the daily routine. We boast self-complacently of the labor saving devices which a busy industry rolls off its assembly lines in bewildering profusion. The housewife is daily assailed by the advertiser's exhortations to escape the "backbreaking" drudgery of homework. Billboards flatter you that "electricity is your servant." Your kitchen and bathroom are choked with gadgets meant to do away with the discomfort of effort and exertion. Educators rack their weary brains to ease the "uncomfortable" task of acquiring school knowledge. Mothers and fathers have learned to shun the discomfort of staying home with their babies. Youngsters resenting the discomfort of rules and conventions are in feverish haste to cast off age-old restraints. I shall ignore the fact that automobiles have abolished the effort of walking, that typewriters have disposed of the inconvenience of writing and that an elaborate push-button system prevents us effectively from working off our unspent energies on household chores and office jobs. All of this may be rated as an unavoidable development, perhaps even desirable in a limited sense. What is more important is that this process of removing effort and creating mechanical comforts is being acclaimed as a value and cultural achievement. We take a childish pride in our "modern progress," extol with boyish conceit our "high standard of living." We class as "backward" and "unprogressive" countries which lack the mechanical comforts which we enjoy. In all of this, the cult of comfort is recommended as the royal road to superior culture. The pursuit of comfort is glorified and the facing of discomfort discouraged. In this modern scheme of life the Will to bear discomfort has no place. If comfort is raised to the level of a value or ideal discomfort is necessarily looked upon as something not to be tolerated and endured, as something that is definitely not part of life, certainly no necessary part of our "modern life."

I do not wish to convey the impression that I am opposed to the use of such mechanical conveniences as refrigeration, electricity and gasoline. If anyone wishes to introduce these or kindred comforts into home or shop he has my blessing. But he will have to know that this type of legitimate comfort is merely useful and not at all valuable. In those departments of life which are governed by valuations the cult of comfort is decidedly misplaced. If you want to maintain the values of health and self-respect, of initiative and determination, of character and self-discipline, what you will have to learn is to bear the discomfort of controlling your impulses, of steeling your Will, of curbing your temper. This calls for an attitude which far from exalting the virtues of comfort places the emphasis where it belongs: on THE WILL TO BEAR DISCOMFORT. When Phil embraced the Recovery doctrine that discomfort, even in our "advanced" days, is a thing to be patiently borne, bravely faced and humbly tolerated he discovered forthwith that his "I cannot" write was nothing but an "I care not" to be uncomfortable. He then revised his distorted valuations, braced himself against that part of life which means discomfort and realized to his amazement that with the emphasis properly shifted things were done more efficiently and life was quite comfortable again.

4

REALISTIC AND ROMANTIC AMBITION

Frances, on the Saturday afternoon panel, reported that when her sister got married not so long ago she was asked to help with the arrangements for the wedding. "I knew that I have a strong desire to run things. So I decided I was going to check that desire because I didn't want to get tense and develop symptoms. But things went wrong at the reception and I got tense anyhow. I felt I had to take a hand and began to run around and gave orders and told everybody what to do. Right then I felt my temples got tightened and my neck was painful. Suddenly I remembered what Dr. Low told us about spotting a reaction and stopping it before it has a chance to produce a vicious cycle. I then spotted my restlessness and sat down and kept sitting. The tightness and pain disappeared in no time. In former days I would have rushed around the hall all afternoon and evening and would have tried to direct everybody and get things done, and I would have believed that all the responsibilities were on me and I would have gotten nowhere except into more tenseness and more symptoms. In the end I would have been exhausted and coming home would have thrown a honey of a tantrum."

What Frances described may be called restlessness or aggressiveness, or a meddlesome disposition, or a tendency to be domineering. But what precisely drove Frances to display her rush of energy and her burst of activity? Was it a chaotic volley of impulses? Or was it rather a well ordered though by no means balanced philosophy? Let me tell you that it was a philosophy, wild, stormy and untamed, but aiming at what philosophies generally aim: to guide conduct and—misconduct.

I told you repeatedly about philosophies (of life) and having studied my writings you ought to be well acquainted with the three philosophies which I distinguish: Realism, Intellectualism, Romanticism. When Frances permitted herself to flit through the reception hall, skipping from guest to guest, pestering the one with unsolicited advice, the other with an uncalled-for direction, messing up things and getting nothing done she answered clearly to my description of the romantic busybody. This type of an eternally rushing and pushing personality, the lively and energetic and mercurial "go-getter," is the ever-present and unavoidable "live-wire" at gatherings, meetings, club functions and receptions, and the power which drives this self-exhausting volcano is called ambition. Why was Francis ambitious to push people, to advise and direct them, to pester and impose on them?

Ambition, well conceived and sensibly pursued, is the breath and spark of life. Mothers are ambitious to train their children "properly." And businessmen are moved by the ambition to take "adequate" care of sales and purchases, of customers and employes. And physicians ought to be guided by the ambition to render the "right" kind of service to their patients. And a hostess' ambition should be to provide "suitable" entertainment for her guests. You see here that ambition means the determination to do what is "proper" and "adequate" and "right" and "suitable" with reference to the job in hand. The job is the goal which you have set for yourself, and unless you are determined to "go about" it with ambition you may not employ the proper, adequate, right and suitable means toward achieving it. Which was the goal Frances set for herself? Did she "go about" it with the proper, adequate, right and suitable means? I may here mention parenthetically that the word ambition is derived from the Latin verb "ambio" which means to "go about" a job, a task, a plan.

I quoted the ambitions of the mother, the businessman, the doctor and the socially active woman. Ambitions of this kind aim at long-range goals, lasting a lifetime or a goodly portion of it. While pursuing his long-range endeavor, a person is bound to strike against obstacles, resistance, ill-will, frustration. It takes strength, perseverance and courage to face and fight these difficulties. On many occasions, the individual faced with a forbidding obstruction to his effort, will become discouraged. Then he needs ambition to bear the strain and continue the march toward his goal. Take the case of the mother. If the children are unruly or ailing or somehow deficient; or, if the mother happens to be self-conscious and timid, doubtful of her capacities or fearful of her responsibilities, then, she may develop a sense of frustration, confusion and discouragement. But discouraged or not, the maternal task must go on. No matter how threatening the obstacle or how severe the strain the mother must continue "going about" her job. For this she needs ambition, the ambition to give the "right," "proper" and "adequate" care to the children and "to do right" by husband and home. You will now understand that ambition is needed for long-range goals. On the other hand, short-range goals, usually of a simple nature and extending over a brief period of time, can hardly ever strain the energies and persistence of a person because they require very little of them. Moreover, short-range goals, as a rule, are of little importance, and if in reaching out for them, your perseverance gives out, no great harm is done. Nothing of significance is involved in the goal of taking a swim, or going to a show, or visiting a friend. And if for some reason you wish to forego or postpone the activity you may do so without any serious consequence. But mothers cannot forego or postpone the task of caring for the children. Nor can physicians or businessmen afford to drop or neglect their business or profession. And even the hostess is not permitted to deal lightly with her social engagements because her club meetings and dinner parties, although in themselves short-range, are woven into the long-range fabric of sociability, reputation and prestige. Summing up: ambition is indispensable for long-range goals, especially if they are important. For short-range goals, an unambitious, carefree attitude will be sufficient and perfectly "right and proper."

Frances, entrusted with a relatively unimportant, short-range task, went at it with an ambition which would have graced any responsible, long-range endeavor. For some reason, presumably irrelevant, she felt that "things went wrong," that she "had to take a hand," and that "all the responsibilities" were on her. This is exactly the philosophy of petty romanticism. The romantic person is intoxicated with his own importance. His feelings, experiences and observations appear to him to be singular, exquisite, interesting; hence, he feels important. Being important, he knows how to do things. He knows what is "proper" and "right" and "adequate." He knows, but the others do not. These others are not important. They do not know how to do things "right." When they try, things tend to "go wrong." When this happens the romantic soul feels impelled and obliged to "take matters in hand," to show people how things are done, to direct them, advise them, push them around.

After Frances had done her quota of directing, advising and pushing, her temples tightened, her neck pained and her muscles tensed. We may be certain that it was not her ambition to accomplish such disastrous results. What kind of results did she expect? What precisely was the object of her ambitious meddling? In order to answer this question intelligently we shall have to realize that ambitions are of two kinds: the one aims at gratifying *personal inclinations;* the other tends to discharge *social obligations.* We shall call them the personal and social ambitions, respectively. Either of them carries its own reward. If you manage to give free rein to your inclinations; if you impose your will on people; if you are successful in pushing them around, directing and advising them; if they meekly submit to your "leadership," you feel vital and dynamic. This gives you a feeling of glamor and grandeur, a sense of power and importance. Nothing more delightful can happen to a romantic soul. Every particle of it craves the thrill of glamor and power. The misfortune is that men and women seldom relish the privilege of being pushed around. They react strongly, resent the intrusion and rebuff the intruder. If this takes place, the illusion of glamor bursts and the sense of power collapses and all that remains is weariness, defeat and humiliation; and if the romantic person, thus deflated, chances to be a nervous patient the final outcome of the romantic adventure is likely to be a storm of symptoms; tightenings and tensings and spasms and pains. This was the reward which came to Frances when she launched out into a reckless spree of what we may now call *romantic ambition.* She exercised glamor and power and reaped humiliation and defeat as reward. The romantic ambition, proceeding from unrestrained personal inclinations, landed her in frustration and agony.

Compare now Frances' romantic ambition with the ambition displayed by the mother anxious to tend her children. This mother feels important because her objective and realistic task is important. She may feel grandeur and glory but only because she conceives of her realistic and objective goal as grand and glorious. You see the difference. In Frances' mind her own person figured as the center of importance, and her own personal qualities appeared to be reflecting glamor and grandeur. The mother derives whatever reward she expects from a realistic accomplishment in a group, in the group of her family. Hers is a *realistic ambition* founded on the proper discharge of social obligations. In contrast, Frances' ambition was romantic instead of realistic and was based on personal inclination instead of social obligation.

In point of distorted views Frances is not alone among my patients. They all are romanticists (or romanto-intellectualists) with romantic ambitions and romantic, unrealistic goals. If there is any realistic pursuit it is health. It is long-range and calls for the exercise of extreme patience and relentless perseverance. But my patients treat health as a short-range goal, demanding instant relief and quick cures. Their sense of importance impels them to crave a ludicrous amount of attention. Their suffering, instead of being borne silently, is continually broadcast as "exceptional" agony. They do not ask for help as humble persons would but demand it as is the right and privilege of important personages. They feel singular and are convinced that theirs is "the only case" of its kind. They think of their frustrations and conflicts as "interesting" and expect to have a prodigious amount of exploring, probing and analyzing wasted on them. Their impulses impress them as so powerful that they consider them "uncontrollable." With all of this, they enter a claim of being "different" from the general run of sufferers. If their claim is not acknowledged they prove the uncontrollability by throwing what Frances calls a "honey of a tantrum." They pamper their feelings, coddle their thoughts, which points to the conviction that their experiences are different, singular, powerful, exceptional, interesting, that is, romantic. After going through training in Recovery, they gradually learn to do what Frances did. They spot and stop their romantic inclinations and engage in a course of action which has due regard for social obligations. After they have learned the techniques of spotting and stopping they acquire a philosophy of life which values realistic goals and scorns romantic ambitions. Frances travelled this road from unrestrained romanticism to disciplined realism with the result that her ambitions are now centered around home and children and husband instead of on chimerical efforts to hunt for glamor, power and self-importance. Her reward is a peaceful life, with health and happiness compensating copiously for the lost illusion of glamor and the self-deception of importance.

5

INTELLECTUAL VALIDITY
AND ROMANTIC VITALITY

Mona, on the Saturday panel, reported that some time ago
before she even knew the name of Recovery she waited her
turn to purchase meat. When the butcher called "next" a
woman answered who had entered after Mona. "I got red in
the face, my heart raced, my throat tightened and I turned to
the woman and told her I was first. She mentioned something about people sleeping which made me mad and spoke
to the butcher in a foreign language which made me more
mad yet. I got so confused that when the butcher called my
name next I could not think what I had come for and bought
a piece of meat that I really didn't want just to get out of the
store quickly. All that afternoon I couldn't forget what
nerve that woman had and how yellow I was. . . . I worked
myself up and became so tense and irritable that when my
little daughter asked a question I pushed her back in anger.
That made me feel more sore at that woman because she had
made me abuse my child. For hours I talked about that
awful woman and told the story to everybody who would
listen . . . ." Mona then added that since she joined
Recovery she has had similar experiences, but she spotted
both symptoms and temper immediately and when she felt
like telling the story to "everybody who would listen" she
commanded her speech muscles not to move.

What Mona described could easily furnish the material for a
big volume. The story it would tell is that of temper producing
symptoms and disturbing adjustment. This would be nothing
new to you. However, two brief chapters of that hypothetical
volume would bear quoting. The one might carry the heading,
"She was wrong." This would be an intellectual judgment. The
other could be fittingly worded, "I was yellow" and would
constitute a romantic declamation. Which adds up to the conclusion that Mona, our dear, plain thinking and soft speaking
Mona, was addicted, in her pre-Recovery days, to the type of
thought which we call intellectual and the type of feeling which
we call romantic. Like Mona, all our patients have been

intellectualist and romanticist prior to their Recovery training and have adopted a realistic philosophy only after they joined our group.

I told you repeatedly that the judgment "He is wrong" cannot be passed except by a duly appointed judge. And in social or domestic "differences of opinion" there is no judge to decide whose opinion is right and whose wrong. But I see already how your eyes flash and your speech muscles twitch to protest emphatically that the woman who edged ahead of Mona was "clearly in the wrong." Does it require a judge to brand that woman's behavior as outrageous and impossible and unquestionably offensive? That woman used unfair means to secure an advantage over a neighbor; she employed aggressive tactics, was pushy, reckless, rudely inconsiderate. How can anybody deny that Mona was right and that woman wrong? Well, I offer the denial and will presently produce the reasons.

At the time of the incident Mona was in the throes of a depression which had lasted close to five consecutive years. She was self-conscious, preoccupied, hardly able to think of anything but her physical torture and mental anguish. Many of you who have gone through a depression know that in a condition of this kind everything is done with the utmost effort. The simplest acts of walking, speaking, thinking, are executed with the greatest difficulty. Finally, even listening to plain conversations and trying to understand what people say becomes a fatiguing exertion. At this stage the patient ceases concentrating on what he hears or sees and is continually preoccupied with his worries and anxieties, his helplessness and seeming hopelessness. With concentration gone he does not attend to the business in hand. His thoughts wander, his alertness suffers. When his name is called he may not hear it. His turn for an assigned task is at hand but he has all but forgotten the purpose of his waiting. That's what happened to Mona in the butcher shop. Preoccupied and with her attention wandering she missed her turn and stood woolgathering. Perhaps "that woman" paused to see whether somebody would step forward and when nobody stirred concluded that she was next in line and quite properly placed her order with the butcher. The order might have been given in a vigorous, sonorous voice which aroused Mona from her preoccupation. When now Mona contended for her "rightful" turn and insisted that she was "wrongfully" passed by, the remark made by "that woman" about people sleeping was rather discourteous, but was it "wrong?"

Mona knew that she tended to be preoccupied, inattentive, dreaming. In the preceding five years she had amassed a prodigious record of tasks neglected, things forgotten, remarks not heard. She knew her defect of not hearing, seeing and recalling properly. When at the butcher's she missed her cue her first thought should have been that something went "wrong" because of her nervous condition; that her attention had wandered again as it had on so many previous occasions. Instead, she jumped to the conclusion it was "that woman" who caused her to lose her "rightful" place. You see, even in this "clear-cut" case there are two sides to the story, and it would take a very wise judge to decide which was the right and which the wrong side. Mona looked at her own side of the story only. The part of the story which could have been told by "that woman" was thoroughly neglected. It is the distinctive mark of the so-called intellectual to emphasize or over-emphasize one side of an issue only, usually his own side, and to look away from the other side. Much of what I have told you in the past ten years about temper can be safely condensed in the one concise formulation: temper is, among other things, the result of an intellectual blindness to the "other side of the story."

When Mona exclaimed, "How yellow I was," she stepped from the sphere of intellectualism into the realm of romanticism. I do not know precisely how the colloquial expression "yellow" came to acquire the meaning of cowardly, low-spirited and faint-hearted behavior. But somehow it must have derived from the idea that a "he-man's" blood must be red and not yellow, or that a man must be able to get "red in the face" or "see red" in order to lick the fellow who dares step on his toes. This romantic view assumes that excitement is the spice of life, that if you want your daily existence to be interesting and stimulating you will have to assert yourself and draw first and strike fast. You must show red blood and not a green yellowish bile. Be that as it may, you will realize that temper is born from the intellectual theory that you are the judge to decide who is right, and from the romantic conviction that a person is not worth his salt if he shirks a fight. If you object that a woman of Mona's type, endowed with a disarming sweetness of manner, could hardly be charged with intellectual rudeness and romantic combativeness I shall remind you that temper has precisely this effect that for the duration of the outburst, it abolishes refinement of culture putting in its place the coarseness of raw nature.

Why did Mona feel the urge to rant about her experience for hours and tell her story "to everybody who would listen?" A story endlessly repeated becomes stale and hackneyed and monotonous. The listener is bound to respond with weariness, boredom and disgust. If Mona's objective was to convince her listeners, to gain their consent and endorsement a concise recital of the episode would have served the purpose far more effectively than the tiresome rehashing of the story which the countless rehearsals were certain to deprive of its freshness and plausibility. Let me state briefly that this ceaseless recounting of experiences is at the root of what may be called the "complaint hobby." My patients are generally addicted to this hobby, and Mona, in her pre-Recovery days, was one of its devotees.

The main pride of the average person is that his views, opinions, plans and decisions are right, sensible and practical. Essentially, this is a claim that the thought processes are solid, that they can be depended on to prove true, in short, that their premises and conclusions are valid. This may be called the *intellectual claim to validity.* A parallel ambition of the average individual is to prove to himself or to others that his heart is "on the right spot," that he is emotionally responsive, ready to fight for his rights and to defend his convictions. His feelings and sentiments, he insists, are generous, noble, vigorous and vital. This is the *romantic claim to vitality.*

The abiding distress of the nervous patient is precisely his inability to trust the validity of his thoughts or to have pride in the vitality of his feelings and sentiments. He states it as his opinion that his suffering is unbearable and is not even listened to. He repeats untiringly that he is doomed, that he is threatened with collapse, but his predictions, failing to come true, are ultimately laughed at. The fact that he cannot secure a respectful hearing is proof positive that the validity of his statements is doubted or ridiculed or rejected. His feelings and sentiments share the same melancholy fate. He protests that his interests in family, business and social obligations are as vigorous and vital as ever; that he neglects them only because of his handicap, but is told to quit being lazy and to use his will-power. With this, his vitality is indicted. He aches to prove that he is both valid and vital, but his words fall on deaf ears and his pleas meet with dull responses. Exposed for years to the skepticism and ridicule of those around him he finally accepts their verdict that he is basically lacking both qualities. Then comes the temperamental spell. It works a miraculous transformation. All of a sudden he is aroused to a fit of anger. He fumes and raves; he is indignant and fairly panting for a fight. What else can that be but strength, vigor and vitality? And that insult that was hurled at him by "that rascal" was clearly and undoubtedly an injustice, an unprovoked attack. That he is right and the other fellow wrong cannot possibly be questioned. In a "clearcut case" of this kind, who but a fool or knave could challenge his premises and conclusions? The temperamental spell re-establishes as with magic his intellectual claim to validity and his romantic claim to vitality. No wonder he is eager to rehash and rehearse and repeat the story to "everybody who would listen." He has found a convincing story and interested listeners, and he is going to make the utmost of the opportunity.

6

THE VANITY OF KNOWING BETTER

Lucille, on the Saturday panel, reported that some time ago she bought an ashtray and "just loved the looks of it." She showed the new acquisition to her sister Martha expecting to be complimented on her good taste. But the sister, little impressed, burst out laughing. "Why," she exclaimed, "that's no ashtray. It is something to hang on the wall. Don't you see it has a hole in it?" An argument developed, Lucille insisting it was an ashtray "for sure" and the sister claiming with equal insistence that it was a wall decoration "at best" and "certainly not an ashtray." Lucille was upset. "I hated to admit that I had made such a silly mistake. But I checked my temper and refused to continue the argument. . . . A few weeks later I was in the same store where I purchased the dish and saw it was still on sale there. Just for curiosity I asked the salesman what kind of an article it was. "Why," he said, "these are ashtrays." I felt the impulse to rush home and tell my sister that she had been wrong but that would have led to an argument again and might have given me my symptoms. When I arrived home I said nothing about my conversation with the salesman and felt proud that I could exercise self-control."

What Lucille and Martha fought about was not the ashtray or its possession or its value. The contest was to decide who of the sisters was more competent in discerning the meaning of the otherwise paltry and insignificant object and finding the proper name for it. As such it was a matching of wits in which the question at issue was: Who knows better? Whose is the superior intelligence? Bursting with contemptuous laughter Martha indicated that in her mind Lucille figured as a dunce, a person who did not know the difference between an ashtray and a wall plate. Lucille, with the humility born of persistent Recovery training, retired into silence, tacitly admitting that perhaps she did not know, that perchance her intelligence had its limitations. To admit one's limitations is humility, to insist on one's superior knowledge is vanity. Martha was vain, Lucille was humble.

I well remember the time when Lucille used to come to my

office complaining about her choking and sweating and palpitating, her air-hunger and pains and numbness. All I had to do was to inquire about her recent experiences at home to find the unfailing source of her symptoms and distress. It was invariably battles with her sister, her son and husband about sheer trivialities in which she was "sure she knew and was right" and the others contested her claim and were equally "sure she did not know and was wrong." From these battles about superior knowledge Lucille emerged regularly prostrate with agony and weariness and torturing symptoms. In those days the vanity of proving her superior knowledge rocked her body with endless turmoil and torment. Today, with a humble awareness of her average limitations, her body is in repose and her mind at peace. Which method effected this transformation of a vain superiority hunter into a humble person mindful of her average limitations?

You who have gone through the process of training in Recovery techniques know that the method is that of spotting. From what you have been taught in Recovery you know that everybody, not only my patients, has the natural impulse to prove the superiority of his thinking abilities (intellectual validity) and to demonstrate the exquisite quality of his strength, forcefulness and prowess (romantic vitality). Both impulses result from claims. The intellectual person claims he knows better how to think, the romantic individual has the equivalent claim to know better how to act. Both insist they "know" and know better. This claim to know better, being a claim, is nothing but a pretense, a vanity. The trouble is that your brothers and sisters and friends have the same variety of claims and vanities, belonging as they do to the same universal tribe of romanto-intellectuals who people this globe of ours. All you have to do is to advance your claim of superior knowledge and they will promptly feel that their identical claim was challenged. Your statement will be hotly contested and stiffly resisted. This merry exchange of claims and counterclaims we call temper, and its essence is that vanities clash and pretenses collide. The violence of the clash and the heat of the collision produce anger; the anger gives rise to tenseness which, in nervous patients, precipitates symptoms. If my patients are to be rid of their symptoms they must learn to dispense with the vanities of claiming superior knowledge and to cultivate the humility of realizing their limited efficiency in thinking and acting. This requires continuous and unrelenting spotting, the pre-eminent method of self-control taught you in Recovery.

In order to spot your temper correctly you must give up your claim to know, to know more and know better. This ought to be easy. It ought to be easy to drop a claim which is nothing but a pretense, a vanity, an illusion. The tragedy is that the illusion of superior knowledge provides you with stimulation, excitement, thrill. It gives you an opportunity to fight, to score a victory, to prove your shoddy excellence and spurious value. Your symptoms make you feel helpless. They deprive you of your vitality, of zest and self-confidence. Dragging along day after day, tired, weary, listless, despairing of ever again experiencing the thrill and rapture of being alert and dynamic you crave the exhilarating sense of being vigorous, vital and self-assured. As it is, with your symptoms straining your energies, with your nervous fatigue sapping your efficiency, you miss the spark of life, the stimulation of interest, the throb of spontaneity. You would do anything to recapture that delightful feeling of being alive, active and forceful. Along comes the occasion for a temper outburst. You feel challenged to maintain your claim to superiority. True, it is nothing but a claim, a pretense and vanity. But if it promises to restore, even for a few minutes, your waning sense of vitality you will plunge into the fray and again live through the rapture and ecstasy of fighting and proving to yourself that your vitality, far from being exhausted, is again brimming with energy, throbbing with life. If a miracle of this kind can be performed by the sheer claim to know better, well, let it be a pretense, a vanity and illusion. It has the mysterious capacity to restore vitality and spontaneity and if spotting it correctly is likely to undo its effect you will strain every nerve to avoid spotting. You will rather retain your symptoms than relinquish the supreme thrill of a rejuvenated vigor.

And memory is fresh yet of the days when I grappled with Lucille trying to persuade her that the thrill provided by the tantrum is nothing but a momentary exhilaration certain to be followed by intensified suffering and aggravated symptoms. She listened and seemed convinced but when the occasion for a temper reaction arose she craved the thrill and yielded. One day she came to my office beaming with joy. She told the story of how she felt provoked by a neighbor, how her temper rose and she controlled it. "After that," she continued, "I was relaxed and as comfortable as never before. I really felt proud of myself." She had hardly completed the sentence when a shadow settled on her face. "Doctor," she said, "if I feel proud of myself doesn't that mean that I am vain instead of humble?" I asked her,

"Is a mother vain if she is proud of her child? A wife if she adores her husband? A citizen if he basks in the glory of his country?" And I went on explaining that to be proud of actual and realistic accomplishments is desirable and valuable. What the mother prides herself on is the effort and labors and deprivations which the raising of the child entailed. She is proud of her self-effacing or self-control. And if a wife is proud of her husband be certain that what she has in mind is his accomplishments which are the result and product of his self-control, and similarly with the citizen extolling the virtues of his nation. These virtues are an index to the labors, successes and exploits of past generations which were secured at the cost of vigorous group discipline and collective self-control. Lucille understood. As I continued my explanations she grasped the fact that every act of self-control produces a sense of self-respect. This self-respect is a form of pride. Another form of pride is vanity. The latter does not point to actual and realistic accomplishments, to no effort or self-discipline. It is merely a claim, pretense and illusion. Lucille learned the distinction between the two varieties of pride, the one realistic, the other illusional. Realistic pride leads to self-respect, repose and relaxation, illusional pride or vanity, to self-torturing, momentary thrill and enduring tenseness. In nervous patients it leads in addition to perpetuation of symptoms.

Many a patient has told me, "I have learned to control my temper outbursts. I no longer want the victories of vanity and prefer the peacefulness of humility. But my fears are still active." With the one patient it is the fear of collapse, with the other the fear of the permanent handicap. These fears do not seem to stem from the vanity of knowing better. To the contrary, a fear appears to be the expression of a shrinking and retreating disposition, hence, to be related to humility rather than vanity. But when I tried to explain to a patient that his fears are groundless; that they are due to a thought of insecurity in his brain; that he can dispose of this thought if he accepts my authoritative knowledge; that he can brave his fatigue and step out forcefully without any danger of collapse; when I tell him that his so-called sleeplessness is a myth; that even if he feels he hasn't slept, nevertheless, he did a good deal of sleeping and perhaps of snoring; when I confront him with the store of my knowledge about these subjects and point to my solid experience of half a lifetime he argues and opposes and clings stubbornly to his notions and engages in insipid verbal fencing and—knows better. He knows he has not slept a wink last night; he knows the fatigue is "real" and not nervous; he is certain his head pressure is the result of hypertension. And when I take his blood pressure and assure him that it is within normal limits and nothing to worry about he is likely to counter with the exclamation, "But doctor, when I am in your office I relax and my blood pressure goes down. I am sure it will go up the moment I step out on the street." You see, whether it is the angry or fearful temper the situation is the same. The patient "knows better." He is an arch romanto-intellectual who knows and is sure and cannot be convinced without a long, drawn-out struggle. If he is to be cured he must be trained to assume a humble attitude and divest himself of the vanity of knowing. The road to humility leads through spotting to the determination to abandon the craving for the divine thrill of knowing better.

7

TEMPERAMENT AND TEMPER

Betty, on the Saturday afternoon panel, reported that several weeks ago she had an appointment to see Dr. Low at his office. "I had to wait from 2:30 to 4:00 P.M. Then I had to go shopping for a belt and a pair of shoes. After that I had to go to the insurance office and to be there before closing time. At the department store I had to spend time picking the merchandise I wanted. Then it took more time yet before the saleslady took care of the purchase. I got to the insurance office just five minutes before closing time. By now I had a severe head pressure, and when I was on the street it occurred to me that I had to get a few things for supper and that after supper I had to attend the monthly Recovery meeting of the panel members in the evening. The head pressure became worse and I felt exhausted. Finally I arrived home, trembling and sweating and palpitating. Then I noticed that my husband had not returned from work although it was past his usual time. My first thought was that something had happened to him. My symptoms became worse. Then I remembered my Recovery training and thought I shouldn't anticipate danger. Instantly I felt better. . . ."

Betty, in an emotional upheaval, summoned forth a slogan she had learned in Recovery and obtained instant relief. Experiences of this kind are now commonplace among our members. They know that all they have to do to stop emerging symptoms is to spot their emotionalisms and to refuse to accept the suggestions of doom and disaster offered by their temperamental lingo. And if Betty managed to secure instant relief from her spotting the conclusion seems inevitable that she spotted correctly and applied the appropriate technique taught her in Recovery. But Recovery techniques and Recovery maxims stem from me, your physician, and if it is true that I ever taught Betty or anyone else not to anticipate danger I must have been dreaming or utterly careless in the choice of my words. How can anybody be alive and avoid anticipating danger? To be heedless of danger is a sure prescription for running straight into it. Just cross streets and turn corners unmindful of the dangers of a busy traffic and I will not want to be responsible for what might happen to you some day. Clearly, Betty applied a Recovery slogan correctly but in quoting it distorted its phrasing.

No wife worth the name can avoid uneasy thoughts and anxious anticipations if her husband is unduly late in arriving at the customary time. The image of an accident, of collapse and even misgivings about foul play must of necessity arise in her brain if she is possessed of affection and imagination. In a situation of this kind the thought of possible danger is the unavoidable and proper response. No teaching of any kind, Recovery or otherwise, will ever be able to eliminate this response which is necessary for life and desirable for human relations. The question is how a person experiencing the response of apprehension will react to the experience. Will he worry with reflective calm? Or, will he work himself up to a burst of emotional hysteria? If he permits himself to become emotional and hysterical, then, the *original response* of plain worry has been "worked up" or "processed" into a *temper reaction*. What patients are taught in Recovery is to curb their tempers and to leave the original responses to run their course, that is, to let them rise and fall, come and go. Temper keeps them rising and coming and prevents them from falling and going.

What I here call "Original Responses" are the ordinary run of thoughts, feelings, sensations and impulses which, in the average individual, come and go, rise and fall. They are inherited and constitutional. A dog jumps at you unexpectedly. You are startled, and the startle is an original response which everybody is likely to experience in an event of this kind. It would be absurd to tell you not to get startled. The response is rooted in your racial inheritance, embedded in your constitution. It is original, natural, hardly changeable. Another example: your ear is assailed by a harsh word or your eye by a disdainful gesture. If you are at all responsive you will feel hurt or insulted or shocked. That is again your original response, just as constitutional and refractory to change as is the startle occasioned by the dog's jump. Original responses of this kind are without number. The pity aroused by suffering, the joy and warmth produced by a smiling infant, the enthusiasm created by a stirring speech, the delight felt at the sight of a friend, the anger provoked by an affront, the impulse to run in the face of danger—these and a multitude of others are all original responses.

The sum total of original responses which a person is possessed or capable of are called his *temperament*. Temperament means that a person is sensitive, receptive, impressionable to events inside and outside him. If your temperament is receptive and impressionable your original responses will be many and varied; if it is dull they will be few and static. It is temperament which responds to events with readiness or sluggishness, warmth or coolness, sympathy or aversion, interest or indolence, thrill or chill.

When Betty, arriving home, found her husband missing the thought struck her that something might have happened to him. Every wife would or should have experienced the same response provided her temperament was endowed with the average qualities of warmth, affection and tenderness. If Betty's temperament was of this description she had to feel concern, worry or misgivings. You see here that when temperament stirs feelings are apt to rise. In the present instance, the feeling was that of worry. Betty might have acted on this natural and original response of worry. She might have telephoned to the husband's place of employment or to any locality at which she could have reasonably expected him to stop on his way home. Had she done that her original *response* would have guided her to a rational, sane, well adjusted *reaction*. Or, she might have analyzed the situation in the light of previous experience and reflected that her husband's arrival had been delayed frequently in the past by overtime work, by a traffic jam or by a decision to have his hair trimmed before setting out on his homebound trip. This again would have led to a rational and sane reaction. Betty would have simply waited, calmly and patiently. But Betty's temperament was not disposed to release the responses of calm and patience. She is or was a nervous patient, and if the temperament of a nervous patient stirs it is likely to develop—*temper*. And you know that temper is incompatible with calm and patience. Temperament raises mild and moderate fears, worries, angers and joys. But temper acts differently. Its responses are always vehement, immoderate, excessive and even explosive. In her pre-Recovery days, Betty responded to disappointments with temper. After she had gone through her Recovery training her responses became again those of her native temperament, calm, even, sane. In former days her temperament led her straightway into hysterical emotionalism. Now it produces feelings of average intensity. Formerly, when disappointed, her temper suggested a grave emergency. Now her temperament merely hints at a possible average danger. To think of danger—calmly—is undoubtedly wholesome and necessary in life in general but particularly so in the hustle and bustle of our metropolitan life. Why, then, did Betty think she "shouldn't anticipate danger?" Obviously, she confused two types of anticipation, those generated by a wild temper and those inspired by a mild temperament. In Recovery she was taught not to entertain hysterical anticipations in response to average dangers which merely call for gentle and moderate worry. When she met with the average situation mentioned in her panel example her temperament produced the original response of concern. But unwittingly and following a year-long tendency she thought of a dire emergency and developed temper. The result was that her "symptoms became worse." Now she remembered her Recovery training, spotted her temper and felt instant relief. She acted correctly but when she reported the event she used a wrong phrasing. She claimed she spotted and stopped her temperament when, in actual fact, she put a stop to her temper. She applied properly the Recovery techniques for curbing temper but misquoted the implied principle when she presumed to have checked her temperament.

My patients will do well to ponder the lesson of this clear-cut distinction between temperament and temper. Afflicted with nervous ailments they are extremely sensitive and the original responses of their native temperament are aroused by actions, statements and events which other people, less impressionable, would overlook and ignore. Somebody maintains silence in their presence. Instantly my patients are likely to construe the reaction as slur or indifference or neglect. Or, they commit a minor blunder or sustain minor losses, failures or defeats. The average person would take these insignificant mishaps in his stride and not a ripple of excitement might cross his temperament. But my patients are apt to respond with self-blame, embarrassment or a sense of inefficiency. This is in itself no calamity and merely indicates that my patients are unfortunately blessed with temperaments which pour forth endless streams of original responses. The responses as such are no wise different from those experienced by men and women not the victims of nervous trouble. Everybody may at any time feel slurred or neglected and may on occasion indulge in self-blame and a sense of embarrassment. With the average person such common inner disturbances are readily forgotten or dismissed. But with my patients there are no minor or common disturbances. Every disturbance has to them the major aspect of an urgent emergency. And if an emergency is thought of emotion is mobilized and temper released. Minor apprehensions are then fanned into major explosions, into panics and tantrums. These dramatic or dramatized developments can be checked if the patient is trained to regard his worries, embarrassments, misgivings and forebodings as what they really are: the innocent outpouring of a temperament which has been sensitized by an endless career of suffering and has acquired the habit of producing an unbroken succession of harmless original responses. The nervous patient will have to learn to be tolerant of his responses and to refrain from processing temperament into temper.

8

TEMPER MASQUERADING AS "FEELING"

Florence, on the Saturday panel, spoke with surprising candor about her marital life. "I was always jealous of my husband," she said. "All he had to do was to invite some girl to ride home with us from church and I became jealous and felt very insecure. Before I joined Recovery I did not know that this was temper. I felt I had a right to ask my husband not to pay attention to any woman but me. But when I got my Recovery training I learned that I was not the judge to decide who was wrong and who right. Today I know that when the jealousy gets a hold of me I feel irritated but nobody is wrong. I have learned to let the irritation run its course, and it does that in a few minutes. And after my jealousy is gone I feel good and feel proud that I am able to control it. In this manner I endorse myself and that makes me feel better yet. In former days when the jealousy came over me it produced a blurring of my eyes and gave me a headache that would last for days and my married life was a mess all the time. Today I have very few of the symptoms and both I and my husband lead a much happier life than we ever did before I joined Recovery."

Florence suffered from jealousy for many years but did not know it was temper. That was before her Recovery training and at that time she merely "felt" insecure. She also "felt" she had a right to be jealous. I shall ask: Who or what did Florence "feel" for? The answer is: She felt for her own security and for her own rights. She showed little if any feeling for the husband's security which was gravely threatened by her jealousy, and for his rights which were ruthlessly ignored when he was forbidden to extend simple courtesies to a fellow church member. And my conclusion is: Florence, in her pre-Recovery days, had feelings for her own dear Self only whenever the jealousy took hold of her. The feelings for the husband were either absent or feebly operating. Yet, the couple had formed a life partnership. They were united in matrimony, and the marital union, assuredly, called for mutual feelings, for sharing, communicating and exchanging. Instead, whenever she was in the throes of jealousy, Florence made her feelings flow out toward her own Self only; the partner's Self was denied its legitimate share of consideration and affection. If the concern about security and rights was at all the outcome of feelings they were certainly self-centered and not group-centered. And self-centered feelings (self-pity, self-blame, self-disgust, self-importance) are temper, of course. For you, the members of Recovery, this is commonplace and needs no explanation.

Florence aimed her jealousy at her husband. Since he was her partner in their marital group the feeling was group-oriented although in a superficial sense only. But it declared the other person as wrong and oneself as right, and that quality stamped it as unquestionably temperamental. Her jealous temper led Florence to be resentful, sullen, suspicious, indignant, perhaps also hostile and vengeful. All these feelings tie in with jealousy, their main characteristic being that they adjudge the other person as wrong and oneself as right. Though they must be classed among the group-directed responses, nevertheless, they are tempers.

Many of you remember the time, some eighteen months ago, when Florence first joined Recovery. None of you realized that she was of a jealous disposition. How could you know? She never showed temper when she was with us. She was unfailingly sweet, considerate, patient, forever willing to be helpful. As a member of our group, she displayed a vast capacity for joy and enthusiasm, affection and forebearance, devotion and selflessness, fellowship and compassion. Needless to say, these were feelings, group-centered with regard to their aim, genuine in intent, sincere in application. As such, they were emphatically not temperamental. Her affection had, of course, no implication of somebody being branded as wrong and herself extolled as right. Feelings of this kind whose exclusive tendency is to benefit and serve the group go by the name of sympathetic responses. They may properly be called the *feelings of sympathy*. By their very nature they cannot be suspected as furnishing the material out of which temper is woven.

You will also remember that at times Florence appeared in our midst with drawn features and a worn look. Her mood was depressed, and her depression, we know now, was largely the result of her physical ailment. In these periods of depression her countenance reflected silent grief, a soft resignation, a touching sadness. But there was no wailing and complaining, no self-pity or self-blame. Nobody was assessed as wrong, nobody as right. She just suffered in placid resignation. Feelings of this kind signify a lowering of the feeling tone, from joy to grief, from sympathy to apathy. They are known as the apathetic responses and may be fittingly called the *feelings of apathy*.

My opportunities for observing Florence were limited to office, classes and meetings. I had no occasion to study her behavior in such casual situations as encounters with sales persons and elevator operators, in chats with neighbors and friends, at card games and on visits to theatres. What was the nature of her responses in these contacts? We know that Florence is a warm person, easily stimulated and eagerly responding. So we may take it for granted that in most instances her reaction was mainly that of sympathy. Occasionally, more particularly when her severe physical ailment dulled and lowered her receptiveness, her attitude might have been that of apathy. But when an idle sales girl, busy with her make-up, kept her waiting impatiently at the counter; when a neighbor was sharp and a friend neglectful; when her bridge partner spoke in a sarcastic vein, or when an unmannered person, with tactless remarks and distasteful noises, prevented her from enjoying a show, we may safely assume that she was a prey to irritation, annoyance or outright anger. Under circumstances of this sort it was more than likely that she was chilled in her sympathy, roused from her apathy and seized with *antipathy*. Was this a feeling? Or, was it temper? The answer is plain: if she was merely irritated and annoyed it was a more or less unadulterated feeling; if she proceeded to condemn the offender as wrong and to exalt herself as right it was temper. You will now understand that feelings are of three kinds: sympathy, apathy, antipathy, either toward oneself or others. Temper is of one kind only: antipathy, against oneself or the other person, plus the judgment of right and wrong. On the basis of these formulations we may sum up the meanings of the various reactions displayed by Florence. When she was moved by jealousy she was resentful, sullen, suspicious, indignant, perhaps hostile and vengeful. This was antipathy plus judgment of right and wrong, hence, temper. When she was free from jealousy she responded with genuine or tolerably genuine feelings of either sympathy, apathy or antipathy with no judgment of right and wrong marring the relative purity of the responses. This was feeling without admixture of temper. As everybody does, Florence expressed both feeling and temper.

Feelings should be expressed. This does not mean they ought to be acted on or acted out. It merely means they should be communicated to or shared with somebody who can be trusted to understand them. If the feelings are those of sympathy their expression will create good-will and, thus, further the interests of the group. If they are those of apathy or antipathy their expression will give relief to the person oppressed by them. Obtaining relief, the oppressed person will be purged of antisocial trends, and the ends of the group will thereby be promoted. This is different with temper. Feelings can be reported. They lend themselves to matter-of-fact discussion and calm appraisal. But temper, involving a claim to being right, cannot be reported objectively, calmly and matter-of-factly. It invariably leads to arguments, debates and rebuttals. Even close relatives and intimate friends, asked to pass a verdict on the justification of a temper outburst, may and frequently do voice disapproval, criticising the uselessness or harmfulness of the explosion. If the temperamental person resents the rebuff a new temper reaction is released, this time involving the relatives and friends. The result is that the temperamental hothead obtains no relief from his tension and group life is disturbed. Temper should be checked and controlled. It should not be given any expression at all. It should merely be avoided or, once it has occurred, it should be prevented from recurring. Feelings call for expression, temper for suppression.

Florence needed training in Recovery to learn that temper is different from feeling. Why did she fail to make the distinction herself? She has a keen intelligence and a refreshing willingness to learn by experience. Her intelligence could have told her that most feelings are noble, that even those that lack the attribute of nobility are not likely to injure the group. By the same token, she could have discovered, by sheer use of her native intellect, that temper, far from being identical with feeling, is its very opposite. It is positively ignoble and disrupting group life. And should she have consulted her past experience she could have easily learned the fact which I mentioned, that feelings, when communicated, give relief while temper has no such effect. How is it her intellect and experience failed her? The answer is that men and women derive their views not merely from their own observations but mainly from public opinion. And contemporary public opinion has fostered a type of thought which glamorizes temper by the clever trick of identifying it with feeling. The trick is of an engaging simplicity. Temper and feeling, in the present-day psychological jargon, are deftly lumped together under the common name of emotion, and emotion is nimbly interpreted as feeling. The next step in the argument, assiduously promoted by modern psychologies, is that emotions, being the driving power in the human economy, are infinitely more important than intellect. And since intellect is generally considered as a valuable function the conclusion drawn by the average person (and by professionals) is that emotions being superior to intellect must also be of superior value. With this, emotion is not only glamorized but also raised to the rank of dignity and nobility. This view, given wide currency by recognized professions, leading universities and philanthropic foundations, has found its way into the channels of communication with the result that dailies, weeklies and monthlies, radio, film and television fairly vie with one another in the gentle art of catering to unbridled tempers carefully avoiding the odious word and slyly substituting the terms "emotion" or "emotional experience." Antisocial impulses, born from dark temperamental dispositions, are then portrayed as "just emotions," as "plainly human," indeed, as of valuable "human interest." True, these emotions (read: tempers) may also be troublesome; they may cause tenseness, maladjustment and symptoms. But the newer psychologies have wisely anticipated this unfortunate inconvenience and provided a suitable remedy by spreading the gospel of "free expression" of "emotional" frustrations and aggressions. That this vicious doctrine of free expression has had a prominent share in the spread of both individual and social tenseness and of all kinds of antisocial trends is plain but will not be elaborated here. What interests me at this point is the deplorable fact that my patients have been exposed to the sinister influence of this modern dogma of the identity of temper and feeling and have been reached by the insidious propaganda carried on by textbooks, by the stage and the press to the effect that ungoverned emotions (read: aggressive tempers) can be cured by the expedient of "free expression." Well, Florence, under the influence of an utterly irresponsible public opinion, gave formerly "free expression" to her temper and almost wrecked her marriage. Today, when through old-fashioned Recovery teaching she has recovered her mental balance, she expresses her feelings but suppresses her temper and with temper curbed, her feelings, properly communicated and shared, spread their warmth and glow over a happy marital scene.

9

TANTRUMS HAVE MUCH FORCE BUT LITTLE FEELING

Ada thought she was rid of the fear of being alone in her home. For years her sister who occupies the apartment next door was not permitted to leave unless she took Ada with her. But "for the past couple of months," Ada related, "my sister left me alone, and I handled myself very well." This splendid record of improvement was suddenly interrupted by that severe reaction which is known to our patients as the well nigh unavoidable setback. On the morning of the panel discussion, Ada's sister announced she was going to a luncheon. Instantly "a ball of fire shot into my face. I felt dizzy; my heart palpitated, and the room was going around and around. I meant to plead with my sister not to leave. But I had too much Recovery training to do that. I rushed to the phone and called Rosalie. She reassured me. But soon after my sister was gone I felt tense and fearful. Before long I had myself worked up into a panic. I dashed at the phone and called my husband. He suggested a walk, but I was so weak I could not drag my body. At that moment I thought of our Recovery training and became disgusted with myself. I felt ashamed that I had practiced such dreadful sabotage. When this thought struck me I felt calm all of a sudden, picked up my sewing and kept sewing till after lunch. And now I am here sharing in the panel, and I am all right."

Ada's experience illustrates three points: (1) that patients after they recover, are apt to have setbacks; (2) that the setback, usually mild, may attain the violence of a panic; (3) that with proper Recovery training, even the wildest panic can be broken in a fraction of a second. I told you frequently that in my very extensive experience I have met few nervous patients who did not suffer from setbacks after they improved. Therefore, it is of the utmost importance for all of you to know how to deal with setbacks, more particularly, how to deal with them if they threaten to develop into a panic.

A panic must be broken, abruptly and decisively. If it is

permitted to go on unchecked the danger is it will leave the patient discouraged and demoralized. He may then give up the fight for health, reflecting that "what's the use struggling if even Recovery cannot help me." The result will be the defeatist belief that once a nervous ailment becomes "chronic" it is incurable. You know that our Recovery language calls this the "fear of the permanent handicap."

In the ordinary man's language, as distinguished from Recovery usage, the word "panic" connotes a condition in which a person is gripped by a violent fear that is overwhelming and irresistible. It is a fierce storm that lashes the organs of the body into a frantic burst of palpitations, sweats, dizziness, air-hunger, tremors, tenseness and weakness. If that storm is overwhelming how are you going to check it? If it is irresistible how will you resist it?

Common language speaks of "irresistible" impulses, emotions, tantrums and spells. Recovery denies emphatically that any inner experience of the nervous patients is irresistible. It knows of situations only that *were not resisted*. This refers to common everyday experiences, the common tantrum, the common crying spell, the common anger and common fear. All of them can be resisted, none are irresistible.

Diseases cannot be resisted. If a patient is seized with a prolonged depression of his mood I shall not tell him to resist the depression. He needs expert medical treatment. But a depression of this kind is not a common everyday experience. A few other experiences may fall into the same category. If a mother loses her child her sadness may have an irresistible quality. This is perhaps true also of the condition of "being in love." Whether human beings, except in certain brain diseases, can develop a truly "irresistible" rage I do not know but I have reason to doubt it. You will realize that the grief of the mother, the infatuation of the lover and the blind rage of the person ravaged by brain disease are not common, everyday situations.

The tantrums and panics which our patients experience in the course of a setback are common, everyday occurrences; they are the result of nothing more unusual than—temper. Ada suffered from an ordinary, commonplace temper outburst and "worked herself up" till she drifted into a panic. Soon she felt ashamed and disgusted with herself and dropped the panic as you would a silly thought.

Thoughts can be formed and reformed; they can be accepted and rejected; they can be retained and dismissed. Feelings are of a different make. You cannot change, reject or dismiss them. They descend upon you, and you must wait until they depart. Ada formed a temperamental idea, worked it up to a pitch, then rejected and dismissed it.

Ada was enabled to perform this feat because of her Recovery training. In the language of Recovery, temper is distinct from genuine feeling. The sadness of the bereaved mother is a genuine feeling. That feeling is original, primary and pure. In contrast, temper is derived, secondary and adulterated. I shall try to explain these terms. Every feeling has thoughts attached to it. A sad person is bound to think that the world is flat and stale. In this instance, the feeling of sadness produces the thought of staleness. It is not so that the bereaved mother forms first the thought that the world is stale and, consequently, falls prey to sadness. The reverse is true: she is first sad and then thinks the world stale. The feeling of sadness is original, the thought of staleness is derived from the feeling of sadness. You can express the same relation between feeling and thought if you substitute "primary" for "original," and "secondary" for "derived." You will then understand that, in the instance of the mother, the feeling of sadness is primary, and the thought of staleness secondary.

The terms "purity" and "adulteration" are easily explained. The mother feels sad, pure and simple. She is not angry, fearful, jealous or envious. She has no desire to dominate others, to be consoled by them. She is just sad, and her feeling is not contaminated by an admixture of other feelings. It is original, primary and pure, i.e., genuine.

Contrast now this genuine feeling of sadness with Ada's temper tantrum. In Ada's own words, after the sister left, "before long I had myself worked up into a panic." The feeling did not descend on her; she "worked" on it, produced it and fanned it into a lusty fire by means of inflammatory thoughts. What precisely was the nature of her thoughts? Ada says it was the idea of being left alone, the idea of helplessness, the idea of perhaps needing help and not getting it. If that was true she could easily remedy the situation; visiting a friend or merely going for a walk, or to a show would have cured the loneliness. Instead, she "worked herself up." We know what that means. It means that Ada now gave herself up to all kind of sinister thoughts. "The nerve to leave me alone. They know I can't stand it. What do they care how I feel? All my sister thinks of is her own pleasure. My suffering means nothing to her. Etc.,

etc." You see, the train of ideas that set temper afoot and keep it growing are the familiar resentments and indignations that find their simple expression in the temperamental phrase, "They are wrong." Dwell on this thought, expand and deepen it, and the sky is the limit to which you may "work yourself up." Ada had the idea of herself being right and the sister wrong. That thought produced a feeling which, being derived from a thought, was not original; and being adulterated with resentment, indignation and vindictiveness, was not pure. Lacking the qualities of originality and purity it was not genuine. A thought produced it, and a thought could drop it.

Ada, a loyal member of Recovery and devoted disciple of its teachings, knows the meaning of temper. She knows that the thought, "I am right, and they are wrong," is an utter absurdity. She has undergone thorough Recovery training and undoubtedly has discarded the arrogant attitude of being a judge on the rightness and wrongness of actions. If she has learned anything she certainly learned the Recovery principle that right and wrong must be no issues in domestic and social contacts. If, in her tantrum, she endeavored to revive a thought that she had discarded she obviously tried to deceive herself into believing something she no longer believed. You heard me frequently state that temper is an effort to deceive oneself into the belief that somebody is right and somebody else wrong. Ada tried to practice the temperamental self-deception but did not succeed. All she accomplished was to "work herself up." The emotional flame which she was able to fan into existence had a great deal of sentimental smoke and verbal fury but lacked the genuine fire of feeling. A mere breath of common sense suddenly remembered from her Recovery training extinguished the weak conflagration, and when cool reasoning cleared away the smoke of excitement Ada noticed that not even embers and ashes were left. She was calm, resumed her sewing and "kept sewing till after lunch." The emotional storm was nothing but shallow and empty self-deception. The feeling that steered it was shallow; the thought that directed it was empty.

Whether pure and genuine feelings exist anywhere in this imperfect life of ours is doubtful, the only possible exceptions being the instances cited above. Even a mother's love for her child is ordinarily adulterated with a sense of possessiveness; the lover's affection is frequently contaminated with some stirring of jealousy or vanity. There is perhaps no purity, hence no genuineness, in the sphere of common human feelings. And if I tell my patients that their temperamental feelings of anger, fear, disgust lack genuineness I merely wish to remind them that their explosions, tantrums, impulses and obsessions share the fate of all human feelings. They are mixed and adulterated with other feelings and overlaid with all manner of thought. Not being genuine they lack the irresistible force that is credited to genuine feelings. Being largely directed by thought they can be originated and dropped at will as any thought can. Keep that in mind, and you will have little difficulty disposing of your temperamental upheavals.

10

GENUINE FEELING AND SINCERE THINKING

Clara, in the course of a panel discussion on "Sabotaging Sleep," commented on her difficulties of sleeping which she experienced prior to her Recovery training. "I would awaken from a nightmare; I was shaking and sweating and my heart pounded and I felt as if nothing in the room looked familiar. I was sure I was dying. The first thought I had was to awaken my husband and ask him to hold my hands. . . . There was no rest for me. I felt scared and was waiting for that something awful to happen. . . . Today when I awaken at night I instantly know that my sensations are not dangerous. I wait and though I am not comfortable I lie still in bed and do not think of waking my husband. In a short time I fall asleep again."

When Clara was "sure" she was dying she asked her husband to hold her hands. Then she waited "for that something awful to happen." But it would seem that if death threatens it would be wiser to summon a physician than engage in the serene practice of holding hands. From this I conclude that Clara was not at all sure she was dying. Indeed, the inference is inescapable that she was "sure" she was not dying. You may question the propriety of casting doubt on Clara's account. Is Clara a liar? Assuredly, she is not. A liar deceives others. What Clara did was to deceive herself. She believed something which, judged by the standards of genuine experience, is impossible. She *thought* "for sure" she was dying, but she did not *experience* the fear of death.

Clara spoke of a nightmare, of shaking and sweating. The look of things had changed and she was scared. All of this points unmistakably to fear. And if I stated that she did not experience the fear of death what kind of a feeling was it that produced all these frightening reactions? It certainly was a fear and most intense at that. Why do I refuse to call it the fear of death?

I told you that Clara with the "certainty" of death in her mind asked her husband to hold her hands. Suppose a baby is seriously ill, and the mother makes ready to go to a dance. You will conclude that this mother has strong feelings for dancing but

none or very dull ones for the fate of her child. How did you
arrive at your conclusion? You observed an *act* (the mother
preparing for a dance) and gathered that a *feeling* (for the baby's
fate) was weak or missing. The point I wish to make is that a
given act may or may not fit into the pattern of its underlying
feelings. Or, acts and feelings may or may not match. Clara's
act (of holding hands) was not properly matched with her pro-
fessed feeling (of fearing death).

An act expresses a feeling and a thought at the same time. The
act of tending the baby, for instance, expresses the mother's
feeling of love and also her thought of what the baby needs or
what is best for it. In this combination, the feelings and thoughts
are the *inner experiences,* and the acts their *outer expressions.* If
an act expresses a feeling in its true and real significance then the
meaning of the act matches the meaning of the feeling. If the
matching is thorough we say that the outer act gave *genuine*
expression to the inner feeling. This is different with thoughts.
They are not judged from the viewpoint of genuineness. Instead, they are considered as either *sincere* or lacking sincerity.
If an act really and truly matches the meaning of the inner
thought the expression is said to be sincere. If act and thought
fail to match the expression is insincere. When Clara, awakening with what she calls the terror of death, roused her husband to
hold her hands did her act of behavior express genuine feeling
and sincere thought? Did her outer act match her inner
experience?

A mother craving amusement while her baby is sick may feel
some sort of affection for her suffering offspring. But her act of
going to a dance does not match the feeling of motherly love. It
matches another feeling, namely, the feeling of boredom and the
love of excitement. If, while preparing for the outside engagement, she explains in so many words that, after all, a competent
nurse is in attendance and the physician within easy reach her
act of speech expresses an insincere thought. That thought is not
focused on the welfare of the baby; it is merely offered as a face-
saving excuse for an inexcusable neglect. The inner experience
and outer expression *mismatch.* The feeling lacks genuineness,
the thought bears the mark of insincerity.

The real meaning of Clara's behavior ought to be clear by
now. The feeling of approaching death, if genuine, can only be
matched by a life-saving act, for instance, an emergency call to a
physician or the instant rush to a hospital. Holding hands is no
such life-saving performance. All it can be reasonably expected

to give is comfort. If what Clara craved was to be comforted her feeling must have been that of discomfort, perhaps a very intense and torturing sort of discomfort. Even if you add that she feared not to be able to stand up under the "terrific" strain, if you add further that the harrowing vision of a night of never-ending torment caused an almost unbearable fear, nevertheless, the feeling was that of discomfort, nothing else. It was not a genuine feeling of threatening death. That Clara was "sure" she was dying contributes nothing to the situation. Feeling and act were decidedly mismatched. Was her thought of death sincere? Well, I have no record of what she expressed in words about the kind of thought which dominated her brain at the time. But it would be easy to reconstruct her thinking process on the basis of experience with a multitude of patients in similar pseudo-emergencies. Their first thought was that the husband will again refuse to believe their protestations, that the reality of their agony will be doubted, that their anxious outcry will not be taken seriously. But with a sincere thought of impending death the only consideration that will match the inner experience is the necessity for securing instant help and not the desire to be believed. No doubt, Clara's feeling of death approaching was not genuine, her thought of life ebbing away was not sincere.

Feelings lacking the mark of genuineness and thoughts devoid of the touch of sincerity are the commonest features in the lives of average individuals who being just plain average are neither leaders nor saints nor heroes. Lack of genuineness and sincerity are indeed the warp and woof of daily existence. And if Clara is frequently insincere in her chats with neighbors and in her dealings with tradespeople, if following the common pattern she displays little genuineness in her devotion to civic virtues and social obligations she is just average with all the failings and deficiencies characteristic of average endeavors. But Clara is a nervous patient endowed with a nervous system that is unduly sensitive to tenseness, and if she practices insincerity and lack of genuineness with regard to her symptoms she will misinterpret discomfort as meaning danger and the result will be panics and vicious cycles. With reference to his symptoms a nervous patient must be genuine in feeling and sincere in thought.

In order to practice a suitable degree of genuineness and sincerity patients must be made to know that their inner experiences if applied to symptoms are woefully lacking these qualities.   To know one's inner experiences means to gain insight, and insight requires spotting.   The very moment the feeling of fear stirs in his body and the corresponding thought of danger rises in his brain the patient must instantly spot the condition as one of severe discomfort with no danger attached. Continuous spotting disposes of insincerity and lack of genuineness.   What Clara demonstrated and demonstrated with singular force was that after a relatively brief training period in Recovery she is now able to spot her frightening inner experiences as being nothing but silly emotionalisms or inane rationalizations.   Having acquired these insights she is in a position to redirect her acts and to match them properly with her experiences.   When she said, "Today when I awaken at night I instantly know that my sensations are not dangerous," she merely indicated that she masters the techniques of spotting and that her outer acts are now well matched to the meaning of her inner experiences.

11

GROUP-MINDEDNESS AND SELF-MINDEDNESS

During a panel discussion on "Temper and Insight" the following example was offered by Bernice: Several weeks ago my husband went with his buddy to a nearby tavern to watch the football game on a television set. I asked him when he would be back and he said about four o'clock. When 4 o'clock came I got dressed as I expected him to be home any minute. Well, 4:30 came and no Bill. Five o'clock came and Bill wasn't home yet. I became temperamental and began to work myself up. I thought he doesn't care how I feel and he thinks more about that d... football game than he does about me. Before long I had palpitations, tightness in the stomach and pressure in the head. I thought of calling up the tavern and telling Bill that I wouldn't stand for the way he treats me. By that time I was very uncomfortable. Suddenly it came to me that this was sabotage. I said to myself you think he is wrong and you are right. But in Recovery we learn there is no right or wrong in domestic life. There are only irritations and discomfort and we must not judge who is right and who wrong. So I said these things will happen in married life and it wasn't worth working myself up over it. Pretty soon I calmed down. About six o'clock Bill walked in. I asked, "Is this 4 o'clock?" He looked at me and said, "When I say 4 you should know I mean 6." I was irritated but I didn't make an issue of it. Before I had my Recovery training I would have told him exactly how I felt, how wrong he was to do that to me and I wouldn't have spoken to him for days. But then I would have developed all kinds of symptoms and would have suffered from them for weeks.

When Bill kept Bernice, his wife, waiting for two solid hours without troubling to call her he was undoubtedly rude. But was rudeness his intention? Did he *mean* to be rude? Most of you know Bill and none of you will hesitate to credit him with a gentle disposition, with the will to please, to help and to make himself liked. And if his main features are as I said why does he neglect to practice them in his approach to Bernice? You may be inclined to be charitable and explain Bill's lack of consideration on the basis of his keen interest in football and television. You will then argue that he became wrapped up in the fascinating spectacle on the screen and—naturally—forgot wife and home. Suppose this is true and the whole incident the result of an innocent lapse of memory. But when in response to his wife's reproach he had the incredible impertinence to proclaim, "When I say 4 you should know I mean 6," no explanation in the world could possibly atone for the crudity of that reply. Then you will no doubt revise your charitable opinion about his being two hours late and will grant that the delay was inexcusable and certainly called for an apology which Bill failed to offer. And taking it all in all you will agree that Bill, our gentle and likable Bill, was rude in the one instance and savage in the other. And the question arises: Did Bill intend and plan to display rudeness and recklessness? Did he *mean* it? Was it his deliberate will to insult his wife, to crush her feelings?

Putting it into different words this is what Bill intended to convey to Bernice: "If I say something I may mean something else. What precisely I mean is my sole concern. I am the boss and I do not have to account for my actions." If you read this meaning into his statement you will understand why I call it rude and savage. Married life calls for sharing, and Bill denied Bernice her due marital share. With this he launched a rude and savage attack on the very foundation of the marital structure. Was that his intention? Did he really mean to muzzle Bernice and to deny her the status as a wife? Was it his deliberate will to wreck his marriage?

Marriage is a Will. It is the will to share experiences, to enjoy and suffer together, to plan jointly and to act in concert. All of it is called companionship which is a Will, the will to be and remain companions. Implying jointness and togetherness and sharing, companionship rules out individualism which implies self-centeredness, inconsiderateness and single-handed action. Nobody can be a companion and an individualist at the same time or in the same situation or relationship. But that's precisely what Bill intended to be. He wanted to be married and single-acting, companion and individualist, all in one piece. His scheme of life was based on two mutually exclusive Wills: the will to companionship and the will to individualism.

I want you to know that everything in life that is of significance and value is a Will. Friendship is the will to have and keep friends. To be and remain on amicable terms with your neighbors calls for the will to cultivate neighborly relations. Citizenship is the will to be a desirable citizen, honesty the will to honest dealing, fairness the will to practice fair procedure. You cannot be understanding unless you free yourself of the will to misinterpret, to find fault, to be captious or literal. In the same sense, thinking is the will to draw correct conclusions from solid premises. There is the will to doubt, to believe, to be well. Even plain possessions constitute wills. Your house expresses the will to ownership, your garden the will to add charm to your life, your automobile the will to enjoy legitimate comforts. Needless to add that religion, education, race, and nationality, and countless other trends, strivings and ambitions are all Wills.

You will readily understand the reason why I stress this matter of Will as a force which permeates all significant phases of our daily lives if you realize that the contemporary and modern tendency is to place the emphasis on emotions, drives and instincts as the main power which governs human action. We in Recovery will have nothing of a theory which relegates life, more particularly life in a group, to blind instincts and capricious drives. We have solidly embraced a viewpoint which considers action as based or capable of being based on deliberate plans and settled decisions, on reasoned conclusions and firm determinations. And plans, decisions, conclusions and determinations are guided by the Will; they are not or do not have to be driven by instincts. This is in the nature of an aside remark, but a very vital sort of an aside.

The wills which I mentioned before are centered around the needs and requirements of group life. They are called group-oriented or *group-centered*. Opposed to them are the wills which are centered around the individual or personal self. They are individualistic or *self-centered*. The desire to be in a tavern instead of at home, to spend time with a chum rather than with one's wife is a self-centered Will. It may be unobjectionable at times, but it is self-centered, nevertheless. In order to be group-centered you must control or hold down your self-centered desires and cravings, that is, your individualistic trends and drives. The control is exercised by the Will.

Once you have declared the will to join hands with another person, in marriage or friendship or business, or even in a mere act of casual conversation or some fleeting and transient endeavor, you have tied your hands and have assumed the obligation to act jointly, to share with the partner and to consider his or her needs, tastes and feelings. Henceforth you are no longer free and independent. You are committed to your obligation and have lost the freedom to enact individualistic behavior. In our democratic order there is ample room for free action and independent conduct. Nobody is forced to work or marry or practice friendship or worship or vote. And if you avoid obligations, partnerships and group ties, then, you retain a good measure of freedom to indulge your personal tastes and your self-centered inclinations provided they do not clash with law or morals. But even in our democratic way of life, while you are free to shun certain obligations, once you assume them you tie yourself and lose your independence. Democracy means freedom of choosing (within certain limits). But after you have chosen you lose your *freedom of inclination* and are bound by the *restraint of obligation*. Bill assumed the marital obligation to share but retained his individual inclination to lead an independent life. The needs, tastes and feelings of the person he had tied himself to were neglected, ignored or shocked. He insisted on practicing contradictory and incompatible modes of living at one and the same time: self-centeredness and group-centeredness, independence and restraint, refusing and sharing, drive and will, individualism and companionship, inclination and obligation.

You remember I asked whether Bill *meant* to be rude, whether he *meant* to rob Bernice of her due share of matrimonial life. This term "to mean" refers to that singular capacity of the human Will to toy and trifle with some activities and to "mean business" with others. A Will which makes group-centeredness its business means the group and not the self. It is then unqualifiedly *group-minded* and ceases to be *self-minded*. If it oscillates and alternates between self and group, then, it toys and trifles with one or with both tendencies. It does not mean business. Bill was a good provider. At heart, he was deeply concerned about his wife's welfare. When Bernice was ill he went out of his way to help her. In a sense, he *meant* to be a companion and to maintain the marital group. But he permitted his personal inclinations to interfere with and frustrate his group obligations. His Will was divided, serving partly the group, partly the self. He was both group-minded and self-minded. Meaning both members of a team of opposites he did not "mean business" with either. Perhaps he did not mean to be rude. Perhaps he meant to share. But whether meaning or not meaning, at all events, he did not "mean business."

Now a word about Bernice. When she felt mortified and decided not to work herself up over it; when she burnt with indignation and concluded that "there is no right or wrong in domestic life;" when she was crushed by humiliation and refused "to make an issue of it," when she did all of this she exhibited a degree of self-control that is truly touching in its gentleness and nobility. In a savage assault on her feelings she used her Will and conquered emotion. She was thoroughly group-minded and self-oblivious, devoted to obligation and forgetful of inclination, in short, the flower and consummation of Recovery's self-help spirit. She had the Will to companionship and the Will to health and *meant* both.

12

SUBJECTIVE WANTS AND OBJECTIVE NEEDS

Annette, on the Saturday panel, recalled an episode from the days when she was ill already but had not yet joined Recovery. The incident referred to an experience in her pre-marital life when expecting a Valentine gift from her present husband, Clem, her expectations were disappointed. "Valentine's Day came," she said, "but there was no gift or card or any sort of a token of attention. I got angry and tense and had a pain in my side and had no appetite for supper. When I made an effort to push down the food, forcing myself to eat, there was a tight feeling in my abdomen. I went to bed, and cried and felt I had been let down. In the middle of the night I awoke and had a strange sensation in the abdomen. I felt nauseated, went to the bathroom but couldn't vomit. Then I began to tremble all over. I felt wretched all the time, I boiled inside and was furious at Clem and worked myself up into a panic. . . About two years after this miserable night Valentine's Day came around again. By that time I had my Recovery training and knew the difference between important things and matters that are trivial. And after dinner I asked Clem calmly, did you forget today is Valentine's Day? He said, 'no,' and went to his coat and pulled out a box of candy. At that moment I realized how I had changed. . . ."

Annette failed to receive a box of candy (Valentine gift), and as a consequence worked herself up to such a degree of excitement that she developed an agonizing night of pain, tightness in the abdomen, nausea, tremors and a "boiling fury" at her boy friend and later husband, Clem. In other words, she disturbed the peace of her inner organs and the harmony of her marital life because of—a box of candy. At the time of the incident, Annette assures us, she had not yet gone through the process of Recovery training and did not know the "difference between important things and matters that are trivial." Some years later she had a similar experience but behaved in accord with Recovery principles, controlling temper and refusing to sacrifice inner and outer peace to—a box of candy. "At that moment," Annette commented, "I realized how I had changed." But does it take the cumbrous machinery of Recovery training to make a person recognize the difference between trivial matters and important values? Between the relative insignificance of a Valentine gift and the supreme relevance of individual well-being and marital happiness? To make this distinction requires nothing more than a modicum of intelligence. From what we know about Annette today she must have had a generous amount of that commodity even before she joined Recovery. And if she insists that she has changed the change cannot refer to her intellectual powers but rather to her sense of values. What Annette learned in Recovery and what all my patients are expected to learn there is to approach things with a proper set of valuations. It is your table of valuations which tells you what is important or trivial, what is essential and what insignificant. In her pre-Recovery days, Annette's table of valuations was in a muddle, contradictory, jumbled, confused. Today it is solid, stable, balanced. And if this is so, Annette must have changed, indeed.

You may object to my manner of simplifying and distorting the story of the Valentine gift. The meaning of that gift is by no means exhausted by calling it a box of candy. As a Valentine gift it was meant to be a token of affection and attention. As such it represented a value, and if Annette felt hurt and provoked because that valuable object was denied her is it fair to charge her with a poor sense of values? Another question may be properly asked: two years after the first incident another Valentine came around and Annette's husband, Clem, arrived home without offering a gift. On that occasion Annette raised no fuss about Clem's seeming lack of attention and affection. Due to her Recovery training, she claims, she now realized that a box of candy was a triviality. But attention and affection can hardly be called trivialities. Was Annette's sense of values now blunted? Was it blunted precisely by that much vaunted thing we call Recovery training? You see here that it is by no means easy to manipulate the sense of values.

Briefly, a thing is valuable if it promotes inner peace leading to contentment, well-being and self-respect; or, if it advances the cause of outer peace resulting in adjustment to family, friends, neighbors, co-workers. If your main aim is to secure peace you are a realist. Then, the attainment of inner and outer peace is your supreme value. Unfortunately, if life is nothing but peaceful it is apt to acquire a note of drabness and monotony, a quality of dull routine with a conspicuous lack of variety and novelty.

People are likely to be bored by an existence that is gently
flowing along in its unruffled course with little change and
newness. Many people crave activities which are flavored and
spiced. They want a measure of excitement, stimulation, adventure. They prefer the thrill of "dangerous living" to a peaceful,
well settled and thoroughly ordered daily round. To them, mere
peace is deadening, flat, colorless and lifeless while excitement,
thrill and adventure are vitalizing, sparkling and energizing. To
many men and women, the supreme value is that which is
interesting, agitating, stirring. If they are romantic they want to
be stirred by emotion; if they are intellectualists they prefer the
thril of bold views and daring thoughts. Summing up: The
realist strives for peace, the romanto-intellectualist for thrill and
excitement. Peace, order and balance are the supreme values of
the one; thrilling excitement, variety and adventure those of the
other. Unfortunately, many persons prefer romanto-intellectualist excitement to realistic peace.

I shall admit that excitement, producing thrills, is the spice of
life. But it is not life. It is merely its spice. If spices are added to
food they contribute nothing to its value as nourishment. They
merely make the food more tasty and palatable, more appetizing
and desirable. But mark here that taste and palatability, appetite and desirability are highly personal and subjective. What is
tasty to me may not at all suit your taste; what whets my appetite
may blunt yours. My palate may be tempted by what yours is
repelled; my desires may run to things which yours shun. Food is
in a different class. You may dispense with spices altogether but
you cannot eliminate food from your life any more than I can. In
other words: food is an *objective need,* spices are *subjective
wants.* Returning to our original subject we may conclude that
peace is the food of life, a value and objective need while
excitement is merely the spice and thrill of life, a desirability (not
a value) and nothing but a subjective want.

I said that peace is a supreme value. This implies the existence
of lesser and lower values. Such lower values are affection and
attention; conversation and conviviality; joy and entertainment.
They go by the name of *mental comforts.* Another series of lower
values is concerned with the various desires for physical recreation, with the stimulation of food and drinks, with the effort to
ease the exactions of the daily routine, and with the craving for
attractiveness in point of personal appearance and personal
property. These go by the name of *physical comforts.* Both the

thrills of excitement and the comforts of the lower values are legitimate pursuits if cultivated in moderation. However, if they clash with the aims and needs of the supreme value of peace they must be suppressed or checked or controlled. To know which thrills to tolerate and which comforts to admit within one's scheme of life requires a delicately balanced sense of values. The sense of values is not born with you; it must be acquired through training. The one to train you is your leader. It may be parents, teachers, ministers or anyone who knows the distinction between values, on the one hand, and thrills and comforts on the other. For the nervous patient, the proper source for leadership is his physician.

My role as a leader of nervous patients is difficult and, in a sense, embarrassing. My patients suffer agonies and discomfort and torture. Hence, they desire quick or immediate relief. This is their subjective want. It is legitimate and should be granted if possible. Unfortunately, a *quick relief,* even if it could be secured, is not a *lasting cure.* As your physician I must insist on the final cure because it alone will restore your health. Relief is mere comfort while health is a value. Health returns you to a useful and valuable life in family and community. Relief does nothing of the kind. I should like to relieve your discomfort but my main endeavor is to regain for you the value of sustained mental health. There is another disturbing element in my function as a leader to my patients. Handicapped by the torments of suffering they are barred from an active social and occupational life. Their existence is, therefore, deprived of the excitements and thrills of stimulating experience, of accomplishment and self-respect. Their daily round is carried on in an emotional void, in an atmosphere of drabness and boredom. In order to fill the void and to escape the boredom they want excitement. And if they cannot secure it in routine channels they hunt for it in devious paths, in endless complaints, in all kinds of devices for attention-getting, in tantrums and tempers. That these excitements are wants and not needs is obvious. Even these excitements might sometimes have a proper claim to toleration. But as your leader I have the embarrassing obligation to emphasize needs in preference to wants.

We shall now be in a better position to understand the meaning of the incident in which Annette disturbed her inner peace through symptoms and her outer peace through a clash with her fiance. The missing Valentine gift meant to her a token of affection (mental comfort) and the anticipation of a surprise (thrill). When the expected comfort and thrill were denied her, Annette threw a tantrum and jeopardized the values of health and marriage. With this she displayed a tendency to favor subjective wants in preference to objective needs. But endowed with a good native intellect it should have been easy for Annette to reason that needs are more important than wants and that peace is more essential than thrills and comforts. Why did her intellect fail her? The answer is that a person's reasoning is powerfully influenced by the values cultivated in his group. And our contemporary group has placed a preposterous valuation on romanto-intellectual wants to the detriment of realistic needs. This statement does not require detailed exposition. All you have to do is to inspect the system of education as practiced in our schools and colleges and you will realize that present-day teaching has the almost exclusive ambition to cater to the student's want of mental and physical comfort, and to pay far less attention to his need for training and discipline. That the modern home has abandoned the effort to train and discipline children is too well known to call for special mention. The average parent of today, encouraged by popular philosophies and psychologies, gives his youngsters ample freedom to express their individualistic wants and to ignore the needs for group control and group discipline. If I add that the newspaper headlines, comic strips, radio, movies and television fairly vie with one another in their sordid occupations to cater to the comforts and thrills of their readers, listeners and viewers I have about completed the circle of the sinister influences which today pervert the tastes and corrupt the valuations of children and adults alike. Our modern media of "education" extol, knowingly or unwittingly, the superiority of wants over needs and the priority of thrills and comforts over discipline and values. Annette, in her pre-Recovery days, could not possibly escape the overpowering pressure of these organs of public opinion and from them imbibed the pernicious contemporary philosophy which favors subjective wants and scorns the value of objective needs. This modern philosophy was largely responsible for her ailment and her torturing symptoms and might have wrecked her marriage had not Recovery intervened and made her revise her faulty sense of values.

13

THE UNCONVINCING COMPLAINT

The panel discussed the subject of "Helplessness Is Not Hopelessness," taken from the October 1946 issue of the Recovery Journal. Caroline mentioned a recent experience in a department store. Approaching the elevator she was preoccupied with her inner difficulties, and instead of pressing the elevator button she pulled a light switch. The store section went dark. "I immediately realized my mistake, felt tense and trembled. But then I applied the spotting technique and knew that average people make mistakes of this kind and if I didn't have the courage to make mistakes in trivial matters I did not consider myself a person of average but as one of exceptional inefficiency. After the spotting I was calm . . . In former days I would have become hysterical, would have thought that surely something was wrong with my mind. I would have suffered awful sensations and would have rushed to the phone telling my husband that was again proof I couldn't get well and trying to convince him that I was hopeless."

Caroline described in graphic detail the striking contrast between her present and her past behavior. In the past, prior to receiving her Recovery training, she felt helpless and hopeless when a minor mishap occurred. Now she feels helpless for a moment; the idea of hopelessness presents itself in a flash but she spots it instantly and commands her muscles not to respond to her silly feelings. This is all in accord with the basic principles of Recovery's self-help system and requires little comment. By now it ought to be a commonplace that our patients are trained in Recovery to deny muscular expression to their feelings of fear and anger and to control their temper through the process of spotting.

There was one phrase in Caroline's account that arrested my attention. In the past, she said, she would have rushed to the phone trying to convince her husband that she was hopeless. A statement of this sort has a weird and uncanny note. It seems to me that were I faced with a hopeless situation I might either resign myself to my fate; or I might make a desperate effort to force the issue, or I might pray for deliverance; or I might yell for help. But the last thought that could conceivably enter my mind would be to want to convince somebody that, really and truly, I am actually helpless and hopeless. Yet, Caroline, in a condition of seeming despondency, had no other thought but—to be convincing.

If Caroline's ambition was to convince her husband she must have assumed that he needed convincing, that he doubted her stories of suffering and agony, at the very least, that he thought them exaggerated or colored or twisted. Her stories were what we call "complaints." And if Caroline's case is somehow representative of nervous patients in general we must conclude that the leading fear in the minds of our patients is that their complaints are doubted, that their sincerity is questioned, in short, that they are not convincing. No wonder they make heroic efforts to compel conviction.

What the patient wants his listener to be convinced of is that he is a helpless victim of his symptoms; that he tries everything within his power to be calm but does not succeed; that he is trapped by his handicap and cannot escape its grip. His tantrums, his bursts of dizziness, his weakness and fatigue, his tremors and palpitations, he thinks, are all of one cast: they are beyond endurance and beyond control. These complaints lack conviction because they are grossly contradicted by the facts of daily observation. The tantrums have a peculiar quality of being enacted at home only, perhaps also in the physician's office, but never at a concert or at a social gathering. The fatigue, unendurable in the forenoon, disappears miraculously in the late afternoon and in the evening. The headache, "splitting" or "killing," follows immediately upon a domestic squabble and vanishes conveniently when a welcome guest arrives on the scene. Several of my patients were unable to stop a jerk in the arm whenever they were at home but kept it under perfect control when they went shopping in the morning or visiting in the evening. Some had vomiting spells in restaurants but never at home or vice versa. I have seen patients whose throat "locked" exactly at 1:00 PM every day. I have seen others who scratched away furiously at an "uncontrollable" itch at home but controlled it perfectly in the presence of friends and strangers. There is the patient who experiences his "unbearable" fatigue on Sundays and holidays only. On weekdays, in the office or factory, he is alert and chipper; or, the girl who vomits in the morning only and at home only, never after 9 AM and never outside the home; or, the woman who is nauseated in the afternoon only after the husband returns from work. On Sundays the nausea persists all day, the husband being home all day. Most suspect of insincerity and most damaging to the patient's reputation is his incurable fondness for monstrously exaggerating the intenseness of his symptoms. If month after month and year after year he clamors that he "simply can't stand it," that "if something isn't done immediately" he is "surely going to end it all"; that he "can't take it any longer"; and that today he is "positively at the end of his rope"; if these hackneyed phrases are repeated monotonously spell after spell and tantrum after tantrum the relatives cannot fail to realize how well the patient "can stand it," how little he is inclined to "end it all," and how the rope has a mysterious way of lengthening without reaching its end. The threats are then ignored and the alarms treated with contemptuous indifference. There is no point multiplying these examples although it would be easy for me to cull additional hundreds or thousands from my records. They all tell the same story: the nervous symptom is not convincing, and if the nervous patient wants to be believed he must make it his supreme goal to compel conviction. That's what Caroline did. In a panic which seemed to shake her with elemental force she did not cry for help but thought of one thing only: to convince her husband that her plight was beyond remedy.

That the patient's complaint sounds unconvincing to the relatives is a calamity. But that calamity turns into outright tragedy if the patient is unable to convince himself. And conviction is denied him irrevocably. The complaint may be a frequency of urination which "forces" him to run to the bathroom every five minutes. "That surely is something I cannot stop," he exclaims or thinks. Then he sits through a show or card game for solid three or four hours without even a passing thought to his otherwise "uncontrollable" bladder trouble. How can he possibly believe his own doctrine of helplessness if a mere card game helps him check his trouble? Another complaint may be that of "unbearable" pressure in the head. "Clearly, that is out of my control," the patient insists. When questioned he admits that the pressure is absent when he is in his office, "but once I step out I have it." Or take the case of the mother who yells at her own children incessantly because they are "intolerably" noisy. With the neighbor's children she is a paragon of charm and sweetness in spite of their equally "intolerable" loud and boisterous behavior. That mother cannot by any twist of logic make herself believe that her temper is out of control. The ease with which she controls it with the neighbor's children stamps her complaint as insincere and renders it unconvincing. Experiences of this kind admit of one conclusion only: the patient has good control but fails to practice it under certain conditions. Fully aware of his ability to help himself he is unable to believe his own protestations of helplessness. And trying to convince his relatives his efforts are stymied by his own lack of conviction.

If a person is unable to believe himself he loses or weakens his *self-respect*. If he is unable to make others believe him he loses or weakens their respect for him, that is, he ruins or impairs his *reputation*. It is difficult to live without proper self-respect. But life becomes an almost unbearable affliction if both self-respect and reputation are wanting or markedly defective. From this vantage point it is easy to understand the tragic plight of the long-term nervous patient. After years of futile and ludicrous complaining his self-respect is in tatters and his reputation torn to shreds. He could restore both should he decide resolutely to give up his plaints and lamentations. If he fails to do that he is doomed to lead a life of indignity and self-contempt, a life of stigmatization and social isolation. An existence of this kind is possible only if somehow, by hook or by crook, the illusion of uncontrollability is maintained and fortified against all evidence to the contrary. The doctrine of helplessness and hopelessness must then be hammered unceasingly and unrelentingly into the patient's own head (to save his self-respect) and into the heads of the relatives (to save his reputation). Hence, the imperative urge to carry on a veritable crusade of convincing, that is, complaining. The proudest achievement which Recovery can claim is the thoroughness with which it has purged its members of their pernicious habits of wailing and lamenting. Trained in the techniques of spotting and commanding their muscles our patients have ceased complaining and are now convincing.

14

PARTIAL VIEWS AND TOTAL VIEWPOINT

Loraine reported her recent setback. She had been well for the past several months but suddenly got back her fears of riding alone on elevator trains and subways. She suffered the "most awful" palpitations, sweats and panics when she took rides. Before long she employed the Recovery techniques of spotting fears and using muscles and controlled her symptoms, manipulating rides without difficulty. But in spite of all her pluck and determination she was unable to relax. She was tense and restless and thoroughly disgusted with herself. She then decided that what was really wrong with her was that she was not sufficiently busy. So she increased her average quota of shows, bowling, swimming and sundry other recreational activities. "I needed something stimulating," she said, "so I wouldn't think of myself all the time. . . ."

Loraine wanted stimulation which indicates that she was bored. Being bored she was disgusted with her Self. And in order to escape boredom and Self-disgust she decided she had to avoid thinking of her Self "all the time." But it seems to me that to think of one's Self ought to be a most stimulating occupation. Why was it irritating and disgusting to Loraine?

To be bored means to be disinterested. You cannot experience boredom while you read an interesting story or attend an interesting show or take part in an interesting conversation. In all these instances, your interest is held, engaged, attracted. If the interest deepens you are absorbed, engrossed, fascinated, perhaps enraptured. In a situation of this kind, most or all of your attention is directed toward the object which interests or fascinates you. But once the interest wanes or the fascination lifts your attention reverts to your Self and is no longer diverted from it. Now you are alone with your Self, not distracted from it but attracted to it. And whether your Self bores or interests you depends on the view you take of it. Clearly, Loraine viewed her Self as something that could not engross her interest, as something that bored her, as something devoid of fascination and stimulation, perhaps as something odious, repelling and loathsome. Beholding that Self which she thought of as detestable and

hateful she became "tense and restless and thoroughly disgusted." No wonder she "needed something stimulating." Her own
Self was "disgusting" and irritating.

I know Loraine; I know her husband, mother and sister; I
know her home life and her social activities, her character and
tastes. With all this intimate knowledge of her conduct, history
and circumstances I cannot share even a fraction of the disastrous view she takes of her Self. To my view, her Self is of good
or fair average; to her own view, it is of the poorest quality, not
fit to be looked at, not suitable to be left alone with. What
precisely makes our views clash so radically?

If you look at an object, let me say a table, you place yourself at
a certain point and take your view from there. This is *your point
of view* or your *view-point*. If the point from which you observe
the table is too distant you will miss many details. Your viewpoint will then furnish you with a *general view* only. If the point
on which you take your stand is too close you will miss the
general features of outline, shape and style. Your viewpoint will
then provide you with a *particular view* only. The correct view
is the one which combines both the particular and general views.
This is the *total view*. Whether your view of an object is more
particular or more general, in either case, it is a *partial view*
only. The total view must combine both particular and general
views.

The object which Loraine viewed was her Self. She noticed
her tenseness and restlessness and concluded that her Self was
"disgusting." She knew what was "really wrong" with it; it
"needed stimulation." With this, she diagnosed the condition
and prescribed the cure. If so, her view-point was that she (her
Self) was a competent diagnostician and efficient healer. She
claimed expert knowledge and made a show of authority, that is,
she paraded her Self as important, highly informed and superior.
You, my patients, know that this is what I call the romanto-
intellectualist attitude.

If Loraine held the view that her Self had the qualities of
excellence and superiority how could she at the same time
subscribe to the very opposite view that it was disgusting? This
is clearly a contradiction which you will not understand unless
you consider what I told you about the difference between
particular and general view-points. If you look into yourself you
will discover within you many features which are excellent,
superior and exceptional. At times you displayed unusual courage, at other times there was an act of singular loyalty, or a
performance of superior skill, or an exhibit of extraordinary

wisdom. If you merely view these isolated instances of your behavior (particular viewpoint) you can easily form the opinion that yours is an exceptional Self. But if you review the broad lines of your past development you are likely to find a great deal of misdirected effort, of goals missed and purposes frustrated. Judged in the light of this general view-point, your record may appear as one of mediocrity and incapacity in which the instances of failure crowd out those of accomplishment. Your particular view-point, focusing the gaze on scattered triumphs, gives you the impression of an exalted and superior Self; but the general viewpoint, surveying the larger field of your past endeavor, offers you the picture of failure and futility and may make you feel "disgusted."

I told you that my view of Loraine's life was decidedly more favorable than was her own. I knew many details of her life. I knew particular occasions when her conduct had been anything but a credit to her. I was acquainted with her tantrums, her temperamental explosions, her craving for attention, her stubbornness and vanity. This was the particular view I had taken of her behavior. Aside from this, I had studied the various aspects of her past history, and my verdict was that it represented a crazy-quilt of good intentions and poor execution, of lofty aspirations and petty performance. This was the general viewpoint I had of her. But in reviewing her record, I judged her neither by the particular nor by the general viewpoint. Instead, I applied the total view. And surveying the totality of her experience I reached the conclusion that it had the average quality of a fumbling, erring and straying existence. But no matter how deplorable was her fumbling, how distressing her erring and how disconcerting her straying, it was all average. Having drawn this conclusion I formed the *average viewpoint* which is based on common sense and ought to be the *common viewpoint* held by everybody. In order to gain a full understanding of this average viewpoint you will have to realize that the life of the average person is punctuated by precisely the features which were characteristic of Loraine's Self: temper, attention-hunting, stubbornness and vanity. Being average, these features cannot, by the wildest stretch of the imagination, be called degrading or disgraceful or "disgusting." If Loraine applied precisely these terms to her Self I conclude that her philosophy was that of exceptionality. She had not yet absorbed the Recovery philosophy of averageness and condemned when she could have condoned, accused when she might have excused. You see here that the total view is closely associated with the *average view*. With the average view to guide you, you will be able to behold the deficiencies of your Self and will judge them as average failings; they will not strike you with terror, hence, you will not be tense; being reconciled to them, you will not try frantically to run away from your Self; hence, you will not be restless. And losing your tenseness and restlessness, you will be relaxed and will enjoy your Self instead of being "disgusted" with it and bored by it.   The average view will teach you to tolerate your Self. Moreover, viewing your own Self as average and acceptable, you will give the same rating to the Selves of others; hence, you will practice tolerance toward them.   And being tolerant of the actions of others, you will not become angry at or provoked by them, hence, you will have little or no temper. No doubt, the average viewpoint which is essentially the total view of life has much to recommend it. If my patients could be induced to adopt it energetically and wholeheartedly, temper, restlessness, tenseness and Self-disgust would be reduced to average levels, and symptoms would not develop into panics and vicious cycles. You will now understand why I stress so persistently the importance of thinking and feeling in terms of averageness. What I have in mind is not a high-sounding philosophy but such down-to-earth matters as symptoms, afflictions and torture.

My patients have the exasperating habit of looking at their symptoms with the partial viewpoint mainly or exclusively. They notice a fatigue sensation and rush to the particular view that their body is exhausted and ready to collapse. They notice that their attention wanders, that their concentration lags, or that on a particular occasion their memory fails them and infer that their mind is unhinged. In all these instances, they observe particulars and base on them a particular viewpoint of doom and disaster. At times they resort to a generalizing viewpoint. They survey the general features of their painful existence, roam across the years of suffering, across their record of frustration and disappointment and exclaim, "What's the use? After these many years, how can I get well?" They shy away, persistently and doggedly, from the total view that their symptoms are of the average variety although more persistent in duration and more resistant to management.   True enough, the resistance and intensity of the symptoms are such that the patient can no longer control them with his own meager resources. But a total view of life could easily tell them that, generally speaking, certain performances of the daily round can be conveniently mastered by the average person while others, more complicated, more intractable, require the services of an expert. If my patients could be made to accept the total viewpoint; moreover, if they were ready to cultivate the common sense of the average viewpoint, suffering and discomfort would be held to a minimum.

Unfortunately, the general trend of modern development has been to disregard, systematically and dogmatically, the total viewpoint. If you listen to our modern forums you will find there groups of persons discussing issues, presumably in order to settle them. However, what they discussed are their particular views, their own pet notions, their own "true" opinions. The theme moves from one particular argument to another or loses itself in a sea of wild generalizations. This has perhaps always been the case and may not be peculiar to our age. But what is decidedly peculiar to our age is the advent of popular psychologies. The exponents of these psychological doctrines seldom if ever touch on the total experience of the average individual. Instead, they prefer to give absurd prominence to particular stirrings and strivings trying to convince you that this particular trend of yours or that isolated disposition is solely and unqualifiedly at the roots of all your ills. With some of these clever coiners of striking and appealing phrases it is the sex instinct which causes your maladjustment, with others it is a mysterious thing which they call collective consciousness, with still others it is a shallow conception termed "inferiority complex." With all of them it is invariably *one thing, one trend, one particular item* of your total experience which is supposed to disturb or wreck your total existence.

Loraine, noticing her tenseness and restlessness, jumped to the conclusion that these distressing but innocent items of her experience needed instant and thorough treatment. Had she taken a total view of her past life she would have realized that tenseness and restlessness had been frequent occurrences in the scheme of her existence and were nothing but average psychological events. But exposed to the defeatist influence of popular philosophies presented to her on screen and stage, in newspaper columns and magazine articles, in lectures and books on popular psychology, she conceived the vague idea that an instinct was running wild, or that a "complex" went beserk, or that a "conflict" ran amuck having broken through the barriers of a so-called repression. All these pretentious and bloated terms are the confused stock in trade preached by modern psychologies. They are based on particular, narrow and one-sided views of life and should have no place in the lives of my patients who, in Recovery, are trained to view events and experiences from the total viewpoint of average experience.

15

BUSINESS AND GAMES; EFFORT AND COMFORT

Lela, on the Saturday panel, spoke of her habit, noticed since early childhood, of correcting mistakes made by people. "We lived in the country and salesmen came by and stopped at our house. One of them spoke of a certain town and said it was in Wisconsin. I knew this was wrong and ran for the map and showed the man it was Minnesota and not Wisconsin. My father laughed and thought it was cute and did not say a word of disapproval to me. This habit of correcting people gave me plenty of trouble. It made me unpopular, worse yet, it made me feel irritated if I could not correct people when they made remarks which I thought were wrong. Today I know, of course, that this desire to prove that people are wrong is temper. It means I am right. In Recovery I have learned to spot the habit, and I think I have it under pretty good control. The other day I stood with a neighbor in front of a yard, and we saw a weed. I asked, 'What is it?' She said, 'Why, it is a ragweed.' I grew up in the country and know ragweeds, and this did not look like any I know. I was about to say, 'It is not a ragweed' but stopped and said, 'Is it?' I was proud of having controlled my impulse and was grateful to Recovery for having trained me to check my temper."

Lela had the habit of correcting people. She loved to show them up as ignorant and to present herself as possessing superior intelligence. This is what you know as the intellectualist variety of temper. You to whom Lela is no stranger will not hesitate to call her a kindly person, gentle in disposition, eager to be helpful and anxious to give no offense. If she was endowed with an amiable disposition, why did she at the same time display a tendency to be aggressive, to trip up people, to expose them as stupid, uninformed, intellectually inferior? Clearly, the two trends are mutually exclusive, the one cancelling the other, both working at cross-purpose. Lela's friendly disposition created good-will, but the good-will thus produced was weakened or dissipated by her disposition to be critical, fault-finding and antagonistic. Which was the "real" Lela? Which was her "real" purpose in life? Was it to win people over with courtesy? Or, was it to repel them with an uncouth manner? The answer is: ordinarily, and as a rule, Lela made it her *business* to make friends. But sometimes, and as an exception, she practiced the *game* of shocking and antagonizing people, thus making enemies. Lela claims that the game of shocking people caused her "plenty of trouble," making her unpopular and giving her a lot of irritation. If so, why did she continue the game? Why did she insist on toying with life instead of strictly tending to its (and her) business?

Life is a business. There is or ought to be time in everybody's routine to play and toy, to amuse himself with games and to divert his attention from the serious aspects of the business of living. Nevertheless, life is not a game; it is a business which must be toiled at and attended to. Its business is to create and maintain values (family, community, education, religion, sociability). The trouble is that values are tender and delicate and easily disturbed. They are likely to be disturbed through destructive forces arising in inner environment (symptoms and temper), or from commotions and convulsions affecting outer environment (strife and dissension between persons and groups). Since strife and dissension usually are the result of temper we may safely assume that the peace of persons, families or communities is threatened by two elements mainly: symptoms which interfere with inner peace, and temper which obstructs both inner and outer peace. To sum up: life needs inner and outer peace for producing and maintaining values. The factors which endanger peace are symptoms and temper. Life's principal business is, therefore, to reduce both symptoms and temper to a minimum.

If anyone deserves the title of a conscientious, serious-minded person it is Lela. She is dependable and generous, has firm convictions and a sturdy quality of character. From what I know of her background there can be no doubt that even in early childhood she was thoughtful and considerate, courteous and tactful, treating people with respect and careful not to hurt their feelings. With all these features to her credit she must have taken seriously the business of her life. Why did she at the same time trifle and gamble with that same business? The answer is that even people as lovely and desirable as Lela have a tendency, at times, to be serious about games and playful about business. They are particularly apt to be so if the game they are engaged in is that of romanto-intellectualist temper. Ordinarily, Lela is a realist taking the business of her life seriously. But at times she feels (or used to feel) the itch of romanto-intellectualism indulging the game of playing with the business of life. And to play with the business of life means to gamble.

If you start a game you are not obliged to continue it. You may drop it because you don't like it, or because it bores you; or because luck is against you; or because you have as trivial a thing as a headache. Conversely, if you engage in business (job, marriage, the rearing of children, helping a friend, civic activities, club work) you are under obligation to continue it, to see it through, to finish what you have started. Headaches, boredom, dislike, strain are no justification for shirking the duty you have assumed or the commission you have accepted. Games are *personal inclinations*; business is *group obligation*. Games are pleasure, business is a *task*. A task may be pleasing which means that pleasure and task can be combined. But if a game, no matter how pleasurable, interferes with the serious task of a business the thing to do is to stop the game and to continue the business. Tasks must have unquestioned priority over games. Lela, going through months of Recovery training, imbibed this supreme principle of Recovery philosophy that in the business of life tasks must invariably take precedence over pleasures. In life, even a plain conversation with a neighbor acquires the character of a task. It imposes the obligation to be courteous, to be friendly, to show humility, to create good will, to avoid criticism and intellectual snobbishness (the desire to show superiority).

In commercial business, there is one goal only: to produce income. But business men are human, endowed with human desires, whims and inclinations. There is the inclination to take it easy, to go off on a trip, to over-expand, to run up debts because of hastily conceived plans. These inclinations are human stirrings and human strivings and as such the direct offsprings of "human nature." It is human and natural to crave an easy life or to long for the amenities of a trip, or to take chances with indebtedness. But no matter how human and natural these desires are, they turn into a wild gamble if they clash with the one and only business aim: to produce income.

Getting well is a business. It is emphatically not a game, certainly not a wild gamble. Unfortunately, my patients have the tendency to play and gamble with their health. They give unthinking and wanton precedence to the stirrings of their "human nature" to the detriment of their only legitimate goal: to get well. It is human and natural to want quick relief, to be impatient with the irksome obligation to wait for the final cure; it is understandable and natural to hate the discomfort of laborious and untiring practice, to want to give way to temper, to play for attention, to crave sympathy and to indulge in self-pity, to complain and to work oneself up. But all of this is gambling with the business of getting well. It is the game of giving in to human nature, not the business of health. The one and only goal of the patient must be to regain his mental health. In order to achieve it the goals and whims and wishes of "human nature" must be held down with ruthless determination.

Games provide relief from strain; they provide diversion, entertainment and relaxation. All of this means: comfort. Business is in a different category. At times, it may be conducive to relaxation, diversion and entertainment. But ordinarily it requires toil and strain, patient application and ceaseless exertion. All of this means: effort. Games are conducted with the *Will to Comfort*; business is executed with the *Will to Effort*. Time was when the Will to Effort was systematically cultivated in homes and schools, on farms, in stores and factories. Men and women were trained routinely to expect of life a great deal of effort and a small fraction only of comfort. In the process, they developed a rugged disposition which means: the Will to Bear Discomfort. Unfortunately, the accent is today on comfort, on fun and entertainment, on making things easy and pleasant. With the Will to Comfort scoring heavily over the Will to Effort people are no longer prepared to endure strain and anxieties and suffering. And when suffering strikes, especially the excruciating suffering of nervous ailments, they expect the cure to be effected with the proverbial ease of a child's play and perhaps in as brief a space of time as the average game may last. This means playing with the illness and converting the business of getting well into a game of trying to secure effortless comfort. In Recovery, you are taught to approach the business of getting well in the spirit of performing a task and meaning business. The business calls, first and foremost, for labor and exertion and self-control, in other words, for the Will to Effort. A good portion of the effort must be directed toward the business of curbing the romanto-intellectual temper. As you know, it is temper primarily which creates and maintains tenseness, and it is tenseness which creates and maintains nervous symptoms. Lela, having learned in Recovery that temper interferes with the business of getting well, decided to take seriously the principles of Recovery training, to keep a vigilant eye on her temper and to consider health as the supreme task to be accomplished by a patient. She is not well yet but is certain to obtain her final cure if she continues as doggedly as she has done to pursue the serious business of realistic health and to avoid the frisky game of romanto-intellectualist comfort. With the Will to Effort effectively curbing her Will to Comfort she is bound to attain her ultimate goal: to get well.

16

INTERPRETATIONS AND CONCLUSIONS

Ada recalled the agonies she suffered for many years when at times her throat suddenly "locked." "The locking happened," she said, "when I became irritated, when my feelings were hurt, or when I became temperamental. I was sure I had a growth in the throat because how could an irritation or upset produce that awful pressure I felt in that spot? When the locking took place I would jump from my seat, my heart would pound and I broke into a cold sweat and I shook with tremors and I was sure I was choking to death. My brother lives with us and when he was present he would grab me and pound me and hit me on the back as one would revive somebody who is choking. If that didn't help as it usually didn't he would drag me on the back porch and continue the pounding there and I made a terrible noise and the neighbors would rush out of their apartments to help. Because of these panics I developed all kind of fears. For instance, I was afraid to take orange juice because the pulp might stick in my throat. I was of course afraid of being alone at home because I might get a spell and nobody around to help me. I was also afraid to go out on the street or visit people because I might be seen in a spell. After I joined Recovery the spells got less and less but sometimes I have them yet. Not so long ago I was sitting at the table reading a newspaper when I picked up an apple and took a bite. Suddenly the throat locked. I got scared and felt like smothering. My brother ran over to pound me but I motioned him not to. I spotted the spell as a sensation and knew it was distress but no danger. So I got up and walked to the kitchen, and when my brother reached me and saw that I had gotten my breath he said, 'Why, I can't believe it. How did you manage to stop the choking? I swear it did not last more than thirty seconds.' I tried to explain and said something about spotting but he did not seem to understand. Finally he said, 'I don't understand what you folks talk about in Recovery. But it certainly works.'. . . ."

Ada stated explicitly that her throat "locked" when she was

irritated or when her feelings were hurt or when she was in temper. This can have one meaning only, namely, that the locking was caused by emotions, frustrations and mental upsets. Receiving this information I was certain that Ada considered her trouble as nervous and psychological and not as organic and physical. If this is so, you will realize how amazed I was to hear Ada continue: 'I was sure I had a growth in the throat because how could an irritation or upset produce that awful pressure I felt in that spot?" In the first pronouncement the condition was declared to be psychological and nothing else; in the second, it was said to be physical and nothing else. How is it that Ada, usually possessed of clear thinking and precise expression, launched out today into such a flagrant contradiction? Did her customary logic fail her? Did her mind "lock?"

What Ada actually did was this: She noticed or *thought* that her throat tightened. The tightening was experienced or *felt* by her as a choking which stifled speech and impaired breathing. What she thus thought and felt produced a panic which gave rise to distressing *sensations* (palpitations, tremors, sweats) and produced the *impulse* to run for life ("I jumped from my seat"). All of this means that when the locking happened, Ada made, in a flash, sundry *observations* about her inner experiences cataloguing them in her mind as a varied assortment of thoughts, feelings, sensations and impulses. She noticed further that whenever the locking occurred it was preceded by irritations, frustrations and temper. From this series of observations she drew two *conclusions*: (1) the cause was psychological, (2) the cause was physical. This process of drawing two contradictory conclusions from one and the same set of observations we call *confusion*.

When Ada, with her throat "locked," made observations and drew conclusions she practiced what is called the process of thinking. This process is an art based on a technique and governed by rules. The technique is that of dependable observation; the rules are those of valid conclusion. When my patients get ready to employ their thinking process for reporting or studying their symptoms they almost invariably bungle the observations and jumble the conclusions. That happened in Ada's case when she observed a tightening and concluded that it was a "locking." The throat is a tube which serves the purpose of letting the food pass through the esophagus and the air through the larynx. Nervous patients experience frequently a tightening in this locality. But it is merely a tightening, perhaps not even a narrowing of the passageway, certainly not a complete closing or "locking." Had Ada, in her pre-Recovery days, been trained in the technique of making pertinent observations she could have noticed that air circulated freely and food traveled unhampered through the tube even if the throat was "locked." She never had an opportunity to observe an actual stoppage or occlusion or obstruction.   What she reported on the panel demonstrates conclusively that she suffered no such thing as a "locked" throat. On her own accounting, when her brother dragged her out on the porch she "made a terrible noise, and the neighbors rushed out of their apartments to help." That "terrible noise" assuredly required a great deal of air.   How did Ada manage to push through her "locked" throat a quantity of air sufficient to produce a "terrible noise?" Clearly, her thinking process had acquired the habit of rushing into hasty observations and jumping to shaky conclusions.

If observations are made and conclusions drawn with regard to symptoms the process is called the art of making a diagnosis. That this art is difficult, utterly complex and reserved for thoroughly trained persons only is generally accepted.   But my patients ignore what everybody knows and when they observe a symptom they promptly rush to supply a diagnosis of their own. They notice a pain in the chest and conclude it means a weak heart. They feel a pressure in the head and "know" it is a tumor. A nervous bladder drives them into endless journeys to the bathroom, and "what else can that be but a kidney disease?" Some of my patients discovered that on some days they had two evacuations instead of one, soft but not at all "running," and on the basis of that flimsy observation they concluded it was a "running bowel," or a "diarrhea" or a "colitis." Experiencing a pulling sensation in the neck my patients are apt to conclude that the pulling "must be done" by a growth, at the very least, by a swollen gland.   Many of them delight in the practice of "observing" themselves in an obliging mirror.   The mirror invariably tells them that their features are drawn and haggard, that the eyes have no luster, that the tongue is coated.   The diagnostic inference is that "there must be something wrong somewhere.   Don't you think so?"   They paw over the entire expanse of their bodies, finding a swelling in the leg, flabbiness in the arms, glands in the neck, a quickened pulse in the wrist and forthwith indulge in a riot of grisly diagnoses.   Their theory is that anybody who is not an outright moron knows how to use the thinking process and for a person of "normal" intelligence it is "no trick" to make reliable observations and draw valid conclusions.   In this, they display an enormous contempt for the complexity of the techniques and rules of solid thinking. Putting it differently, my patients approach their symptoms with the philosophy of shallow intellectualism, rushing headlong into uncritical observations and jumping recklessly to immature conclusions. It is the particular mark of the petty intellectual that he has a boundless disrespect for the pitfalls which beset the utterly complicated process of correct thinking. He is smart, and his intellect, he is convinced, has a native sharpness and quickness. So why bother about clumsy techniques and cumbersome rules.

Observations are of two kinds. You observe either the world outside you (with your senses) or the world within you (through introspection). The one furnishes outer experience, the other inner experience. Suppose you meet a man on the street and observe through your senses that he is walking at a leisurely pace, carrying a briefcase and looking straight in front of him. You advance toward him, offering a friendly greeting, and he responds with a smile and the assurance that he is glad to see you. There is hardly any possibility of bungling this series of outer observations. Everybody whose eyes and ears are not damaged by disease or injury is qualified to make them without previous training in technique and rules. The difficulty begins, however, the moment you go beyond the domain of *observation* and pass into the area of *interpretation*. After observing the smile on the man's face you may ask yourself, for instance, what precisely that smile means. It may mean warmth of feeling and joy of seeing you. The proper interpretation, then, would be: fellowship, friendship, good will. Or, it may mean nothing more than conventional politeness. That would be: indifference. If the smile is associated with strained features the proper interpretation might be: annoyance or resentment of your intruding. And finally, the smile may have an expression of irony or sarcasm. In that case, the proper label would be: haughtiness, disrespect and perhaps hostility. This simple example indicates that the pitfalls of thinking reside in interpretation rather than observation. The trouble is that once you have made an observation you feel an imperative urge to interpret it. And if interpretation is difficult even in outer observations, the atempt tto apply it to inner experiences increases the obstacles to such an extent that only a mind trained in the techniques and rules of the thinking process can be expected to conquer them. When Ada experienced the tightening in her throat her observation played on an inner experience. Had she merely stated that she felt a tightness, hers would have been a plain observation secured through introspection. Like everybody, Ada was in a position to make such introspective observations. But when she interpreted the sensation as one which "locked" her throat and stopped the free flow of air, she lacked the qualification to employ this very difficult part of the thinking process. After reaching her dismal interpretation she had no choice but to conclude that something terrible had happened and that a grave emergency was set going. The result was a panic with the attendant vicious cycle and the unavoidable commotion and confusion.

While doing her disastrous piece of interpreting and concluding Ada was not aware of the fact that in doing so she had the temerity to engage in the subtle art of diagnosis. To her untutored perception, this was merely the innocent act of "thinking about" her symptoms. And Ada, being a child of this most modern of all ages, had on many occasions been exposed to the contemporary slogan that a grownup person has not only the right but the solemn duty to "do her own thinking." But I am not at all interested in the philosophical profundities of this so horribly advanced age of ours, and whether my patients have the right or duty to "think for themselves" is a question which concerns me not in the least. My supreme and only duty is to relieve my patients of their agonies. And if their panics and vicious cycles result from their faulty use of the thinking process I shall advise them to throw overboard the rubbish of modern slogans and let me do their thinking in the matter of interpreting and concluding with regard to symptoms. My thinking process has had the benefit of many years of thorough training and disciplining and my thinking about symptoms is not likely to rush into interpretations and jump to conclusions. What you, my patients, have to do is to let me, your physician, teach you how to exercise your thinking process when you attempt to apply it to your symptoms. This is what I have described as "spotting." Spotting means for you to be perpetually on guard against your inveterate tendency to "do your own thinking" when observing a symptom and its accompanying temperamental reaction. It means a ruthless determination to eliminate self-diagnosing and thus to do away with panics, vicious cycles and endless horrors of agony. Ada reported an instance in which the resort to spotting was almost inhumanly difficult. It was of such stupendous difficulty that her brother refused to believe that it could be done. But even that skeptical brother had to admit that "it certainly works."

17

SYMPTOMS, FELLOWSHIP AND LEADERSHIP

In a recent panel discussion on Imagination, Temper and Symptoms, taken from the December 1946 issue of the Recovery Journal, Kenneth made the significant statement: "I was always troubled with self-consciousness, and down at work about four months ago some of the girls at the office were laughing and joking and for some reason I decided they were laughing at me. I got very tense about it and my eyes got blurred and my throat got choked and the first thing I decided was that Recovery was no good and it did not help me and I was going to drop it . . . I was so disturbed that I decided it would be better to join the army again. I had no symptoms there . . . ."

Listening to the panel discussion I was struck by Kenneth's remark and attempting a hurried analysis I noticed three main points in his utterance: (1) Kenneth traced his self-consciousness, and I may add, his symptoms, back to early childhood; (2) his self-consciousness has made him so sensitive that the innocent giggling of bantering girls was likely to exasperate him; (3) while he was in the army he lost his self-consciousness and with it his morbid sensitiveness and his symptoms.

Let me first tell you that many of my patients, concealing their past record of a nervous or mental ailment, enlisted in the armed services. They all seem ready to subscribe to Kenneth's thesis that life in the army provided a mysterious tonic for jaded nerves and that the supposedly peaceful routine of civilian existence meant constant grating and grinding for the same nerves that relaxed so beautifully in barracks, dugouts, under air bombardments and artillery barrages. While in the army, close to four years in the Pacific theatre, Kenneth had his due share of privation: jungle, insects, heat, humidity, monotony, worry about an uncertain future, threat to life aplenty and menace of dreadful disease galore. But he felt relaxed and secure all the time. There was incessant danger to his *physical person*. But his *social personality* was protected and sheltered. What was it that secured this protection for the personality of the soldier while he was in the army? Which was that factor in military life that made the nervous patient feel that he was basically sheltered?

The answer is this: in the army there is *fellowship* and *leadership*. The fellows make for contentment and relaxation; the leaders supply certainty and assurance. A person who is accepted as a fellow in his group and enjoys the leadership of men endowed with stability of character and steadfastness of purpose feels secure and loses his sensitiveness. If he is a nervous patient he also loses his symptoms.

If this is true, it will be important to know why the singular benefits of fellowship and leadership are so stubbornly denied our group of nervous patients. What is a fellow? What is a leader?

A fellow is a person who shares your activities, habits, tastes. He may also share your views and beliefs. If he does not he respects them. A leader does not have to share your life. His part is to tell you what to do and how to do it. He gives you plans, instructions and directions. They are based on principles, standards and values. Suppose the set of habits and tastes which you shared with your fellow comprised in the main such joint activities as visiting one another, going to shows together, bowling and swimming. All of a sudden the fellow conceives a dislike for sports and shows, preferring races, card games and taverns. Unless you follow suit and adopt the same interests and tastes fellowship will be disrupted. We conclude that *fellowship rests on stability of habits*.

Consider now the matter of leadership. A leader guides your conduct by means of the principles, standards and values which he imparts to you. He gives you the policies and patterns for your daily activities and sets the goals for you to aim at. Suppose now that the men to whom you look for leadership change their principles, standards and values as it may suit them, a few or many times in succession; the policies which guided you and the goals you aimed at will become shifting, capricious and whimsical. And without stable principles, firm policies and steady goals there is no leadership. We conclude that *leadership rests on stability of principle and policy*.

Let me be brief now. In the army habits and tastes hardly change, and principle and policy remain almost unvarying. Fellowship and leadership are there founded on the rock of stability. Caprice, whim, passion for frequent changes have little or no place in its rules and patterns. The physical person of the soldier is perpetually confronted with novel and perilous situations, with incessant shifts and changes. But his personality is thoroughly stabilized by the twin influences of the fellow's adherence to stable habits and the leader's commitment to firm policies. In such a moral climate the nervous patient finds security and relaxation. His person is in continuous danger, but his personality is solidly sheltered.

It is the curse of our modern life that stability of habits has become impossible. Everything around us is in constant flux. We have drifted into a mode of life in which change, under the guise of "progress," has been turned into an ideal. Home life is continually changing. Moving from one district to the other has become a mania. Furniture that served its purpose last year is no longer wanted the coming year. Automobiles are traded in although they may be in working condition, just because a "new" model is wanted. We have adopted the pernicious philosophy that the "new" is desirable and the "old" obnoxious. Stable tastes and habits are impossible under a system of this kind which glorifies everything that has no other distinction than its novelty and scorns the value of things for no other reason than that they are no longer modern. Fellowship is dying or withering under the impact of a system which idolizes novelty and modernity.

If we "moderns" contented ourselves with merely changing furniture, homes and automobiles the threat to our personalities would be serious enough because novelty hunting interferes with fellowship. Far more fatal, however, is our modern craving for scrapping time-honored principles and exchanging them for recent "advanced" and "progressive" patterns of life. What I refer to here is our tendency to discard with a callous ruthlessness well established systems of education, to rush at "reforms" with unholy haste, to display a contemptuous attitude and ouright ridicule for ancestral standards, to condemn the past as "Victorian" and to extol present-day endeavors as the inspiration of "advanced thought." All of this digs the grave for principle and values and standards. It casts stability of policy into discard and establishes the prerogative of caprice, whim and erratic impulsiveness. And with caprice, whim and impulsiveness to guide our action there can be no firm policy. And without settled policy there can be no leadership. And without leadership the nervous patient is bound to be victimized by the sense of insecurity, tenseness, self-consciousness and symptoms. No wonder Kenneth felt at home in the army and helpless and lonesome after he returned to his home community. In the army he had fellows and leaders. At home he was thrust into a stream of life whose stabilizing influence had yielded to the disintegrating effect of novelty and modernity.

Kenneth, noticing the reappearance of symptoms, felt desperate and despaired even of Recovery. But he is here among us today, and his mere presence, apart from his participation in the panel, testifies to his abiding faith in the Recovery system. He knows that in Recovery there is stability of habits, hence, fellowship, and stability of principle, hence, leadership.

18

LEADERSHIP VERSUS INFORMATION

Gertrude, during a Saturday panel, spoke of her condition prior to joining Recovery. "My main symptom," she said, "was the fear of death. I had palpitations and felt weak and could hardly eat and lost weight and I was sure I was just dying away. Dr. Low asked me whether I was afraid of riding in an automobile and I told him it didn't mean anything to me to race 60 or 70 miles an hour, and he said, 'Well, one thing is sure, you are not afraid of death in an automobile accident.' That reminded me that I did other things which were dangerous but I didn't fear them. I wasn't scared at all when I went on high rides in Riverview Park. And where I live I have to pass three cemeteries every day to get to where I work. And in the evening, coming back from work, I pass the three cemeteries again, frequently late at night. That doesn't frighten me a bit. When I told Dr. Low all of these things he said, 'What you are afraid of are your own thoughts and impulses and sensations. You don't fear physical death.' That was hard for me to understand and I don't know whether I understand it much better today. But one thing is sure: I have learned to spot my fear as distressing but not dangerous and since I don't attach the idea of danger to my palpitations they bother me only once in a while and when I have them they go as fast as they come."

Gertrude was given an explanation about the nature of her fear and did not understand. Then she was given instructions about spotting her inner experiences and she promptly learned to practice a rule and to dispose of symptoms. My theoretical explanations failed, but my practical directions succeeded. When I offered explanations I was a teacher; when I gave directions I functioned as a leader. Gertrude reacted poorly to my teaching but responded magnificently to my leadership.

What I tried to teach Gertrude was the simple fact that what appeared to be an outer danger may be an inner threat. There is nothing mysterious or obscure about a statement of this kind. It is plain and simple and ought to be grasped without difficulty.

Why was Gertrude unable to understand this obvious and not at all complex explanation?   As I see it, the substance of my teaching was clear in language and transparent in meaning.   It certainly had greater clarity than the rather complex directions I gave her when I acted as leader. As such I told her to employ our spotting techniques.   Assuredly, the principles of spotting are far more difficult to manipulate than a simple sentence about inner and outer dangers. And if Gertrude is still unable, even today, to understand my teaching but ready to accept my leadership I suspect that it is not so much a matter of understanding but rather one of preference.   Whether she knows it or not, the fact is she prefers dynamic leadership to pale and dry teaching.

I wish that all my patients shared Gertrude's preference for leadership. Then, I could tell them what to do in order to control their temperamental leanings, how to curb their romanticisms and intellectualisms, how to check their sabotaging trends and how to eliminate their fondness for self-diagnosing. If that came to pass, suffering would be reduced to a minimum, and improvements might rise to an optimum. But unlike Gertrude, the general run of my patients have an absurd hankering for explanations and probings, for discussions and arguments. At the time they consult me they are in a state of confusion. For Gertrude this confusion was a source of untold agonies. In the morning she felt exhausted and "beaten up" and had the desire to stay in bed but knew that it was her duty to prepare breakfast for her husband. Duty conflicted with desire. Should she tend to what she conceived as her health? Or should she discharge what was clearly her marital duty? The dilemma confused her. To the physical torture of the symptoms was added the mental torture of not knowing what was right and what wrong. Life appeared to her as an unbroken series of confusions. When she was petrified by the fear of death and dreaded being alone, she rushed out of the house, hurrying in a senseless haste to her mother or sister seeking comfort and assistance. But, on arriving, the panic was gone and what was left was a crushing sense of shame for acting like a baby and causing distress to those she loved. Was that proper? Was this not evidence of inconsiderateness, even of cruelty? It was all so puzzling, so perplexing. At times her husband reprimanded her in harsh terms, insisting on her using her will-power. To her this appeared to be a lack of understanding. She was resentful and felt ugly impulses rising within her. Was she getting irresponsible? Could she no longer trust her impulses? How confusing! Then the racing of thoughts, the inability to concentrate, the difficulty of following her own trend of thought or of "taking in" what others told her. Did that perchance mean that her mind was slipping? Confusion was with her all the time, in every place, on all occasions. If she only knew what it all meant. If she could only understand. This was her state of mind when I first saw her. Every fiber in her ached to get understanding, to be shown what was right and what wrong, to escape her doubts, to relieve her ignorance. And doubts can be cured, she thought, by explanations, ignorance through knowledge. That called obviously for teaching, discussion, exploration and talk. In this, Gertrude acted the part of the intellectual. It is the intellectual's way of thinking that problems, issues and perplexities are the result of ignorance, and the proper remedy is education which he calls enlightenment. Confusion, reasons the intellectual, is created by darkness, and darkness is dispelled by light, and once the individual "sees the light" impulses become docile and sensations turn reasonable. The scheme, I admit, is easy to understand; it represents the purest logic and the most attractive reasoning. But does it work? Is it successful?

It is possible that I lack the astuteness and logical skill of an intellectual. Perhaps I am deficient in the art of devising snappy formulas and trim slogans. And so it happened that when I offered Gertrude what I considered solid explanations about sensations and impulses she was not at all relieved and her confusion was not lifted. "That was hard for me to understand" was her way of indicating that my attempt at re-educating her had miscarried. Plainly, she was not impressed with the quality of my teaching. This is the verdict of the majority of my patients. Few of them take kindly to my explanations. Most of them "find it hard to understand" what I tell them. Yet, I am certain that what I tell them is about as substantial and lucid as explanations can reasonably be expected to be. It is not true that my teaching is "hard to understand." The truth is that patients cannot be taught by teaching alone. What they need is teaching supplemented by leading. Gertrude failed to understand what I taught her, but when I added leadership to instructorship her confusion gave way to clear vision and her puzzlement to firm grasp.

Nervous patients suffer from fears and must learn how to conquer them. Learning suggests education, but education is by no means identical with teaching. What teaching does is to give you information. Many things can be adequately acquired through information. If you wish to gain knowledge in history and geography or in languages and literature mere information will or may fill the need. The teacher in geography or literature need not be a leader. This is different if you want to learn a trade. The foreman who teaches you must supply leadership besides technical information. He will have to make you translate into practice what he taught you through information. To make a person practice what he is learning is the essence of leadership. In making you practice the leader will insist on patience, perseverance, self-discipline. While you practice your attention will frequently wander, your effort will lag, your courage will ebb. The leader will then, through precept and example, revive attention, redirect effort and restore courage. He will watch your performance and correct mistakes. He will demand numerous repetitons of part acts until the total act will be mastered. You will understand now why I say that to lead means to make one practice. In Recovery, my patients receive a prodigious amount of information, in meetings and home gatherings and in the profuse literature which I have provided for them. In this, I am their teacher who dispenses information. But when I make them practice, unremittingly and untiringly, the information which I gave them I am their leader who supervises the practical training. Like all my patients, Gertrude secured for herself the benefit of both information and leadership. And since she succeeded in conquering her symptoms leadership must have been effective and information helpful. Why, then, did she conclude that what I told her was hard to understand? Why was she doubtful whether she even understood it "much better today?" Apparently, my brand of information, although thoroughly effective, did not appeal to her and does not appeal "much better today."

I know that what I teach my patients lacks appeal. They do not relish the thought that they suffer "just" from inner threats. They insist that what they fear are outer dangers, "nothing less." They do not take kindly to the dictum that their symptoms are "merely" distressing but not dangerous. They resent emphatically my instructions to step out boldly when their muscles feel exhausted or to lie quietly in bed when they cannot sleep because their body is rocked by tenseness and shaken with agony. These items of information and principles of leadership do not suit their fancies. They sound too simple, even childish. They lack the glamor of sophistication, subtlety and complexity. In

their unadorned and naive phrasing my instructions are a positive insult to the intellect. And when my patients come for their
first interview they are intellectualists, and judged by the standard of intellectualism, my information and my leadership must
be found wanting. What Gertrude found difficult to understand
was my temerity to offer simple information for a suffering so
singularly deep and so exquisitely complex. She had not yet gone
through her training in Recovery, and steeped in the philosophy
of intellectualism, was shocked by this rude insult to her
intelligence.

I told you repeatedly that the romanto-intellectualist tendencies of my patients are fostered by contemporary thought. And
our age is hopelessly addicted to the worship of sheer information. Present-day men and women receive the bulk of their
education through the channels of information, especially after
they have reached adolescence or adulthood and are eligible for
what is called "adult education." Then they are given the
doubtful benefit of lectures and forums, book reviews, popular
expositions on science and psychology, advice in child rearing
and family management, instruction on how to make friends and
influence people. The implication is that correct information is
the surest way to correct action and that all a person needs for
improving his habits is to be told how to do it. Training,
practice, leadership have been radically, and perhaps joyfully,
discarded in this weird scheme of life in which grownup persons
are expected to repose childlike faith in the magical power of
theoretical knowledge. The scheme has produced such absurdi-
ties as the quixotic plan to reform criminals through psychology,
to prevent delinquency by spreading the information that "crime
does not pay," to convert races and nations to democracy by
teaching them the advantages of the democratic way. The
notion that by some trick information can change action and
direct impulses has gripped the imagination of the age. We in
Recovery refuse to believe in magic, and if we want to change
our action we devise proper counter-action, and if our impulses
need controlling we provide for adequate means of checking
them. Our method is that of patient practice supervised by a
leader. In our old-fashioned scheme, information is merely the
preliminary to training and practice, not a substitute for leadership. Gertrude demonstrated the effectiveness of the system. As
long as her mind was focused on the questionable blessings of
information she paid dearly in terms of tenseness and symptoms.
After she decided to accept leadership she was rewarded with
relaxation and freedom from suffering.

19

THE PASSION FOR SELF-DISTRUST

Margaret, taking part in the Saturday panel, reported an experience which she had while attending an auction in one of the Loop galleries. "I was tense," she said, "the auctioneer was handling things too fast for me. There was noise; the people were talking and laughing. I intended to bid but was afraid I might do it at the wrong time. But I made myself sit it out and when some cocktail forks were offered I put in my bid. A girl came to collect the deposit for a three dollar bid. I was confused and felt a tightening in my chest. Finally I got up the courage to ask the girl how much of a deposit was required but she did not answer. Maybe I didn't hear her. I became more confused and the tightening in the chest got worse. I fumbled in my pocketbook and took out a five dollar bill. The girl said she did not have the change. I looked for a dollar bill but in my confusion pulled out a ten dollar bill. Realizing what I had done I put it back only to pull out another ten. By this time the confusion got worse and I could hardly see. I was doing what Dr. Low calls processing and realized that I was busy working myself up to panics and vicious cycles. So I collected my wits so to speak and made up my mind to look calmly for a one dollar bill and if it wasn't enough the girl would tell me. Several months ago before I had my Recovery training I would have been sure I was losing my mind. My confusion would have grown worse and that would have made it surer that my mind was going. . . ."

Margaret, fumbling in her pocketbook for a one dollar bill, pulled out five and ten dollar notes in three successive attempts. Noting the three times repeated error she drifted into a confusion which was so intense that it made her head swim with dizziness, threw her muscles into tremors and created a vicious cycle which threatened to precipitate a panic. In former days, she said, "Before I had my Recovery training I would have been sure I was losing my mind." But errors are the most common occurrence in everybody's experience. Indeed, there would be no sound and tested experience unless errors were made, and made repeatedly and then corrected. It is precisely the correction of errors which gives correct experience. If this is so, then, errors are a necessary and desirable and wholesome part of life even if they are repeated three times and dozens of times and hundreds of times. What made Margaret think that the commission of errors is an indication of a mind crumbling?

Margaret has the record of many years of faithful and efficient service in a government office. She is married, has friends, belongs to a church and holds membership in various civic groups. In all these spheres she has witnessed numbers of mistakes made by multitudes of people. Yet, it never occurred to her to suspect this blundering humanity to suffer from mental deterioration because of the innumerable errors chargeable to it. Whenever she was faced with an "erring soul" she knew that "to err is human" and viewed errors, failures, neglects and oversights as what they are: an acceptable and unavoidable "part of life." Why did she assume that erring must not be permitted to be part of her own life? Why did she practice gentle tolerance with others and was preposterously intolerant with herself? To put it differently: when Margaret observed occasional slips in other peoples' mental activities she did not conclude that their minds were slipping beyond repair. But when she noticed a similar temporary weakness in her own mental function she instantly jumped to the conclusion that her mind was going or gone. She has an abiding trust in the mental constitution of others but an abysmal distrust in her own mental capacity. This attitude of wholesale self-distrust is a common feature among nervous patients who as a group are afflicted with the PASSION FOR SELF-DISTRUST.

My daily life is crowded with occasions in which I fumble and falter. While walking on the street I sometimes stumble or bump into another person. Occasionally I slip or fall on the wet or icy sidewalk. At times I actually hurt myself. Nevertheless, I do not conceive a violent distrust of my Self but consider the misstep or mishap as part of my life. The same holds true for numerous other experiences of my daily round. It happens frequently that I talk to people and fear I said too much. Or, I feel I did not say enough or said the wrong thing. Or, I fall into the trap of a slick salesman who, taking advantage of my preoccupation, tricks me into an ill-considered purchase. In all these instances my Self, physical or social, fails me but I do not lose trust in it.

My patients are of a different cast. They spill water and conclude their coordination is badly damaged. If misplacing an object they have difficulty retrieving it they are "certain" their memory is gone. While reading a magazine their attention may wander and they are "sure" they lost the power of concentration. They may make a wrong decision in some paltry endeavor and it is "clear" to them that their judgment is unreliable. There is the matter of forgetting a name, the inability to recall an event, the difficulty of collecting their thoughts for the purpose of writing a letter, or the sudden "freezing up" when called upon to voice an opinion at a club meeting. In all these situations, and in a thousand others, they are "certain" and "sure" and "positive" that their functions, physical and mental, are disintegrating and cannot be trusted. If I try to persuade them that their errors and failures are sheer trivialities, trite and meaningless, they launch into a fierce argument laboring heavily to convince me that it is "clear" and "plain" and "obvious" (and "how can anyone doubt it?") that their mental and physical capacities are utterly beyond redemption and that their Selves cannot be trusted. It is this insistence on the "clear evidence" and "certain indication" and "positive proof" that stamps their attitude as the "PASSION FOR SELF-DISTRUST."

To have trust in one's organs and functions is to be spontaneous. Spontaneity means many things. It means, for instance, that you have an intention and your muscles carry it out, promptly, without hesitation, with precision and determination. This happens in the ordinary performances of your daily routine. You decide to go shopping. This involves a running series of part acts: dressing, walking to the next street car stop, boarding the coach, paying the fare, entering a store, giving orders to the sales person, riding back home. Take the item of the street car ride. You enter, pay the fare, take your seat, chat with the neighbor until you finally arrive at your destination. During this time you performed hundreds of movements and spoke thousands of words. Your muscles acted and spoke without your active intervention. No coaxing, prodding or urging was needed. You passed your intention on to the muscles and they went ahead and implemented it. This gave you the feeling of *vitality and accomplishment*; it gave you the *sense of "I can."* There was no doubt in your mind that the muscles were competent to perform the task. The absence of doubt made for *self-confidence*. Since no watching or checking was required you drifted into a state of *relaxation*. The relaxation caused an *absence of tenseness*. With no tenseness to irritate your nerves the activity gave you *enjoy-*

ment. You felt like an active, living, dynamic personality. Life was pleasure, perhaps bliss and abandonment.

My patients have gone through months or years of torture and in the process developed sustained tenseness and symptoms attending it. Their weariness, their pains, fatigues, pressures and spasms have made them self-conscious in the extreme. Hence, they lack the feeling of vitality and accomplishment; they have lost their self-confidence, are unable to relax or enjoy things. Required to formulate plans and intentions they are instantly gripped with the fear that their muscles will fail them, that they will not be ready to carry out what they are asked to do. Being the victims of an unrelenting self-consciousness they question their capacities, watch and check every one of their moves and perform with hesitation and anxiety. Their attitude is that of an abiding pessimism; they feel whipped and defeated; their guiding philosophy of defeatism has hardened into a settled conviction. They are "sure" and "certain" and "positive" that acting is impossible, that their muscles will defy orders, that their power to get things done is lost, that their personality functions are doomed. Their philosophy of "I can't" has assumed the status of a dogma; it is implicitly believed, hotly defended and fondly sheltered.

The calamity is that the relatives and friends do not share the patient's defeatism and refuse to subscribe to the cult of "I can't." They look at the sufferer and notice a blooming complexion, a strong voice, a lively facial expression. They observe the patient in a fit of his frequent tantrums and witness a display of force and energy which belies the claim to invalidism. Their conclusion is that the patient *could* but *would not* do the things which are to be done. The idea is forced on them that he is *unwilling* instead of *unable* to perform his function. They upbraid him, urge him to make an honest effort and with this they accuse him of shamming disease, of playing a game, of practicing deception. They indict his character, his honesty; they charge him with deliberate neglect of duties and obligations and fasten the label of irresponsibility on him. This strikes at the root of his self-respect, of his personal value and social position. This savage assault must be repelled. The patient feels he must bend every ounce of his energy to the vital task of convincing the others that he "really" can't, that he is "truly" incapable of acting, that he is "positively" helpless. The patient is now a crusader for the philosophy of "I can't." He concentrates on the effort to win over the others to his dogma of defeatism, to make converts, to spread the gospel of his incurability. In order to convince those about him, including the physician, he must engage in a veritable campaign of complaining, wailing, lamenting. In his interminable moaning and groaning he is compelled to overemphasize the utter unreliability of his organs and functions. His body is forever about to crumble, his mind is constantly ready to disintegrate. As he continues on this career of self-denunciation he fairly gorges himself with the idea of distrust and in the end develops the PASSION FOR SELF-DISTRUST. His untiring crusading for the philosophy of "I can't" has netted him one faithful and unswerving convert: himself.

20
THE COURAGE TO MAKE MISTAKES

Mildred reported on the Saturday panel that all her life she had a perfectionist attitude. "I set a standard for myself that an Olympic champion could not approach. I work at top speed and try to do everything at once and drive myself to finish my job in half the time it would take an expert to accomplish it. But then I get tremors, pressure in the head, a feeling of falling apart as though my arms and legs don't belong to me and some sort of sensation in which space has become a solid wall and I must push my way through it every time I move. When this happens I become panicky and feel sure I am losing my mind. The other day I was in the basement washing clothes. I had meat cooking upstairs on the first floor, the vacuum connected on the second floor ready to use, and the washing machine in the basement. As if this were not enough I went out into the yard starting to untangle a hopelessly gnarled clothesline, blaming myself all the time for messing up my work and accomplishing nothing. I had hardly untangled the clothesline when it began to rain. I became confused and frightened and felt I couldn't move across the yard because the solid wall was there instead of space. Suddenly I remembered my Recovery training and spotted my frustration as an attitude of perfectionism. I realized that my rushing from one job to another was the desire to do more than an average person can do and that my confusion was a sense of disappointment at not being able to do the exceptional job. So I stopped the rush, calmed down deliberately and made up my mind to do one job after the other. In an instant the confusion went and the fear of losing my mind stopped. Before my Recovery training I would have kept on working fast and would have gotten into the vicious cycle of fear, self-blame and the depression that went with it. The vicious cycle used to last for months and at one time lasted three years."

Mildred, in a confusion which threatened to unhinge her mind, "calmed down deliberately" and decided to give up her ambition to do the perfect job. "In an instant," she says, "the confusion went and the fear of losing my mind stopped." But if a mere decision is sufficient to put an abrupt end to a long-standing confusion my patients ought to have no difficulty getting rid of their perplexities, vicious cycles and tortures. What Mildred did all of them ought to be able to do.

What was it that troubled and confused Mildred? There was cooking to be done on one floor, cleaning on another floor and washing in the basement. A fourth job was waiting to be finished in the yard: tending to the "hopelessly gnarled clothes-line." The issue was: should all four jobs be carried out at once or one after another? If the tasks were done coincidently Mildred would have the sense of pride, of outstanding accomplishment, of perfection and excellence. If they were done singly and successively the job would be of average quality, lacking the glamor of top performance and peak achievement. Reduced to these simple terms the choice and decision which Mildred was to make was between two discrete philosophies: to be average or exceptional.

I spoke to you about philosophies on several occasions. It is precisely your philosophy (of life) which tells you which decisions are correct and which acts are acceptable. You will remember I mentioned three main philosophies which are current among human beings: realism, intellectualism and romanticism. The intellectualist claims superior powers of reasoning while the romanticist boasts of his exquisite capacity for vigorous feelings, interesting sensations and strong impulses. The one strives to be recognized as being distinct from the "ignorant mob"; the other as being apart from the "vulgar crowd." Their philosophy is decidedly that of exceptionality. They fear or hate to be rated as "just average." The realist, on the other hand, does not view the members of his group as mob or crowd. To him they are average persons, not perfect by any means, not exceptional on any count, but worthy people of average efficiency and average solidity. Their averageness may be of good, plain or poor quality but essentially they are average in the entire sweep of their daily existence. And so is he, the realist. He is average in thought, feeling and action. He claims no glory or glamor, no excellence or exceptionality.

Mildred subscribed to the philosophy of exceptionality. This is nothing uncommon. There are very few people who do not think of themselves as being of a superior breed, as ranking above the "common herd," that is, as being exceptional. With most of them it is merely a dream, an ambition and aspiration. They hope to be exceptional but know they are "nothing but average." In their dreams and fancies they are romanto-intellectuals but in actual practice they behave as realists. Their sense of exceptionality is properly controlled by their knowledge of being average. If you keep this in mind you will realize that most if not all people embrace both the philosophy of exceptionality and that of averageness. The average person adjusts and balances the two philosophies in such a manner that the one (averageness) is leading and controlling, the other (exceptionality) is led and controlled. If this is done, then, decisions and actions are balanced and adjusted on a practical level while dreams and fancies are given free play on an imaginative level. Mildred had no leading philosophy of realistic averageness to tell her which of her decisions were correct, which of her actions were feasible. In her mind, the two philosophies were not held apart, they were not properly distinguished the one from the other; they were permitted to merge and fuse. The free fusion of the two philosophies produced a confusion of the mind. What directed her behavior were her dreams and hopes, her wild aspirations and vague ambitions. With these unrealistic leads to guide her reactions her decisions became fantastic (to act at one and the same time on four separate jobs in four separate places). As a result, her actions became tangled, involved and as "hopelessly gnarled" as was her clothesline. In the end, she despaired of ever reaching the correct decision and became lost in a sea of confusion.

The daily round of the average individual consists in the main of such trivial performances as reading, conversing, working on a job, cooking, washing, cleaning, telephoning, shopping. The person with a settled sense of averageness does these routine chores with hardly any thought wasted on them, without hurry, without anxiety, without the harrowing fear of possible failure. Considering them as routine he knows they involve no danger and is happily at ease, poised and spontaneous while engaged in his work. It is only on those relatively rare occasions when highly important or emergency reactions must be faced that the person possessed of a sense of averageness may become tense and may suffer a decrease in his spontaneity. Spontaneity means that you are not self-conscious, that you are not on your guard for fear of making mistakes. Spontaneity means the COURAGE TO MAKE MISTAKES. In trivial or routine activities no calamity arises if perchance a mistake occurs. This is the reason why realists, that is, men and women of average aspirations go about their daily tasks with due caution and circumspection, it is true, but without any marked fear of making a mistake. Mistakes made in trivial performances are trivial themselves and their possible consequences are just as trivial and not to be feared. With the fear of mistakes largely removed from the mind of the realist his decisions are reached with ease and his actions initiated without undue hesitation. All of this is the result of spontaneity and, in turn, favors its development.

This is altogether different in the instance of the perfectionist or the person consumed with the desire to achieve exceptionality. To him every puny endeavor, each trivial enterprise is a challenge to prove and to maintain his exceptional stature. His life is a perennial test of his singularity and distinction. For him there are no trivialities, no routine performances. He is forever on trial, before his own inner seat of judgement, for his excellence and exceptional ability. He cannot achieve poise, relaxation, spontaneity. He cannot afford to have the COURAGE TO MAKE MISTAKES. A mistake might wipe out his pretense of being superior, important, exceptional. With no margin left for mistakes he is perpetually haunted by the fear of making them. The fear paralyzes decision, hampers actions and confounds plans. Striving for indiscriminate peak performance and confronted with his pitiful record of jobs undone, unfinished and hopelessly bungled he is horrified by his cumulative inefficiency and becomes confused.

Mildred, a confirmed exceptionalist, turns realist embracing averageness as her leading philosophy. She did that after she joined Recovery. There she learned that romanto-intellectualist dreams and fancies must not be permitted to express themselves recklessly but must be led and controlled by an average and humble attitude. She also learned that this must be done through a system of persistent spotting, thorough self-control and relentless self-discipline. It was not easy for Mildred to accept and absorb the idea of control and discipline. She is a product of our modern age and as such was subjected all her life to the contemporary doctrine of unrestrained expression of feelings and impulses. Impulses and feelings are precisely those elements in our experience which balk at being rated as average. They are singularly private and intimate and personal and give you the impression that through them you are set off and distinguished from the others. And if you think of yourself as different from others you are inclined to consider the others as common and ordinary and average and yourself as distinct and exceptional. With nervous patients this tendency to set themselves off from the others is apt to assume ridiculous proportions. If you emphasize your feelings, their importance, and intensity; if you are forever suspicious that they are not properly understood; if you constantly fear and complain that they are deliberately ignored and cruelly hurt; if you pamper and coddle them and, thereby, work yourself up to a hysterical pitch, then, your emotionalism and impulsiveness may easily reach such a fury that they impress you as exceptional, indeed. You will now understand that our modern tendency to favor unrestrained expression of feelings and impulses overemphasizes individual differences and personal distinctions and thus promotes the sense of exceptionality.

Modern education is only one of the factors which promote the philosophy of exceptionality. Another factor is modern machine technique. A machine leaves little or no room for average performance. A machine loses its usefulness if it fails to work at top speed and record efficiency. It must be perfect within the sphere of its application. The numerous gadgets introduced these days in kitchen, shop and office are worthless unless they conform to the "highest standard" of performance. Their work must be faultlessly smooth, perfectly safe and of top flight productivity. In our mechanized existence the machine has become the symbol of perfection. Mistakes are no longer tolerated in this modern scheme of mechanical excellence. If mistakes happen as, for instance, in an airplane or railroad accident the engineering tribe loses no time shifting the blame from the "flawless" machine and placing it where it "properly" belongs: the "human element." The machine can do no wrong. It is always "perfect." It is man, that miserable, as yet unmechanized, backward and bungling creature who is at fault. Man and human nature have become an anachronism, a relic of that unspeakably imperfect "horse and buggy age" which to the modern mind is the epitome of clumsiness and ineptitude. In spite of the "marvelous" advance of technique man is still in a deplorable state of imperfection. It is he who has failed to measure up to the matchless efficiency of the machine. We of Recovery have no use for a system which preaches perfection as an ideal to be achieved through the blessings of a machine-regulated existence. If our mortal state of imperfection can only be redeemed through the "faultless operation" of lifeless machines, well, we are old-fashioned enough to renounce the machine and enjoy our averageness and spontaneity. Mildred, trained in the philosophy of Recovery, learned to scorn faultless operations and perfect performances. In the process, she acquired poise and relaxation and is now in the happy position of doing jobs efficiently (not perfectly, not faultlessly) by the simple procedure of practicing the COURAGE TO MAKE MISTAKES in the trivial affairs of her daily round.

21

PREDISPOSITION, PARTNERSHIP AND PARTISANSHIP

In a panel discussion on "The Illusion of Superiority" Alice made the following comment: "Some day last week I was waxing the kitchen floor and my husband sat by the phone watching me. Suddenly he said, 'Honey, that chair I painted in the basement must be dry. Will you bring it upstairs and then get Charlie on the phone for me?' Automatically I started for the basement and then stopped. 'He is bossing me,' I thought, 'and then he is almost twice my size and can get that heavy chair himself. Besides he is right by the phone and can get Charlie himself, and anyway I am busy.' I felt hurt and was good and angry and in former days I would have given him a piece of my mind. But this time I spotted my resentment as temper and said to myself that my feelings are not so important and I laughed and said, 'I'll help you carry the chair, and you can make the phone call yourself.' I expected an outburst on his part and was already prepared to hold down my temper if that should happen but he merely said, 'O.K., it's a deal.' After that I felt proud of myself and there was no temper and so I had no tremors and pressures or nausea, and on top of it I felt fine because I had asserted myself without temper."

What Alice reported was an incident in which Edward, her husband, took the position that he was the boss, and the wife took the contrary position that she was not going to be ordered about. But if two partners to a joint enterprise take opposite positions the result will be that temper will thwart action. In the present instance, Alice turned her Recovery training to good account taking the final position that temper is something ridiculous and a healthy compromise the only way to establish peace and cooperation in married life. You see here that whether a partnership is marred by temper or aided by a workable compromise depends on the nature of the positions habitually taken by the partners.

It will be important for you to know that every act of yours, no matter how trivial, is preceded by a *position*. Before you take a swallow of your soup you have already decided, that is, taken the position that the food is not poisoned, that it will cause no indigestion, that it is the proper kind of nourishment to take. You may not be, and usually are not, aware of having taken that position but you took it nevertheless; you took it intuitively and unreflectively. Positions of this kind are taken in advance of every move you make and every sentence you speak. No person in his right mind makes a motion or voices a phrase unless he has first determined or taken the position that the coming action is devoid of danger and the planned statement free from risk. You will understand now that every act of behavior is preceded by a position. What kind of positions you will cultivate depends on whether you are sentimental or realistic. If you are sentimental your positions will prepare you for emotional excitements; if you are realistic they will favor peace and compromise.

Another thing you will have to learn: a position is invariably preceded by a *disposition*. If your present disposition is belligerent it will give rise to a series of fighting positions and your subsequent behavior will be aggressive, threatening, provocative. If it is peaceful your positions will be favorable to a courteous, conciliatory and compromising attitude. Alice and Edward were belligerent in disposition and when issues arose in their marital relations their positions were likely to be those of the angry temper: sharp, antagonistic, unyielding. After months of Recovery training Alice changed her dispositions, shelved her temper and tended to take realistic and compromising positions. Her action was calm and peaceful, and the change in her behavior laid the groundwork for a workable and satisfactory marital union.

How did Alice manage to alter her dispositions? Which method did she use to bring about the change? Is such a method available? On first thought it would seem hardly thinkable that a method of this kind could exist. Just reflect for a moment what the word disposition implies. You enjoy a thing because you are inclined or disposed to like it. You hate a person because you are inclined or disposed to hate him. If you swim, eat, walk, speak, rest, work—all of this is done only if you happen to be moved by a corresponding inclination or disposition. Leaving aside purely automatic behavior, there is no act that could conceivably be released without proceeding from an appropriate disposition. And if every act of yours requires its proper dispositional preparation it must be clear that disposition is the very breath of your life. It is the basis of your existence, your fate and destiny, indeed, your nature. Can nature be changed?

I do not presume to know whether physical nature can be changed. I hope it cannot because I love nature just as it is. I shudder to think that the modern magicians of atomic energy may yet succeed in their ruthless attempt to tamper with the grandeur and majesty of physical nature. I fervently hope that even the frightful inventions of modern technology will find physical nature unchangeable. But what I know for certain is that human nature, that is, human dispositons, can be changed at will and with ease whenever it is convenient, desirable or mandatory. When you are at home, alone with your family and no outsiders present, your nature may be that of an ugly disposition, cantankerous, quarrelsome, demanding and domineering. Suddenly you decide to go to the corner drug store to buy the evening paper. No sooner have you reached the street than your nature undergoes a miraculous transformation. Your disposition is now that of affability, good will, grace and courtesy. You meet the policeman on his beat or the delivery clerk from the nearest grocery store, and the grouch with which you left your home is gone; your disposition is fairly oozing sympathy and geniality; your nature has changed from domination to service. It did that in a fraction of a second, prompted by no more dramatic an event than the decision to step outside the house. You can observe the ready changeability of human dispositions in your daily experience where you will notice that abrupt transitions from one natural trend to another are carried out with ease, moreover, without reflection or formal decision. The subject has been treated in great detail in the various chapters of volume 3 of the "Self-Help System" dealing with the temperamental disposition.

Out on the street or at a social function or in the company of your co-workers, you are well-behaved all the time and your temper is under rigid control under all circumstances provided you are a person of manners and not a boor. The man near you disturbs you with unnecessary questions or unwelcome interruptions. You are irritated but retain your courteous disposition. Another man slams the door and you feel provoked by the lack of consideration but your disposition remains calm. You see, outside the home your dispositions are even, always controlled, unconditionally checked. Conversely, at home your dispositions may be at any time uneven, temperamental, ill-controlled. This is due to the fact that dispositions are governed by *predispositions*. Arriving at home you are likely to assume the predisposition to domination with the result that henceforth all or most of your dispositions will be of a domineering nature. On the other hand, once you step out into the street or join a group anywhere you will instantly summon your predisposition to service and will be disposed forthwith to mold your behavior in the spirit of accommodation. The change from one predisposition to the other takes place in a fraction of a second which means that human nature can be changed with lightning-like rapidity, without conscious effort, without deliberate decision, "quite naturally."

Alice shifted her predispositions by means of conscious resolution. In Recovery she had learned to spot the nature and quality of her reactions. Spotting the meaning of her positions she always knew which set of dispositions were about to take command of her muscles. If they pointed to a temperamental predisposition she knew that a shift to a realistic predisposition was in order. She effected the *predispositional shift* and her "nature" changed instantly from temper to controlled behavior. As I mentioned, the ordinary person produces similar shifts routinely without benefit of special training. But what he does is done spontaneously, hence, fumblingly and unsystematically. What Alice did was done with a systematic effort of will, hence, consistently and methodically. What the man in the street does with the aid of vague intuition Alice was trained to accomplish with conscious determination. Learning to spot her positions and to stop her dispositions her Recovery-trained will scored over her "natural" impulses.

What precisely Alice learned in Recoery is this: Human beings are always members of a group. They are wives, husbands, friends, neighbors, citizens, co-workers, schoolmates, executives, employes. If the members of a group are predisposed to realistic cooperation they act as partners. The spirit is then that of *partnership*. If they are predisposed to temperamental explosions they act as partisans and the resulting spirit is that of *partisanship*. Partnership promotes the purpose of the group, partisanship disrupts it. When Alice and Edward joined hands for the purpose of a marital union their aim was a close partnership. But temper intervened and turned marital life into a sharp partisanship. Their marriage was clearly headed for the rocks but was saved from disintegration when Alice, racked by nervous strain and tortured by symptoms, joined Recovery. There she was made to realize that temperamental positions can be tracked down by spotting and that the predispositon to partisanship can be checkmated at will, with ease and with the promise of unqualified success. Recovery had cured a patient and saved a marriage.

PART III

THE PRINCIPAL METHODS OF SABOTAGE

1

SABOTAGE METHOD NO. 1

Literalness

The concept of sabotage is basic to the philosophy of Recovery. The nervous patient sabotages his own health, his social adjustment, his efficiency and equilibrium and—most pernicious form of sabotage—the physician's authority. The trouble is that the patient, engaged in a systematic effort of obstruction, plies his trade in such a subtle and almost underhanded manner that he is not aware of his own plottings and machinations. In former days the author believed that the patient weaves his obstructionist plots from the depths of subconscious motivations. This absolved him of all suspicion of deliberate conspiracy. Gradually, however, it became increasingly obvious that a good deal of conscious contrivance was at work. The patient asks the innocent-sounding question, "Don't you think my condition could be the result of a glandular trouble?" That this is a diagnostic statement and therefore an attempt at sabotage is clear to the physician. But is it equally clear to the patient? Is he conscious of the fact that his question challenged the physician's diagnosis? It is safe to say that at the precise moment when the inquiry is made the thought of antagonism or obstruction may be absent from the questioner's mind. But if we survey the patient's mental activities beyond the immediate scene and trace his meditations no farther back than to the bus trip which he made to the doctor's office the picture changes radically. While on the bus he was preoccupied with the diagnosis given him on the occasion of his previous visit. He was told then that his condition was of a nervous nature, that it implied no danger, that the combination of office treatment and group management would eliminate his complaints. Now, on the bus, he views the physician's pronouncements with a critical eye. It seems preposterous to him that his "unbearable" fatigue should be labelled "just nervous," i.e., innocent and harmless.

Why then was he asked by other physicians to take a rest, to stop working? True enough, his present physician is competent, highly recommended and undoubtedly successful. But Drs. J. and F. were no numskulls, either, and the one diagnosed a mild anemic condition, and the other blamed the fatigue on a low blood pressure. And the doctor who writes the health column in the morning paper suggested yesterday that fatigue states are frequently caused by a lowered metabolism which, in many instances, can be traced to a glandular deficiency. Why should all these possibilities be ignored? The ruminations continue in this vein until the train of thought is interrupted by some incident that diverts the patient's attention. The sabotaging activity is no longer pursued. Leaving the bus, the patient enters a restaurant to take his lunch. He reads the paper, gives some fleeting thought to all kinds of topics and observations, and the subjects of complaints and diagnosis sink to a lower level of consciousness. When he faces the physician his diagnostic doubts may still be removed from the upper strata of his conscious awareness. But are they buried in the subconscious? They were mulled over and rehearsed just half an hour ago and are quite active and fresh in memory although not in the forefront of conscious meditation. They wait merely for the proper occasion to be revived. When the physician opens up with the introductory question, "How are you today?" the patient's slumbering antagonism is quickly aroused, and the thoughts recently rehearsed during the bus ride are promptly sprung on the physician. That antagonism may not at the present moment be glaringly conscious. But it was in the limelight of awareness a short while ago. It did not have the time to sink down to the subconscious level. We may safely call it half-conscious or quasi-conscious.

Clearly, if sabotage is to be controlled and eliminated it must be stopped at its source and origin. It originates at times and in places outside the physician's office, in the bus, at home, on the street, in the workshop. In the presence of the physician the sabotaging thoughts burst forth spontaneously with little reflection and hardly any deliberation. But in the absence of the physician the sabotaging is done reflectively and deliberately. If a person is spontaneous, his utterances are blurted out and poured forth impulsively. Usually there is neither time nor incentive to revise the spontaneous performance. On the other hand, when the patient sabotages in clear reflection he has the time and occasion for correction provided he has also the incentive to correct. Recovery, with its untiring insistence on a total effort, supplies the patient with the needed incentive. But the patient's endeavor is bound to be vague, groping and ineffectual unless he is supplied with adequate insight into the devious ways in which his own sabotaging tricks operate. Armed with both incentive and insight he will be properly equipped for the long-drawn-out and gruelling battle against his sabotaging propensities, the ENEMY NUMBER ONE of mental health. Of the many disguises behind which sabotage hides the most important ones will be mentioned in the present volume. As may be expected, the most common form is one which is frequently encountered in ordinary conversation: Literalness. Essentially, this device makes use of the technique of rejecting a statement made by the speaker without opposing it openly.

Example 1. The patient reported that at a card game his mother corrected him every few minutes. He was provoked, threw the cards on the table and precipitated a violent argument. He slept poorly that night and awoke in the morning all exhausted. He was told to avoid drawing the temperamental conclusion that he is right and mother wrong. His reply was "I think that mother is wrong but not that I am right." It was not easy to make the patient see the obvious truth that the question raised in an argument is who is right and who is wrong; that if the one party to the controversy is declared to be in the wrong it follows inevitably that the other party must be right; that if he thought the mother was wrong it was obvious that he felt he was right. "Can't I think the one thought and not the other?" the disputant continued. "Not any more," he was told, "than you can think of light without darkness, good without bad, love without hate. Once the one pair of the team of opposites is thought of the other pair is called up automatically." The patient was then shown that he could have used his own common sense to realize that he was literal and listened to the letter instead of to the meaning of the physician's statements. If he had done that he would have demonstrated a will to conquer his temper. Instead, he distorted common sense and debauched logic and sabotaged the will to get well.

Example 2. A lady exclaimed in utter frustration, "I can't plan. I get flustered when I begin and then I do not know what to do next." The physician remarked, "Of course, if you say you cannot plan . . ." but was unable to continue because the lady interrupted him sharply, "I don't mean to say that I cannot plan. It is merely difficult for me to make a decision because I have no determination." She was told bluntly that her manner of reasoning was devoid of logic; that the sharp distinction which she chose to make between planning, making decisions, and having determination was superficial sophistry, a literal differentiation meant to confuse the issue instead of clarifying it. Being a college graduate and possessed of such keen logic as to be an artist at word juggling, she ought to employ her logical capacities to analyze her own statements in terms of sabotage. Her aim ought to be to get well, not to stage a senseless and futile debate with her physician. The result was that she produced a new literalistic perversion of logic. She shouted, "I do not mean to debate with you, I merely wish to make you understand my point of view." Whereupon she was told politely but firmly, "Whether I understand or misunderstand you is of no significance. The thing that counts is that you make every effort to understand me."

Example 3. A patient turned in an urgent message of distress over the telephone. He complained in a voice quivering with excitement that his tenseness was "simply unbearable." "What can you suggest for my relief?" he inquired. He was asked to come to the office that same evening. "But I don't see how I can stand it that long, " he replied. He was assured that there was not the slightest danger in a tenseness of this kind and there was no reason for being alarmed. "I am not alarmed, doctor," he shouted, "but I feel something is going to happen if I don't get help. Can't you let me come to the office right now?" The man is a government official of considerable rank and could easily see the identity of meaning between "alarm" and "feeling that something is going to happen." He had been given a number of private interviews but resented being considered a psychoneurotic person. He protested forever that his distress was physical in origin and was annoyed by the physician's insistence that it was emotional in nature. The words "fear" and "alarm" were tabu to him. Taking them in their literal sense he wiped them out of existence by using a phrase with a slightly different connotation.

Example 4. A patient suffered from an itch on the scalp for over five years. In the course of time he developed a marked self-consciousness and tenseness which interfered with his general well-being and his occupation as a drummer in an orchestra. For the past two years drumming had become an obsession with him. He was compelled to drum incessantly on the table at which he sat, on the outer aspect of his legs when he stood, and on the walls of houses when he passed them. The members of his family claimed they "went almost crazy" because of the perpetual drumming. After several months of private and class treatment the itch was under good control, and the tenseness and self-consciousness had given way to a satisfactory measure of relaxation. But the drumming persisted. The patient was asked, "Why don't you stop that drumming? You got rid of the itch by learning to ignore the discomfort and by controlling the muscles of the hands when they 'itched' to scratch. You can control the drumming by exactly the same procedure. Whenever you feel the 'overwhelming' impulse to drum you can check the impulse and can command your muscles not to carry out the drumming movements." The patient replied, "Drumming is music to me, and I like music." He was promptly reprimanded for daring to offer a nonsensical explanation of this sort. "You know as well as I do," the physician said, "that you do not maintain the drumming for its musical value. You know, it is nothing but noise." "It is rhythm, though," the patient replied. After some sparring he finally admitted that his attempt to identify compulsory finger movements with music and rhythm was nothing more than sabotage made possible by a literal misinterpretation of the physician's words.

Example 5. A patient who had lost many of her symptoms continued to complain of blurred vision which had been declared frequently by the physician to be of nervous origin. "The blur still bothers me," the patient said, "I don't see things clearly." The physician renewed his assurance that the symptom was of a nervous nature and nothing to worry about. "I don't worry," insisted the patient. "I merely thought you might want to examine me again." The eyes were re-examined and the patient told that there was no evidence of any defect. The patient persisted, "Don't you think an occulist ought to look at them?" "I do not object to examinations," the physician replied, "but your solicitude indicates that you worry about your vision." The patient then exclaimed with obvious irritation, "But doctor, I assure you I don't worry about my eyes. But, of course, I wouldn't like them to get worse. After all, a person may go blind." The literalistic quality and sabotaging character of this kind of word juggling requires no comment.

Brief examples: A woman patient reported in astonishing frankness about her wild temper outbursts. She related a series of uncalled-for acts of spite and vengefulness, interlarding the recital with comments as, "Of course, I know it's my fault . . . I am just a nag . . . What I need is a good licking, I guess . ." When the examiner warned her not to indulge in an orgy of self-blame she burst forth, "I don't blame myself; I am just telling my story."

A patient was told not to get sore at herself because that was her main form of temper. She replied, "Doctor, I don't get sore at myself. I am just disgusted with myself." Another patient was warned not to be irritable whereupon she rejoined, "I am not irritable. I am just upset by what my daughter says."

A patient remarked, "I have been coming here several weeks, and I don't see any results." Examiner: "You must not be discouraged." Patient: "I am not discouraged. But of course if one does not see progress . . . ." This patient could have easily told himself that "not seeing results" and "not seeing progress" is identical or synonymous with "being discouraged."

Patient: "When I go shopping I wait and wait and have trouble making the purchase." Examiner: "So, you are still having difficulty making a decision?" Patient: "No, I merely cannot get myself to pick the merchandise I want to buy." The identical meaning of the phrases "having trouble making the purchase," "having difficulty making a decision," and inability "to pick the merchandise I want" ought to be obvious, but nothing is obvious to a person bent on perverting meanings through literal distortion.

Examiner: "I hope I did not hurt your feelings when I said that." Patient: "No, I just don't agree with you, and, frankly, I don't think you have a right to tell me that. It just makes me mad if everybody jumps at me."

The patient developed a mild depression consequent on the mother's death. Examiner: "You must avoid guilt feelings." Patient: "I don't feel guilty. I didn't do anything wrong." Examiner: "You blame yourself for not having done enough for your mother." Patient: "This I do." Examiner: "Doesn't this mean feeling guilty?" Patient: "I thought guilt is crime." This literalism is rather naive but variations of the theme are frequently encounterd with patients steeped in the practice of sabotage.

Patient: "Yesterday I had something like a daze." Examiner: "You don't have to be afraid of that." Patient: "I am not afraid. The only thing, I wouldn't like to have to go to the hospital again." She feared "to have to go to the hospital again" but was not "afraid!"

In all the situations quoted in the examples the patients display a tendency to block the physician's effort, to combat his views, to reject his suggestions by means of a literal misinterpretation of the words he uses. Once the patient's attention has been called to his favorite methods of sabotaging he is in a position to correct his habits. In Recovery, corrections of this kind are made frequently and effectively.

2

SABOTAGE METHOD NO. 2

Ignoring or Discrediting the Initial Improvement

Sabotage is the attempt of an individual to thwart the purpose of a group, usually that of his own group. In this sense, the child sabotages the educational purpose of the parental group when he opposes the effort to make him eat, wash or go to bed. Sabotage is also practiced by the soldier who reports for sick call when, in fact, he is merely lonesome or discouraged or disgruntled. That soldier sabotages the national purpose. There is no end to the multitude of occasions which lend themselves to sabotaging practices. The member of a parliament who offers needless amendments to legislative proposals, the employe who absents himself without good cause, the member of a club who stalls on an assignment, they all sabotage the purpose of the group to which they belong and to which they owe allegiance. The purpose that is most commonly and most consistently sabotaged is that of the family. This type of sabotage takes the form of domestic temper and was amply discussed in the "Techniques of Self-Help," volume 3.*

The child is, as a rule, a frank and forthright saboteur. There is little or no equivocation, duplicity or deceit to his sabotaging performance. In most instances, he opposes an order and rejects the parental purpose in candid rebellion. Children, provided they are not sophisticated, do not affect loyalty to the group purpose of good manners and self-discipline. They simply refuse to accept the educational purpose. If they sabotage it they do not thwart their own purpose. They do not practice self-sabotage.

In all other instances which were cited the sabotage is directed against a group purpose which is solemnly accepted and perhaps cherished and worshipped by the sabotaging person. The soldier, the parliamentarian, the employe, the club member and the quarrelling relative level their sabotaging activities against purposes with which they identify themselves. They sabotage endeavors which they endorse and approve. The purpose which

---

* The Techniques of Self-Help in Psychiatric After-Care, 3 vols. Chicago, 1943, Recovery, Inc.

they obstruct is their own, accepted and valued by them. Theirs is self-sabotage.

That the patient who opposes the freely selected physician sabotages a self-chosen purpose needs no explanation. He has adopted and accepted the purpose of health and has appointed his physician to help him realize the purpose. If he obstructs the physician's efforts he frustrates his own purpose and, by this token, is a self-saboteur.

The situation is clear and transparent in the instance of infantile sabotage. For some reason, the child has no inclination to adopt the group purpose of self-discipline. Carrying out rules and obeying standards is obnoxious to him. It gives him discomfort to have to wash; going to bed in due time is reacted to as an odious imposition; eating spinach may be unmitigated torture. If the group purpose makes the child perform these offensive practices he logically tries to foil that purpose. What prompts him to resort to his sabotaging behavior is his desire to preserve his personal and individualistic comfort. His own purpose of individualism revolts against the foreign purpose of group standards. The individualistic craving for comfort locks horns with the group purpose of self-control. As a general rule, the child's struggle against "the tyranny" of group standards is plain, transparent, straightforward and aboveboard.

The adult saboteur proceeds differently. Take the case of the disgruntled soldier reporting for sick call. He complains of dizziness or "sick headache." The army physician, as the representative of the national group purpose, examines him and declares him well. But the soldier feels keenly his distress. His individualistic purpose is directed toward relieving the personal discomfort. Hence, he pleads for a day of rest and exemption from fighting or drilling. The group purpose, on the other hand, insists on continued discharge of duty. If the soldier now engages in arguments, contending against the physician's opinion that he is sick and disabled, he fights against the group purpose which he himself has adopted and accepted. This he can do only if he fortifies himself with "good reasons." He must justify the inroads into the approved group purpose in a manner that will satisfy his own conscience. Since there are no such "good reasons" he is compelled to manufacture them. The manufactured reasons are rationalizations. They are a weird compound of half-lies, truth-twistings, forced excuses and tortured evasions. The struggle of the adult saboteur against group standards is anything but plain, transparent, straightforward and aboveboard.   It is a mixture of self-trickery and self-degradation.

The case of the nervous and former mental patient is similar to that of the complaining soldier. He has "enlisted" in the physician's group of patients and has by implication obligated himself to pursue the health aim of this group with the vigor of a total effort. The patient accepts at first this group obligation and incorporates the purpose into his own set of values. Then he pleads the case of his own personal comfort and claims exemption from health exercises and health drill. He argues and quibbles with the physician, opposes his individualistic purpose of physical comfort to the physician's insistence on self-discipline. His procedure is characterized by the same disreputable resort to twists, distortions and evasions as practiced by the battle-weary soldier.

The reasons why the patient sabotages his physician are many. Some of them will be mentioned in due course. Surpassing all in importance is the sense of being stigmatized. The patient resents having his complaint considered "nervous" or "emotional." He feels his character is indicted as weak by the diagnosis. If all he needs is insight or assurance, then he is declared to be lacking qualities which everybody else possesses. He resents the implications of intellectual and moral inadequacy and embarks on a process of sabotage. His aim is to convince the physician and others that his trouble is of a physical nature.

In order to get well it is imperative that a patient upholds his courage or morale. The prospect of getting and keeping well is directly proportional to the vigor with which morale is maintained. But the sabotaging patient is not at all interested in getting well if the only way to health is that of psychological explanations and moral education. Since his main concern is to convince his physician and others that, in fact, he is suffering from a physical ailment, the self-help system of regaining his health is not at all pleasing to him. Should he recover through the methods of will-training and self-discipline the charge that for years he neglected his will-power and practiced self-indulgence would be unanswerable. To get well would be an admission that his relatives and friends were correct when they attributed his complaints to a weak will and lack of self-control. He senses keenly the danger to his self-respect should he get cured through will-training and morale-building. The topic of morale is repulsive to him. What he wants is vitamin-medication, administration of hormones, perhaps a minor operation, but no morale-lifting. In Recovery he is, nevertheless, caught up in an atmosphere of high morale, reassurance and encouragement and responds instinctively to the new influence. He improves; the symptoms get milder; the prospect of getting well increases. This gives him a subtle scare. He has visions of accusing fingers pointed at him, of a sneering voice bellowing self-righteously, "I told you it was all up to you." Morale is now his enemy. He will have none of it. And if the present state of improvement is an index to a final cure, well, he is going to see to it that the process of improving does not proceed too fast nor too far. Perhaps he cannot stop the process, but at the very least he can ignore or deny it. The saboteur is now thoroughly committed to a well-conceived plan of ignoring or discrediting the initial improvement. Examples of this type of sabotaging activities will now be cited.

Example 1. A lady's main complaint was a marked anxiety which at times assumed the proportions of a terrifying panic. She slept poorly, had no desire for food and was troubled with a severe headache. The condition had persisted for several years, but in the past six months it had become "almost unbearable." She was unable to attend concerts and shows because of an "irresistible" impulse to stampede out of the theatre the moment the lights were turned off. She was also afraid to be alone and to drive her car. After four weeks of private and class interviews her panics and headaches were gone, sleep and appetite were satisfactory, and the fear of automobiling and attending shows had all but disappeared. When at this point she was asked about her condition she disclaimed any noticeable improvement. "I am tense all the time," she said, "I can't stand the slightest irritation, and sleep hasn't been at all good for the past three nights." On inquiry she admitted that even on these three occasions sleep "wasn't as bad as it used to be." She also agreed that she no longer suffered from panics and that the fear of driving the car and sitting through a show were under control. "But doctor," she hastened to add, "that tenseness and irritability just drive me mad. There must be something radically wrong with me." She was told, "When you first consulted me you were just as tense and irritable as now, perhaps more so. But the main source of your agony at that time were your panics and fears. Since they are gone you ought to be happy beyond description. You ought to derive a new courage from the realization that most of your symptoms cause you no more trouble. Instead, you are despondent because of some remaining minor afflictions. Suppose you had suffered from a gastric ulcer for several years. Therapy was ineffective until a new treatment was instituted. After a few weeks you notice that the pain decreases considerably, the bleeding stops entirely, the anemia is checked, weight increases. But some gastric distress is still present and the tenseness and irritability that were caused during years of suffering are still producing difficulty of sleeping and poor relaxation. You would, then, in spite of the remaining tenseness and irritability, take courage in the thought that your vital wish to get well is on its way toward fulfillment. Your morale would improve and would leave no room for despondency. A patient who shows no appreciation for the quick relief from year-long suffering indicates plainly that the relief was not the object of dreams, hopes and desires. A patient of this kind has no genuine will to regain health and is what I call a saboteur."

Example 2. A woman patient has suffered for the past nine years from "intolerable" tenseness, restlessness and irritability, pressure in the head, difficulty of falling asleep, extreme fatigue and gagging when eating. She had consulted numerous physicians and cultists and was emphatic that no treatment ever helped her. She had spent several periods of weeks and months in hospitals, rest homes and sanitariums without obtaining anything but fleeting relief. When a course of electroshock treatment was instituted she lost practically all her symptoms in a surprisingly short time. The former extensive list of her complaints was now reduced to an insignificant headache which she considered quite tolerable. When the question was asked, "Are you not glad you came to the hospital and received the treatment?" she replied, "But doctor, that head pressure is still there and as bad as ever. I wonder whether I'll ever feel just myself." When reprimanded the patient promptly realized the unreasonableness of the complaint and admitted freely that she did not quite relish the thought of improving. "If I were sure I am going to be cured it would be glorious," she remarked, "but a mere improvement frightens me. I always remember how I get worse after improvements." This explanation is frequently given by patients who realize that their reaction to the initial improvement is the outcome of sabotage. They have gone through the ordeal of the "setback" and dread it. To avoid the thought of the setback they try to ignore the early signs of the beginning cure.

Example 3. A former college student who contracted a mental

ailment in his sophomore year was seen two years after leaving the hospital. He presented an inexhaustible list of residual symptoms. The most outstanding complaint was fatigue, procrastination, tendency to remain in bed till afternoon, lack of spontaneity which made him carry out with extreme effort even trifling performances; a constant feeling of hopelessness, tenseness and irritability; difficulty of sleeping; dizziness; annoying habits of twitching and grimacing; forgetfulness; self-consciousness, etc. After obtaining a well nigh startling improvement in the course of a few months of private and Recovery training he stated, "I have a vague fear that I am doomed. Recovery cannot help me. I may be carrying on for six months but I'll never get well." After he recognized the sabotaging character of his statements he volunteered a plausible explanation. He said, "Should I get well this year or in five years I'll have the thought before me that all these years were wasted." Translated into the language of the stigma this means he feared improvement because it would make him feel stigmatized before his own conscience.

Example 4. A woman patient had the common garden variety of neurotic complaints; poor appetite, difficulty of sleeping, palpitations, crying spells and air-hunger. Crawling sensations, numbness, contractions of the throat, nausea were less regular but equally distressing when present. The complaints dated back some fifteen years when a high school boy friend had taken indecent liberties with her. Although she knew nothing had happened, nevertheless, she could not shake off the thought of having been "contaminated." In the past year she had been tortured by the fear she might do harm to the baby. Coupled with the other complaints this made her suffering "unbearable." After about six weeks of combined office and class treatment she reported that the thought of "contamination" had practically disappeared, that the fear of harming the baby was no longer of any consequence, and that the sensations were "much milder." The physician remarked at this point, "So, you made a nice improvement." "Do you really think I have?" she replied, "I am still tense and have quite a bit of trouble in concentrating, and I want you to know, doctor, that I still have the sensations." It was explained to her that her refusal to admit improvement in the face of positive evidence of good progress meant that she discouraged herself and lowered her morale. She then conceded that the amelioration of most of her symptoms was a sign of good improvement but continued, "Why can't I get rid of the sensations? I can't help thinking that is more than just nerves." She was one of those patients who resented being stigmatized as being "just a nervous case." She was unhappy over the initial improvement because it seemed to clinch the diagnosis of a psychoneurotic condition. And that diagnosis she considered a blot on her character.

Brief examples: A lady suffered from a depression of mood. She did everything with great effort, sleep and appetite were poor, interests were at a low ebb. A good improvement took place after three weeks. When seen at the office she denied feeling better. The following conversation developed: Patient: "I don't feel a bit better." Examiner: "How is your sleep?" Patient: "I must admit sleep has been better." Examiner: "Do you still do everything with effort?" Patient: "I have to drive myself quite frequently. But yesterday I felt the desire to go to the movie for the first time in six months." Examiner: "Do you do your cooking and shopping with more zest?" Patient: "Yes, but I can't get myself to take care of the baby." She knew she had improved but brazenly denied the fact of improvement ignoring and discrediting the evidence.

A patient exclaimed, "I had a bad week again." He was asked, "How is your fatigue?" The reply was: "I walked close to twenty blocks today. It really was a surprise to me. *But* last Sunday I was awfully tired all day." When questioned about his fullness in the head he said, "It does not start right in the morning any more as it used to, *but* I am always afraid it will be worse in the afternoon." And this record of good initial improvement was summed up in the phrase, "I had a bad week again." In Recovery, patients of this description go by the name of "but-knockers." Their stock phrases of self-knocking choose the verbal pattern of "My headache is better, *but*. . ." The improvement is affirmed in the first statement but speedily denied in the second.

Another "but-knocker" stated, "I had a couple of good days last week, *but* this morning I felt nauseated again . . . I had a good day, *but*, of course, I kept busy, and that helped me . . . My palpitations are better, *but* I don't understand why my appetite is still so poor . . ."

3

SABOTAGE METHOD NO. 3

Disparaging the Competence or Method of the Physician

If sabotage is directed against a purpose it will be useful to the sabotaging patient to know something about the manner in which purposes operate.

In common language the purpose of a house is to give shelter, comfort, and privacy, the purpose of a garden is to supply vegetables or flowers, the purpose of an automobile is to provide transportation. In this loose sense, the house, garden and automobile are conceived as having or being endowed with purposes of their own. This is not correct. The house, garden and automobile merely serve the purpose of their owners. The owner has or is endowed with the capacity for craving, wanting, needing shelter, comfort, privacy, vegetables, flowers, transportation. These various purposes are served by house, garden and automobile. An object that serves a purpose is a means toward achieving it. Objects, having neither needs nor wants, cannot have purposes of their own; they are means through which purposes are realized or accomplished.

A workman, wanting or needing wages for subsistence, works for the purpose of sustaining himself and his family. The maintenance of a family is his purpose, the particular kind of work he performs is the means serving the purpose. The purpose is set; the means may be subject to change. For some reason the workman may decide that cessation of work (strike) may serve his purpose better than continuation of his activities. Means may change according to circumstances, expediency or policy. Purposes are set, either for a limited time or for life.

The industrialist for whom the worker toils has essentially the same purpose as his employe. He maintains his establishment primarily for the purpose of providing for his own needs and those of his family. For both the purposes are set and stabilized by the needs and wants of their families. This is the reason why the institution of the family is credited with exercising a stabilizing influence. It sets the purpose for the individual, makes for constancy of purpose and counteracts flightiness of endeavor.

Unlike the worker, the owner of the factory cannot change at will the means that serve his purpose. Closing the plant may at times be necessary due to circumstances, but it will hardly ever be beneficial to the family purpose. If the manufacturer wishes to maintain his family he will not be permitted to shut down his establishment for a long period of time. For him both purpose and means are set and stabilized.

There is also a marked difference between worker and owner with regard to the work done in the factory. The worker may tend to the commodity to be manufactured. But the stock room and heating plant are not his concern. To the manufacturer, on the other hand, every part of the factory is important and essential. His concern extends over all buildings, all departments, all activities. If the owner is to accomplish his purpose he must exert a *total effort*; the worker may attain his purpose (weekly paycheck) by engaging in a *part-effort* only.

Another significant feature of a purpose must be mentioned. The owner of the factory may be sincerely devoted to his family. But suppose he is addicted to gambling and fritters away his fortune. He is then *divided* between two purposes and not *unified*. The division is between an individualistic purpose (gambling) and a group purpose (family). Everybody is the seat and repository of individualistic and group purposes. In the adult person who has achieved maturity one group purpose, usually that of the family, is expected to *take the lead* over all other purposes and to guide action towards unified behavior. The dominant group purpose supplies *leadership*. Every purpose which conflicts with the leading group purpose must be checked and prevented from exerting itself. In this manner the natural conflict of purposes is controlled. If leadership is not established two antagonistic purposes act against one another producing the condition known as *cross-purpose or dual purpose*. An individual possessed of a unified purpose is said to represent an *integrated* personality. He is endowed with the qualities of leadership.

The patient suffering from a nervous ailment may be and frequently is an integrated personality with regard to the purposes of family, citizenship and vocation. But with regard to his own body he has lost leadership. His impulses, sensations, feelings and thoughts embark on action independent of his dominant purpose. The purpose of fellowship may suggest a visit of condolence or his presence at a wedding, but his heart sets up palpitations suggesting to him the fear of impending collapse. The group impulse to exercise the obligations and sentiments of friendship or neighborliness is thwarted by the individualistic impulse to cater to sensations and fears. The inner functions of the body are no longer under control. They are discharged suddenly and unpredictably without relation to the dominant purpose of the personality. Leadership is utterly lost because no leadership is possible under conditions of fears, panics and vicious cycles. The patient may make a half-hearted attempt to help himself. But that attempt is in the nature of a muddled and confused part-effort guided by the dual purpose of endorsing the group impulse toward self-discipline and catering to his symptoms at the same time. Rocked by a conflict of purposes he is no longer wholly unified and lacks the qualities of a fully integrated personality. Having lost control over the functions of the nervous system the patient consults the physician asking him to supply the leadership that he himself can no longer provide. Physician and patient are now forming a partnership in which a unified purpose is set and defined by the physician and accepted by the patient. In this partnership the physician represents the group purpose of mental health and self-discipline. The patient accepts it and pledges himself to employ all the necessary means to attain the end. But before long a setback is experienced. The rebellious sensations, impulses and fears reappear making their individualistic demands and insisting on compliance. The resulting panics induce the patient to ignore and neglect the physician's instructions. The patient demands instant relief, and the physician points to the necessity of self-discipline. The unified purpose of the partnership is now disrupted. Should the partnership be dissolved? Or should it be continued? The decision is not easy. Changing physicians would not be difficult. However, if for some reason the patient continues his visits to the office he demonstrates clearly that he considers the physician competent, that he thinks his knowledge expert and his instructions pertinent. But if the one partner is well qualified the failure of the common endeavor disqualifies the other partner. If the patient is to retain his self-respect he must find a way to disqualify his physician. How can he do that if he continues his visits? The fact of the continued visits emphasizes the physician's qualification. How then can he be disqualified?

The task is not easy. The patient must prove to himself that his physician is qualified and unqualified, expert and inept, proficient and unskilled at the same time. This requires subtle twists, half-truths, shams and sophistry. The dilemma is solved by a simple trick: the physician's competence is asserted explicitly but solidly denied by implication. The patient's conscience is now saved. Continuing his visits he demonstrates explicitly that he trusts his physician. But using phrases with disparaging implications he denies the physician's ability to cure him. Tactics of this kind permit the patient to maintain the illusion of accepting the physician's leadership while at the same time disputing and opposing it. The partnership is then officially maintained but rendered ineffective by crafty maneuvering. The precise manner in which this sabotaging technique operates will now be described.

Example 1. A woman patient had been in and out of hospitals for the past thirteen years. Her case was diagnosed as dementia praecox. She was dreaming, untidy, given to explosive outbursts of violence. The mental contents showed numerous delusions and hallucinations. On the occasion of her fifth period of hospitalization she was given a combined course of insulin and electro-shock treatment which resulted in a fair degree of improvement with satisfactory insight. She admitted feeling better but added, "Of course, when the weather is more friendly I always feel better." She then continued, "What I really need is to go to work. I should take up my painting. A trip to the country would do me good, too." These statements were too obviously calculated to disparage the physician's method to require comment. The patient refrained from asserting bluntly that the treatment was ineffective. Instead she pointed out by implication that other methods were superior to those employed by the physician.

Example 2. The patient was in the grip of a deep depression for close to two years. She complained of lack of interest, deficient sleep and inability to do things except with the utmost effort. She thought her inner organs were rotting. She disclaimed experiencing any feelings. The brain was a blank, the abdomen felt like an empty container. Eating was done mechanically and the bowels "would not move." She accused herself of having "committed the unpardonable sin." A course of electro-shock treatment produced prompt improvement. At this stage she was asked, "Don't you think it was a good idea to bring you to the hospital?" The patient replied, "Of course, the rest and being away from home and child . . ." The physician's efforts were disparaged, and credit was given to events and circumstances uncorrelated with technical treatment.

Example 3. The patient, ill for six years, had consulted

numbers of physicians without obtaining sustained relief. When first seen she suffered from various phobias and compulsions. She was afraid of fainting in the street and had to be accompanied by her husband whenever she ventured out of the house. When performing a task she was unable to stop and had to repeat the manipulation endless times. Making beds thus consumed hours because the tucking and straightening seemed never done to satisfaction. Thoughts "repeated themselves" interminably in the brain. If she asked a question it had to be repeated over and again till finally she felt she had found the correct formulation. There were other disturbances: procrastination before retiring and after arising, fatigue, twitches, poor appetite. After several months of combined private and class treatment the major symptoms were gone. She was now able to do things without hardly any repetition, took care of her home work without much waste of time and manipulated long walks without fear. Finally she even mustered the courage to move to a large home confident that she would be equal to the task of tending to a considerably increased schedule of work. She was sufficiently improved to do all the cooking and cleaning without undue repetition. When she was then asked, "Don't you think that is a good improvement?" she countered with the remark, "Of course, I improved because the new house keeps me busy." The physician's effort was disparaged.

Example 4. A patient suffering from a depression of mood for upward of three years had been the beneficiary of all manner of treatment with no success. She received three electro-shock treatments and attended classes thereafter. Before long she regained her spontaneity and was able to do her work without having to drive herself. Sleep and appetite improved and the mood became balanced. The improvement had set in during the first month and had continued progressively during the subsequent four months. She had a vacation coming but hesitated to make use of it because in the past three years she had suffered agonies whenever she spent time in resort places. When she finally went to the country it was done mainly at the physician's insistence. After she returned she was asked how she felt and said, "I feel so much better. Of course, the vacation picked me up." The physician's part in her improvement was flatly denied, Recovery's share was ignored, and the influence of class instruction was "forgotten."

At times a patient will employ less subtle means of expressing his disapproval of the physician's competence. He will then indicate plainly and directly that a different therapeutic approach is better suited to the exigencies of his case. The instance of the patient was mentioned who inquired whether glandular treatment was not preferable to attendance of classes and Recovery meetings. The same patient suggested on different occasions that what he needed was psychoanalysis, shock treatment, change of occupation and scenery. He once exclaimed "I think I ought to get married. Nothing else will help me." When he was told there was no objection to his choosing a mate he remarked, "How can I get married if I am not cured?" The thought of marriage was obviously meant to sabotage the physician. It was no settled plan, it was no thought at all; it was merely a fling at the physician, intended to disparage his method.

Another patient who had been experiencing night terrors for many years said, "My trouble goes back to childhood. Don't we have to dig in my past?" She was told that her past had been dug up so thoroughly both by her present and former physicians that few patches of ground were left untilled. She snapped back, "You ask us to get well through self-help. But it seems that a patient should be helped by the physician." Subtlety was here thoroughly discarded in favor of a bouncing slam at the physician's system in its entirety.

One patient, assiduously active in Recovery and indisputably loyal to the physician, was asked what she thought most instrumental in bringing about her recovery. She remarked, "I spoke to Annette and Rosalie. Of course, the classes helped me a lot. But Annette and Rosalie more. They have experience because they went through the same trouble." The physician inquired, "Does that mean that I have no experience?" The patient, noticing her blunder, corrected with more fumbling, "Oh no, but they are sincere." The physician pressed the argument, "Do you think I am not sincere?" The patient explained, "Well, one never knows whether the doctor is going to tell the truth. He may hesitate to tell me he can't help me."

4

SABOTAGE METHOD NO. 4

Challenging the Physician's Diagnosis:
Outright Insistence on Change of Diagnosis

A student may speak of the examination for which he is preparing himself as being either his present purpose or his goal or his aim. Similarly, a housewife on a shopping tour, may claim that the purchase of vegetables is the purpose, goal or aim of her present endeavor. In all of this, the terms purpose, goal and aim are treated as having identical meanings. Much of the confusion attending plain conversation or important debates can be traced to this careless manner of using the three discrete words and juggling their underlying concepts.

The nervous patient must not permit himself the luxury of employing a confusing terminology. To him it must be clear that the PURPOSE AIMS AT ITS GOAL. He must then be shown with unquestioned clarity which is the purpose that moves him, which the goal he has set for himself and what is the degree of determination with which he must aim at the goal.

The nervous patient here spoken of is an average individual. His purpose is that of the average person, i.e., the establishing and maintaining of a family. There are confirmed bachelors and spinsters, isolated trappers and roaming hoboes whose activities are not centered on the family purpose. There are individuals who devote their lives to religious, scientific or artistic pursuits escaping or actively avoiding family ties. All these groups, no matter how numerous they may be, do not fall within the scope of average existence. Their lives are fashioned on exceptional patterns, and the purposes which move them are not pertinent to the present discussion. Within the limits of the present discussion the central purpose of the average person is focused on the family. It is fixed by average constitution, anchored in original predisposition and favored by nature. That purpose is *given,* not *chosen.* It is stable, practically unchanging, and hardly subject to deliberate manipulation, provided it is embraced and not ignored or rejected as in the instances quoted.

The purpose, itself largely unchanging, chooses or sets its goals. They are the means toward accomplishing the purpose. One person may think a profession is the best means of caring for his future or present family, another may choose a business career, a third politics or agriculture or military service. Once the goal has been set (profession, business, politics, etc.) all significant action must be so contrived that it aims at the chosen goal. The aiming must be effective, i.e., straight, direct, sustained, determined, energetic. It must not be wavering, ambiguous, capricious, hesitating, irresolute.

The student working for the examination aims at a degree, let us say, the medical diploma. This is an *intermediate goal*. The *final goal* is to attain efficiency or prominence in the field of his chosen medical profession. A great number of intermediate goals must be aimed at after the successful passing of the examination: internship, residency, renting of an office, purchase of equipment, marriage, education of the children. By means of these intermediate goals the central purpose (of the family) aims at the final and supreme goal.

While aiming, the individual must be able to analyze the nature of his intermediate goals in order to be certain that they really and actually lead toward the final goal. Otherwise, the aim deviates from its target. Campaigning for an electoral contest, for instance, would be good aiming for the final goal of the politician. The conferences with election workers, the addressing of the public, the canvassing of neighbors and friends are intermediate goals that aim straight and undeviatingly at the final goal of victory at the polls. But if the physician should choose electioneering activities as his intermediate goals he may frustrate his final goal of establishing a solid practice in his community. Aiming must be direct and undeviating, and in order to keep the aim straight the individual must be in a position to analyze and diagnose the nature of his intermediate goals. Faulty diagnosis of intermediate goals leads to defective aiming at the final goal.

If a physician starting out in medical practice engages in politics, the chances are he is guided by a fondness for the limelight. His action is based on or influenced by personal inclination, emotional craving, ill-controlled impulses, unreasonable desires, in short, by *subjective feelings*. In order to prevent the aim from deviating in improper directions an individual must train himself to base his action on sane premises, sound conclusions, cool reasoning and good common sense, in short, on *objective thought*. Subjective feelings divert the aim from its proper target; objective thought tends to keep the aim straight in the line of the target.

The nervous patient vitiates his purpose by allowing himself to be deflected in the direction of improper intermediate goals. The physician diagnoses the condition as one of emotional imbalance and prescribes the sustained practice of self-discipline as the final goal to be aimed at. But the subjective feelings of tenseness, distress and panic intervene to suggest that instant relief is needed and that patience and self-discipline are futile remedies in an emergency. If the sufferer yields to the dictates of his feelings his aim will be deflected from the objective goal of self-restraint to the subjective goal of self-indulgence. The deflection is occasioned by the fact that the patient disregards the physician's diagnosis of an emotional imbalance and substitutes his own diagnosis of a physical emergency situation. An emotional imbalance calls for self-restraint as the goal to be aimed at. An acute emergency may require self-indulgence as the proper aim.

The difficulty would not be serious if the patient limited his faulty aiming to the occasions when he finds himself in a panic. Unfortunately, the regrettable practice tends to persist after the panic has passed. When the patient challenges the diagnostic ability of the physician during the acute distress of the self-diagnosed "emergency" the results carry over into the more quiescent periods when the symptoms cause merely mild discomfort. When, during the panic, he discards the diagnosis of an emotional imbalance the physician's authority receives in the patient's mind a severe blow from which it does not recover easily. His diagnostic ability stands challenged and the propensity for challenging it gains momentum with each succeeding setback. The final result is a policy of consistent aiming in the direction of self-indulgence by insisting that the condition is one of a physical ailment and not, as the physician puts it, one of an emotional imbalance. The policy sabotages the physician's authority and prevents effective cooperation. In the process of pursuing their sabotage efforts some patients do not hesitate to voice their challenge with outspoken frankness while others employ more subtle and indirect methods. The precise manner in which these forms of sabotage are practiced will be demonstrated in the following illustrations.

Example 1. A young woman had been suffering from innumerable frightening sensations for over six years. She complained of a crawly feeling over the head, a numbness of the limbs as if they were paralyzed. The eyes felt as if they were being pulled in. She felt a pressure on the nose as if a ton was weighing on it. She had spells of air-hunger in which she felt she was going to suffocate. There were all kinds of pains, pressures, dizziness and dimness of vision, and many bizarre sensations. One day she reported that "out of a clear sky I felt that something blew up in my head. I thought I was gone." On another day she had a burning in the muscle as if "electric wires passed through them." Her head seemed to be falling forward, the body felt as it if were "floating in space." She knew that the symptoms were precipitated by emotional upsets and disappeared in response to emotional relaxation. One day she volunteered the statement that "of course, it's all nerves. I know that. But that does not help me." She was a loyal member of Recovery indicating that she considered her condition subject to treatment through self-help and self-discipline. Nevertheless, she frequently protested that suffering of this severity could "not possibly be of a nervous nature." Once she said, "If I turn my head it cracks in the neck. Then the pain shoots right up to my hip. How can this be nerves?" On another occasion she remarked, "I get that pain when I do the simplest thing. All I have to do is to peel an orange, and the pain is there. How can nerves do that? . . . I am so weak I cannot cut an apple. That weakness must be physical." She craved medication. She was willing to submit to an operation. Her aim was directed toward the intermediate goals of physical therapy and was deflected from those of self-discipline.

Example 2.   A woman whose main symptoms consisted of pressure in the chest with "awful palpitations" was obsessed with the fear of a sudden collapse. The condition had been progressing for fully 17 years before she was seen at the office. After a brief period of combined class and individual treatment she experienced a considerable improvement and had sequences of good days and even good weeks "the first time in years." She was an untiring Recovery worker and seemed to relish the idea of self-help. But whenever she appeared at the office shortly after going through setbacks the thought of the physical ailment reasserted itself. One of her numerous symptoms was heaviness of the eyelids. "Couldn't that be astigmatism?" she asked. She also suffered from severe abdominal spasms. "Why couldn't that be an ulcer?" she asked. The aiming was deflected from the intermediate goals of self-discipline toward those of self-indulgence. What she aimed at were prescriptions, diets, operations, bed rest, eyeglasses.

Example 3.   A male patient had been maladjusted all his life as far as he could remember. He was always fatigued, pepless and devoid of ambition. At home he was explosive in temper, on the outside meek and timid. He suffered from a profound sense of inadequacy, felt flustered in the presence of people and blushed easily. Having attained expertness as a mechanical engineer, he was unable to capitalize on his professional competence because of his abiding self-consciousness. In social contacts he was clumsy and awkward. When addressed he had difficulty formulating a proper sentence and felt choked when he made an effort to speak. In the presence of girls he was particularly bashful. He had been engaged for over three years to a young lady whom he loved dearly but could not muster the courage to get married. After several months of treatment, his self-consciousness improved considerably, but his explosiveness persisted. Finally he decided to go through with his marriage plans. He established a home and felt happy. Unfortunately, his periodic temperamental bursts marred an otherwise compatible marital life. He realized that his temper could only be cured by self-discipline. He had studied the volumes of Recovery's Self-Help System and attended classes regularly. He knew the distinction between subjective feelings and objective thought, was well aware of his tendency to sabotage the physician's authority. Nevertheless, whenever he was seen after a domestic temper outburst he advanced alternative explanations for his inability to control temper. "If I am argumentative," he said, "I am sure it is because of my high blood pressure." The blood pressure was on the upper level of the norm, not significantly elevated. One day he asked, "Couldn't my excitability be due to a thyroid condition?" He was currently deflected from his final goal of self-discipline in the direction of intermediate goals of self-indulgence.

Example 4. A male patient had gone through alternating spells of depressions and elations of mood for the past thirty years. In the intervals between the attacks he was well enough to make a moderate living but was haunted by the sense of being stigmatized. He was unable to throw off the feeling that he was essentially incurable. During the last spell he was given a course of electro-shock therapy, and the hospital treatment was to be followed up with a well prepared program of participation in Recovery activities. Like so many manic-depressive patients he did not relish a system that places the main emphasis on self-help and self-discipline. He cooperated grudgingly and mainly on the energetic insistence of his wife. For several weeks after leaving the hospital he complained of a number of residual symptoms. He still suspected that people watched him, felt fatigued most of the day and slept poorly. Before long he learned to ignore the fatigue sensations and to reject the suspicions about people watching him. Finally he mastered the difficulty of sleeping by imbibing the principle that the so-called "insomnia" is no danger to health. At this stage he felt grateful to Recovery and joined the activities with a better spirit of cooperation. Nevertheless, he still resented having his residual symptoms termed "nervous." "My sensations feel real," he insisted, "they are physical, not nervous." Soon thereafter he decided to quit Recovery for a while. "I think it would do me a world of good to spend several weeks without talking about my symptoms." The physician's diagnosis was challenged and his method of treatment disparaged. Aiming was deflected toward intermediate goals that ran counter to the final goal of overcoming the sense of stigmatization.

Brief examples. A woman patient who had attended classes for many months had lost most of the sensations she had complained of originally. After a setback she said, "I went through an awful ordeal . . . I still have a pain in the right foot. How is it it does not disappear? That has certainly nothing to do with nerves."

A lady suffered from all kinds of disturbing sensations, foremost among them a "sick headache." She improved and seemed to appreciate the desirability of practicing the self-help methods she had learned in classes. After a setback she reverted to her previous practice of suggesting physical methods of therapy as the proper means for relief. "I am still troubled by these sick headaches," she said, "don't you think I should have my glasses changed?"

Another lady had received a course of insulin treatment for a mental ailment. She recovered and was given after-care in Recovery. She "just loved" classes and meetings and boasted of practicing self-help "just as the doctor wants it." After a setback she asked, "I still have that headache. Is that nervous, too? And I have pain in the legs. Is that anything to worry about?"

A woman who was being treated for a psychoneurosis of long standing suffered a setback which was characterized by all manner of disturbing sensations. She was in a marked state of anxiety which she insisted on calling "confusion." Because of a difficulty of concentrating she anticipated a mental collapse. She knew about sabotage and admitted practicing it. "But, doctor," she exclaimed with a show of emotion, "that panic I had yesterday was just awful. You can't call that nervous. It looked the nearest to a mental collapse."

5

SABOTAGE METHOD NO. 5

*Challenging the Physician's Diagnosis: Implied Insistence on
Change of Diagnosis*

Once the physician has made the diagnosis of a nervous ailment a goal is set for the patient to aim at. The patient is given detailed instructions how to manipulate the aiming. He is told by word of mouth and through books and pamphlets that the object is to ignore his disturbing inner experiences, his threatening sensations, his overpowering impulses, his obsessing thoughts or deranged feelings. Above all, he is directed to command his muscles not to do the bidding of the temperamental lingo and the symptomatic idiom. The instructions are clear. The patient is perfectly able to understand them. Moreover, they are endlessly repeated and currently illustrated with telling examples in classes and meetings. There can be no doubt that the patient fully grasps the nature of the goal, and the proper means of aiming at it. Why, then, does his aim stray so persistently from the goal set by the physician?

The goal is that of self-discipline. What must be disciplined is the patient's behavior, particularly his behavior toward his inner experiences. His heart sets up frightening palpitations, and if they are to be controlled thought and muscles must be trained not to respond to the threat of the symptom. But in past years the patient has developed the habit of indulging himself. He has for many years yielded to the impulse to call for instant relief, to summon the physician, insisting that he cannot "stand it one minute longer." He has for years made use of his panics for the purpose of alerting the house, clamoring for emergency measures, making everybody jump and rush, turning the home into a madhouse, keeping all relatives in a frenzy of suspense and excitement. These reactions have hardened into stubborn habits of self-indulgence. And if the patient is asked to exchange his present set of habits for those prescribed by his physician; if he is told to discard self-indulgence and to replace it with self-discipline the task seems to be exacting indeed. The goal scares him, and there is no possibility of a steady, energetic, fearless aiming if the very target inspires fear, weakens the energy and shakes steadiness into quivering agitation. If thus affected, the patient will be inclined to cling to his old habits of self-indulgence. The goal set for him by the physician will strike him as unrealistic, impossible of achievement; he will question its value, will view it with skepticism if not with outright ridicule.

If the patient is skeptical that means he is not disposed to accept the goal. Yet he accepts it in a sense. The fact that he does not change physicians indicates that he subscribes to the diagnosis of a nervous ailment and pledges himself to practice what he is told to do. But the pledge is given with reservations which find their expression in the statement, "I'll try my best." The "best" to which the patient commits himself is nothing but a weak half-effort, a lukewarm cooperation, a disposition to give up should the first trial prove unsuccessful. Essentially it means the goal is accepted partially only. It is neither fully rejected nor wholly accepted. But without full acceptance of the goal there can be no thorough aiming.

In the foregoing chapter an account was given of defective aiming on the part of the patient who challenges the diagnosis. The examples quoted there referred to outright rejection of the physician's opinion. The patients there described actually substituted a diagnosis of their own. They asked, "How can nerves do that? How can this be nerves? That weakness must be physical." This is about the nearest a patient will come to an outright rejection of the physician's authority if he continues to patronize him at all. This type of sabotage was characterized as "Outright Insistence on Change of Diagnosis" which meant an unqualified challenge of the diagnosis. In the present chapter the case of the patient will be discussed who, avoiding open defiance, rejects the diagnosis by implication rather than straight denial.

Examples: A woman had been suffering from fatigue, poor sleep, headaches, dizziness, chest pressure and all kinds of other threatening sensations. Most annoying was a sensation felt in the abdomen of churning and tremulousness which was present all day every day. The churning became almost unbearable immediately after taking a meal. As a result, eating became a continued and dreaded torture. In time, the patient almost loathed food. She was seen by a number of physicians, was hospitalized several times with no effort spared to arrive at a diagnosis. All tests were negative, and the diagnosis was invariably that of a nervous condition. She was seen in the fourth year of her invalidism and made considerable headway in response to private interviews and class treatment. Nevertheless, she insisted that the constant churning must have a "cause." This term "cause" is frequently mentioned by patients who resent having their disturbance classified as nervous. Nervousness, to them, means a condition for which there is no "cause." It means a trouble which has to do with lack of will-power, self-pampering, refusal to get well, in short, poor morale and weak character. The "cause," if found, would instantly redeem the moral status of the patient, and the stigma of low morale would fall to the ground. The patient in question was untiring in her assertion that her symptoms must have a "cause." "I always have diarrhea. There must surely be a cause for that." When questioned about the character of her evacuation she gave the information that she had two movements, sometimes three on the days in which the diarrhea was present. When asked whether the stool was solid, soft or liquid she said, "Today it was solid in the forenoon and soft in the afternoon." And this was called a "diarrhea" which "surely must have a cause." In this instance, the physician's diagnosis was rejected by implication. It was implied, not mentioned explicitly, that in labelling the ailment as nervous the physician had neglected to look for the "real and true" cause. The diagnosis was challenged by an implied insistence on physical ailment.

Frequently these patients will quote other physicians whom they consulted in previous years reciting some diagnostic statement which may be reproduced correctly or incorrectly. "Dr. H.," a patient said, "warned me that vomiting of the kind I have may be due to a beginning cancer." Another patient quoted or misquoted a previous consultant as stating that he found a "thickening of the folds of the sigmoid. He put me on a rigid diet and warned me to keep my bowels regulated. He must have had some reason for doing that."

Another patient exclaimed, "I have an awful pressure in the head. There must be a cause for that." He was told that this was a quest for a change in the diagnosis and meant sabotage. Whereupon he replied, "Dr. C. said, 'You are on the borderline. You go to the hospital and rest your mind.'" This man was one of those patients who insist that theirs is a mental and not a nervous ailment. This insistence on the diagnosis of a mental condition seems to have gained currency since the introduction of shock treatments. To some patients the prospect of shock treatment is more promising than mere psychotherapy. It holds out the promise of quick relief. One patient had her hopes pinned on electro-shock therapy because she knew it had given quick aid to many suffers she met in Recovery. She was told that her condition was of such a nature that shock therapy would not be successful. This did not discourage her. She replied, "But I am afraid I am a mental case and I need shock treatment. Dr. S. told me people develop bad habits and they stay with them." And this flimsy statement was made the warrant for a change in diagnosis and for the choice of a treatment which entails a great deal of hardship and may even have serious consequences. Some patients, inspired by the desire for quick relief, go even to the length of pleading for the diagnosis of a brain tumor. Any diagnosis seems to them more hopeful than that of a nervous ailment. A brain tumor they view as a possibility for an operation and a rapid deliverance from suffering.

A rather common attempt to reject the diagnosis of a nervous ailment is the recourse to heredity. A nervous ailment, the patient thinks, means lowered morale. This label cannot possibly be attached to a condition which is due to a hereditary predisposition. The patient cannot on any account be held responsible for a difficulty inherited from his ancestors. One patient, immediately on being told that her complaint was undoubtedly due to a nervous disturbance replied, "I hope my son will not get this condition. My mother had exactly the same complaints I have." Another patient said, "My mother was like me. Is that hereditary?" There is certainly no glory in a hereditary ailment. There can be scant consolation in the thought that one's ancestors were "tainted." But anything sounds more hopeful and more comforting than the bleak prospect of having to undergo training in self-discipline. Even brain tumors, mental ailments and hereditary "taints" are preferable to that dreadful indictment as being a weak character and needing training in self-control.

6

DISCOURSE ON VALUATION

Goals are of two kinds: short range and long range. The process of bringing up and educating children extends over twenty to twenty-five years. It takes the greater part of a man's adult life to establish a reputation, to acquire unquestioned mastery of a profession, to build up a smooth-running business enterprise. Such long range goals, requiring prodigious amounts of time for their development and ripening, tax the patience, endurance and determination of the individual. Short range goals are less or not at all exacting. The purchase of a garment, the writing of a letter, the trimming of the lawn or the visit to a friends' home are goals of this description. They call for a minimum of patience, endurance and determination. They are usually accomplished in little time, with scant effort and with negligible risk of failure.

Long range goals, as a rule, carry considerable responsibilities. If you neglect the cutting of your lawn you will not be likely to suffer the tortures of self-reproach. But let the thought obsess you that you neglected the education of your children, and your peace of mind will be gravely affected. You will suffer pangs of conscience and bitter despair. Short range goals permit leisurely, relaxed aiming. But long range goals demand steady concentration and strained attention. They leave little room for relaxation and diversion.

If your goal is of the short range variety you will be able to aim at it correctly if you make use of the proper tool and command the requisite skill and technique for using it. You will do a good job at cutting the grass in front of your home if you employ a suitable lawnmower with moderate skill and a smattering of knowledge about its technical construction. This is entirely different if your aim is directed at a long range goal. Tools, skills and techniques alone will be of little significance if your ambition is to secure a good education for your children. A goal of this kind demands patient application, sustained effort, unflagging determination, and above all an unshakeable sense of duty and responsibility. To be brief: short range goals must be aimed at with *skills and techniques*, long range goals with *character and will power*.

The fact that you set yourself a given long range goal indicates that you prefer that goal to another. You might have chosen a business career but you decided on a medical education in preference to trading or manufacturing. The preference placed a valuation on your choice. You value your activities as student or practitioner of medicine. Your aim is now directed at a *value*.

A physician may value a multitude of things and activities. Hunting, traveling and golfing may be valuable for his recreation. Card games, radio and movies may be of value to him in point of relaxation and diversion. To be expensively dressed, to own a high priced automobile and to acquire membership in an exclusive club may be of value to his reputation or to his vanity. He may, of course, value material possessions, and if in the pursuit of wealth he engages in stock market or real estate speculation be certain that the thrill or the mere prospect of amassing a fortune will be valuable to him. But clearly, the faithful devotion to a noble profession and the greedy scramble for money cannot possibly have the same value. Obviously, valuations must be of two kinds. How are they to be differentiated?

An overcoat is of value as protection against rain and cold. If keeping dry and warm is your present goal the overcoat will be a suitable means with which to aim at the goal. Generally speaking, every means or tool which enables you to aim at your goal is of value for this particular goal. If your goal right now is to escape the summer heat a swim will be of value. If your goal is to still your hunger a hamburger or frankfurter will be objects of value. Since everything may at times become the suitable means of aiming at a goal the possible range of values is limitless. The question is not, however, whether a given means or tool is of value to a given goal. The more important question is whether the goal itself is one of value.

A goal may be of value to the individual or to the group. Whether an overcoat satisfies your desire for protection against the weather and whether a dish of meat relieves your hunger is of no direct interest to the group. These goals serve your personal comfort and are individualistic in nature. They are *individualistic values*. On the other hand, if you bend your energies to educating your children the group will recognize your endeavor as being valuable to the community and will class it as a group value. Needless to say that when we speak of values we mean *group values* only.

In order to guide the conduct of the individuals belonging to it the group has set up a *table of valuations*. All group values, that is, all valued or preferred group goals are there ranged in proportion to the importance they bear to the group purpose. The individualistic goals of personal comfort, vanity, emotional and temperamental dispositions and competitive ambitions are reasonably tolerated within the framework of the table of valuations but are not included in it. To put it otherwise, the group permits a moderate degree of indulgence in gambling, drinking, frolicking. It sanctions certain emotional drives and temperamental leanings. It may even grant a modicum of license to greed, unwise speculation and sharp competition. But all these activities are strictly classed as individualistic and are denied a rating in terms of valuations.

A group strives for stability first and foremost. Short range goals could never guarantee stability. They are pursued for a short time until mood, caprice, disposition suggest other more convenient goals. If stability is to be maintained the group must insist on reserving its table of valuations for long range goals only. As was mentioned, aiming at long range goals calls for steadfastness, determination, patience and sustained effort. In other words, it calls for character. Character is opposed or indifferent to mood, caprice, disposition. Everything that is purely individualistic and personal is outside the sphere of character.

A person endowed with character aims at his long range group goals (values) either with rigid, unyielding *principles* or with elastic but firm *policies*. Principles admit of no exception, policies do. It is unprincipled behavior to steal or cheat even once. But it may be a good policy to relax discipline frequently in dealing with children or employees. Principles call for relentlessness, severity, perhaps even for fanaticism; policies call for a flexible strategy, for maneuver and careful adjustment to the requirements of the just prevailing situation. But no matter how fundamentally different they are with regard to rigidity and flexibility both principle and policy defeat their purpose unless they are acted on with steadfastness, determination, patience and sustained effort.

Health, it would seem, does not figure in the average table of valuations. The group holds its members responsible for their character and, for instance, frowns on dishonesty and lack of responsibility. But it does not set up a code that obliges the individual to tend to his health. There are other important functions which though they represent undoubtedly long range group goals are not included in the table of valuations. Parenthood is one of them, sociability another. The group unquestionably values them but refrains from regulating or supervising them. The reason presumably is that the vast majority of people can be depended on to take adequate care of health, children and social contacts without any prompting on the part of the group. Be that as it may, the fact is that health does not seem to be considered a value in its own right. The other fact, however, is that without health there can be no proper aiming at long range goals and their corresponding values. The functions of loyal service, religious devotion, patriotic duty, parenthood, friendship, sociability, civic-mindedness cannot be accomplished if the individual is crippled, bed ridden or otherwise seriously handicapped. That functions of this order cannot be properly discharged if they are continuously frustrated by frightening sensations, panics, and anxieties needs no comment. Mental health particularly is not only a value. It is a necessary prerequisite for the unhampered functioning of all the values represented in the table of valuations.

7

SABOTAGE METHOD NO. 6

Failure to Practice Spot Diagnosis

Whether or not health is part of the general table of valuations, to the patient it cannot be anything but a value. As such it must be aimed at either with rigid principle or with a firm policy. A principle is not permitted ever to deviate from its goal. A policy may at times, but if it is to remain firm the deviations must be held to an unavoidable minimum.

A physician treating a confirmed drinker will have to insist on principle. He must instruct the patient *never* to imbibe even a single drop of liquor. Should the drinker deviate even once from the goal of total abstinence the deviations are certain to be continued. For the nervous patient such a rigid adherence to principle is not necessary. If suffering from "nervous fatigue" he is directed to take brisk walks in defiance of his physical discomfort he may at times weaken and stray from the goal of self-discipline. In other words, he is permitted to sabotage his goal occasionally. His health practice must be persistent but not continuous. In his case, a performance based on rigid principle can be dispensed with. A firm policy will finally accomplish the end.

In order to hold down the deviations, that is, the acts of sabotage, to a minimum the patient will have to know the nature of the diagnosis and the acts which constitute sabotage. The diagnosis of a nervous condition establishes that the patient suffers from disturbing sensations, feelings, impulses and thoughts. These symptoms may occur numbers of times every hour of every day. Each time any of the symptoms appear the patient must have in mind the diagnosis given him after the initial examination. At that time the physician surveyed the broad field of the patient's reactions. His final diagnosis covered the sum total of the symptoms, the various circumstances in which they may occur, the domestic, social or vocational influences that may precipitate them, the emotional background, the time most favorable for their release. Covering the entire field of their operation the diagnosis was a *field diagnosis*. This field diagnosis the patient must now apply to every occasion and every spot where the symptoms may be noticed. His part in the diagnostic scheme is to practice *spot diagnosis*. In order to perform the diagnostic function assigned to him he will have to acquire skill in *spotting* each symptom as it arises and each sabotaging trend as it emerges. The symptoms will have to be spotted in their initial stage before they reach their peak of intensity. At the moment the "fatigue" begins to stir in the morning the spot diagnosis of a harmless nervous disturbance must be made instantly. Likewise, if worry or alarm supervene the spot diagnosis of sabotage must immediately dominate the patient's mind. If the spotting is done promptly both the symptom and the sabotage will spend themselves without leading to a vicious cycle. In the beginning the spotting will have to be done consciously and laboriously, but with continued practice and experience the process will become relatively automatic and spontaneous.

The spotting practice is not easy. The chief difficulty is that symptoms frequently acquire the tendency to shoot forth with the rapidity of a trigger reaction. The palpitation or air-hunger are there before the patient "even had time to think about them." The trigger symptom is not only abrupt in its appearance, it is also extremely intense, overwhelming, threatening, terrifying. Once its terror grips the patient he will be thrown into a panic and will be caught in a relentless vicious cycle. The terror will instantly suggest that these are "the worst palpitations I ever had," and that "if I don't get my breath quickly this is sure to be my last gasp." The trigger symptom has now set in motion a whole train of sabotaging thoughts, the thoughts of a heart disease, of a tumor in the chest, the fear of impending collapse. The sabotage sweeps aside the physician's field diagnosis and aborts the patient's spot diagnosis.

Clearly, the trigger symptom must be spotted before it has an opportunity to generate the panic and the vicious cycle. This is possible only if the spot diagnosis is established in the split-second when the trigger reaction is born. Stating it otherwise, it means that the spot diagnosis must acquire a trigger quality. The thought "this is nervous and nothing else" must shoot into the patient's mind precisely at the moment when his body fires off its palpitations. *Trigger-spotting must coincide with or follow immediately on the eruption of the trigger symptom.* That spotting of this kind calls for a firm policy needs no emphasis.

Some symptoms have undoubted trigger quality. But most of them are preceded by ordinary tenseness and irritability and gain momentum only because of the temperamental attitude taken by the patient. He becomes provoked at himself or others, indulges in an orgy of self-pity or attention-demanding, and it is this process of "working-himself-up" that finally leads to panicky reactions. This situation which is by far more common than the "out-of-a-blue-sky" reaction demands a firm policy of temper control, that means, *temper spotting.* Contrary to what might be expected, the average patient encounters greater difficulty spotting his temperamental reaction than he does in the process of spotting the symptom. Even the trigger reaction is more amenable to spot control than is temper. The reason ought to be clear: the symptom scares and creates distress. It is experienced as painful, unendurable. Its capacity for creating severe suffering carries with it the powerful incentive to eliminate it. Temper is neither terrifying nor painful nor unendurable. Instead, it is stimulating, vital, energizing. If it provides any incentive it is for prolonging the stimulation and pleasure it affords. It is temper mainly that resists the diagnostic spotting necessary to avoid panics and vicious cycles. Temper spotting calls for an extremely firm policy. In a sense, it might require rigid principle to curb it successfully.

The suddenness with which nervous symptoms are apt to strike is frightening, of course. Anything that occurs suddenly and unexpectedly has this tendency to scare. You strike against an innocent object in the dark and you get scared. A dog jumps at you and instantly your heart palpitates and your knees shake. Let anybody tap you on the shoulder from behind and you will start. The scare caused by the suddenly erupting symptom fits into this common pattern. Anyone would be frightened if his eyes suddenly went dim or when his legs were stricken with a sudden limpness. But the patient must learn to deal with the abruptly emerging symptom as he does when a dog jumps at him unexpectedly. In the case of the dog he gets scared but immediately realizes that, after all, it was nothing but a dog. In this instance, the momentary scare is followed immediately by the correct spot diagnosis. The latter establishes the fact that the scare was produced by an innocent, harmless event. After the spot diagnosis is made the fright disappears. Why is correct spot diagnosis done after ordinary scares but not after the scare produced by a symptom? The answer is that correct spotting is easy in the examples quoted but extremely difficult in the instance of nervous symptoms. If a dog is correctly spotted as the cause of an upset there is nothing to contradict the fact that it was the dog who caused the damage. The thought of another possibility can hardly arise. But after a symptom has made its appearance the patient's thought processes swing into action. Thinking about a symptom means to appraise it, to assess its significance, its danger, its likelihood to recur, and all of this means making a diagnosis. If at that moment the patient makes the physician's diagnosis the symptom will be spotted as merely nervous. Unfortunately, the diagnosis is usually taken from the patient's previous knowledge, and that knowledge was gathered in years past either from his own misconceptions about how symptoms operate or from misinterpreted statements of other physicians or from popular notions current in the community. No sooner has the symptom struck than the patient recalls in a flash the wild diagnoses that have come to him from sources other than his physician. He now indulges in a veritable orgy of self-diagnosing, preventing the correct spot diagnosis, and precipitating a flood of self-scaring reflections. The diagnosis gathered from foreign sources sweeps aside the spot diagnosis recommended by his physician, and the self-scaring ruminations give rise to that variety of temper which, leading to defeatist auto-suggestions, is nothing but plain hysteria. The patient now finds that the present dizziness is "worse than ever." He has "never before" experienced such a furious bout of dizziness. How can the doctor call a dizziness of this kind nervous if it "just drives me mad?" Or, a patient notices that the room swings around him. "I never had that before. It's something new. And the doctor made his diagnosis without knowing about this symptom." Or, the patient experiences that "awful head pressure," and "this time it is real, it is not merely a sensation." Or, the patient is the victim of palpitations and air-hunger. Suddenly he recalls a recent newspaper notice that an acquaintance of his collapsed on the street and died from a heart ailment that had not been diagnosed by the physician. And so the hysteria runs on, releasing a veritable hurricane of defeatist thoughts, sabotaging the field diagnosis handed down by the physician and frustrating any attempt at applying the spot diagnosis. The vicious cycle dominates the scene, multiplying symptoms and pyramiding temperamental outbursts.

Examples: A woman patient complained of a soreness in one of her lower teeth. The condition had been in existence for over ten years alternately affecting different teeth or some part of the gums or cheeks. Most of her teeth had been extracted in deference to her urgent demand to have something done to eliminate "that unbearable pain." She was certain that an abscess or tumor was causing the soreness. She demanded incessantly to be placed in the hospital "for a checkup," insisted on X-Ray studies, tooth extractions, surgery. When she described her pain, she hardly ever missed remarking "This is the worst pain I ever felt. It just drives me crazy. There is a pressure against the root and I am sure it is a tumor." Patients of this kind are given the following explanation: you compare the present pain with a previous pain which you had weeks or months ago. Then you conclude that today's pain is the worst ever. But you must realize that the present pain is actually *experienced* right now while the pain which you had weeks ago is merely *remembered*. Of course, a pain felt right now is always worse than one that is merely remembered. Every experience fades in memory. The pain is remembered but its intensity is softened and mellowed in recollection as everything softens and mellows if viewed in the perspective of time. As a matter of fact, if your present pain were the "mildest ever" it would figure in your mind as the "worst ever" even if you compared it to the most excruciating experience you had in the past. An experience, no matter how mild, is always more intense than a recollection, no matter how severe.

The "worst ever" theme has its variations. Some patients do not merely refer to one single symptom that is felt as having "now" reached its worst intensity; they experience their total condition as being "most" deteriorated today. A patient who had numerous periods of severe depressions to his record was seen on a day when he suffered from a mild condition that only remotely resembled his previous episodes. He "felt blue," but appetite, sleep and initiative were hardly affected. He admitted that he had no difficulty eating and sleeping. He agreed also that he did not have to drive himself as he knew he had to in his severe spells. Nevertheless, he wound up his account with the statement, "I don't see what sleeping and eating have to do with this. I don't think I've ever been that bad."

Another variation of the "worst ever" complaint was furnished by a lady who had for years experienced a sort of tenseness in the abdomen. She called it variously "tremor," "dancing" or "shaking." One day she declared that the shaking was now "worse than ever. It has never been as continuous as these past weeks." Continuity was substituted for intensity in point of being "the worst ever."

Once a patient confers the epithet "worst ever" to a symptom it is no longer spotted as nervous. It is conceived of as something new in intensity, as something that the physician has not considered when he arrived at his field diagnosis. One part of the field had not been sufficiently covered. The patient then supplies the deficiency arriving at the diagnostic conclusion, that "if it is that bad how can it be nervous?"

Some patients content themselves with pointing to the newness of a symptom without touching on its "worse" or "worst" quality. A male sufferer who listed a bewildering host of complaints in his repertory exclaimed, "Yesterday, out of a blue sky, I suddenly felt an electric current through my chest. I never had that before." The patient was an "old-timer" with numerous office visits to his record. The examiner fetched the patient's folder from the files and had no difficulty pointing to several notations concerning electric currents in various parts of the body. The patient was far from convinced. His comment was: "Maybe I had currents before, but that was the most awful experience I ever had."

Patients frequently emphasize the "first" occurrence of a symptom. If it is a complaint which they "never had before," they hasten to add, "Can that be nerves, too?" In many instances, the experience is by no means new and "first," as was easily demonstrated in the case of the patient with the "new" electric current. But new symptoms are, of course, common in psychoneurotic conditions. If they occur they offer the patient a welcome opportunity to engage in his favorite game of sabotaging the physician's field diagnosis. Whether the symptom is the "worst ever" or the "first ever" it is invariably seized upon for the purpose of avoiding the correct spot diagnosis.

8

SABOTAGE METHOD NO. 7

Failure to Spot Emotionalism

If the patient is to spot his temperamental reactions he will have to know those of his acts and statements which give expression to his temper. The coarse varieties of his temperamental expressions ought to be known to him if he took the trouble to read the various chapters of the "Techniques of Self-Help"* which deal voluminously with the subdivisions of the fearful and angry temper. The descriptions there given were concerned with the temperamental behavior which precedes and precipitates symptoms. If a patient develops a spell of choking and dizziness immediately following a heated squabble it is hardly necessary to remind him that his symptoms are the result of his temper. The relation between the two elements is here patent, obvious, self-evident. All that is required to understand occurrences of this kind is plain common sense. The precise meaning of both temper and symptom reveals itself to anybody's native and untutored intelligence and calls for no detailed instruction. This is different with the temperamental behavior which the patient releases *after* a symptom has set in. The symptom may have appeared spontaneously, out of nowhere, without provocation, perhaps at the very moment the patient awoke in the morning. No commotion of any kind preceded it. No sooner were the eyes opened than a heavy pressure settled on the chest and air-hunger produced gasping and choking. The patient is now scared. The scare is originally nothing but a startle, exactly as in the case of a dog suddenly leaping at a man. The startle would spend itself in a few seconds if the patient had the determination to spot the symptom as what it is: the harmless expression of a nervous imbalance. If the symptom is left unspotted the scare may persist, and the likelihood is the patient will now drift into a process of "working-himself-up." Essentially this is a procedure in which the patient talks or

---

* Low, A. A., The Techniques of Self-Help in Psychiatric After-Care, Chicago, 1943, Recovery, Inc. 3 vols.

thinks himself into a mixture of fear and anger which may be prolonged indefinitely just as long as the sufferer cares to maintain his favorite pastime of self-torture. Since the "working-up" process follows the symptom it properly goes by the name of *"post-symptomatic* temper." Its counterpart is the situation in which temperamental behavior precedes and precipitates the symptom. Preceding it, it is called *"pre-symptomatic* temper." The latter is patent and obvious and needs no or little spotting. The former is subtle and elusive and calls for a consummate art of spotting skill.

The practice of "working-oneself-up" follows well defined patterns. The patient may give himself up to a paroxysm of fear or anger. Then he emotionalizes his predicament. He anticipates endless torture; he is certain he is utterly incapable of coping with this "frightful" pressure and visualizes disaster, fatal consequences or outright collapse. After hours of whipping himself up he may realize that nothing fatal or disastrous has happened or is likely to happen. Then he concentrates on the element of suffering and rages either against himself and his own helplessness or against his relatives and their indifference in the face of his agony. All of it is *emotionalism,* a crazy quilt of senselessly exaggerated fears and angers, either overlapping or following one another. After a while, the emotional raving may cease, and another reaction may take its place in the form of *sentimentalism.* If this takes the lead, then, the patient releases an outburst of self-blame or self-pity, deploring his fate which makes him a coward, a burden to his family, a social outcast and professional incompetent. He laments the fact, tearfully and dramatically, that he is deprived of the privilege of discharging his duties and responsibilities, sets himself down as a pernicious example for the children and a disgrace to himself and his relatives. He indicts his moral weakness which robs him of his will power, and his defective intellect which prevents him from understanding the physician's instructions. Frequently, emotionalism goes hand in hand with sentimentalism, the one providing relief through angry explosions, the other furnishing exoneration by putting the blame on fate and destiny or on one's weak constitution. Both employ subtle and indirect reasoning which requires prompt spotting if symptom and suffering are not to be prolonged indefinitely.*

---

* For a more precise formulation of the concepts of emotionalism and sentimentalism see the following chapter.

What is here described represents an extreme expression of the emotional and sentimental character of the "working-oneself-up" process. Even in this extreme development it is common enough. More common, however, and far more damaging to nervous health are its more moderate versions which, keeping this side of outspoken hysteria, follow the line of specious reasoning and transparent sophistry. The patient tries to convince himself or others that he does his best to get well but he "simply does not know" why he cannot throw off his obsession. He claims he makes an honest effort to ignore danger but the sensations persist. What can he do about it? It is his fate to be suffering and to make others suffer. Along with it goes pious protestations that it breaks his heart to see the poor wife distressed, the children not properly provided for and the standard of family life declining. The emotionalism is voiced in soft, timid phrases, the sentimentalism couched in suave, tepid language. No excitement, commotion or hysteria, rather calculation, shrewd strategy, and a good measure of cunning. It is these subtle and devious manifestations of combined emotionalism and sentimentalism that call for a maximum of skill in temper spotting.

Examples: A patient gave an account of the ordeal she went through the day preceding the visit to the office. "I was terribly nauseated ... Then I felt a heat wave ... When these heat waves get me I feel very, very hot. It gets so bad I can't stand it any longer and have to call my husband ... " This is a moderate degree of emotionalism. The language is undoubtedly defeatist, exaggerating the intensity of the experience ("terribly nauseated," "very, very hot") and overstressing its paralyzing effect ("cannot stand it," "have to call").

Another patient delivered herself of a report which, in point of urgency and dramatization, pushed to distinctly dizzier heights on the scale of emotionalism. "This pain," she panted, "just drives me crazy. It's really a pain, it's a sickly feeling, really, it's not my imagination ... My hands are so clammy. They feel like ice. The fingers and toes are real cold. I shake like a leaf ..."

The following description is in a similar vein of forceful dramatization: "I had a chill. My feet got blue. They were almost black. I couldn't even feel them. I had it at least for five hours. And when I got up I felt so weak I could not move. I am still awfully weak. I can hardly eat. Even warm milk hurts my stomach. Couldn't that be a tumor?" One patient exclaimed with flashing eyes and tremulous voice. "That pain is just unbearable ... I was almost out of my mind ... Honestly, I don't see how I can go through this again ... I am sure if that happens again it will be the end ... If my husband hadn't come home in time I don't know whether I wouldn't have done something to myself."

That this emotionalizing language fortifies defeatism, that defeatism intensifies and perpetuates symptoms and that the protracted fury of the "working-oneself-up" process leads to panics and vicious cycles has been explained so frequently in these pages that a renewed discussion of the topic would be tedious. What must be emphasized, however, is that patients of this kind are in the habit of supplementing their verbal emotionalism by equally emotional muscular behavior. They "notice" the "gas pushing against the heart" and clutch the throat and chest, and feel the pulse. They rush to the mirror and scan their features. Then they discover that the eyes have lost their lustre, that a dark shadow skirts the lower lid, that the cheeks are hollow and the face looks wan. One patient said, "My eyes are bloodshot, my tongue is coated. I look in the mirror, and the eyes look weary and beaten down." Many of the tribe continually touch and paw their skin and muscles and promptly discover what they are looking for: hardened glands, flabby tissues, swellings, dryness, moistness and what not.

At times the emotionalism is callously made use of for the purpose of keeping the members of the family in a state of commotion. One such example was furnished by a patient who stated, "I am disgusted with myself. I can't control my temper. The other day it was so bad that I cried out 'I am sick and tired of living.' Of course, they were alarmed. I knew they would be."

9

SABOTAGE METHOD NO. 8

Failure to Spot Sentimentalism

If a patient is to spot his emotionalisms and sentimentalisms he will have to acquire a working knowledge of what are emotions, sentiments and feelings. The first thing he will have to know is that these three varieties of inner experiences are particularly likely to *affect* the functions of the body. Any of them may cause the muscle of the heart to speed its action and to produce palpitations. They may throw the digestive organs into a state of excitement and give rise to vomiting, nausea, belching or gas formation. The muscles of the bronchi may be affected and air-hunger and chest pressure may be the result. They may affect the muscles of the extremities and cause weariness and heaviness, that is, "nervous fatigue." Affecting the functions of the body, emotions, feelings and sentiments have been properly called affections or *affects*.

Everybody has feelings and sentiments every moment of his life. What he feels can be expressed in two terms: a sense of security or insecurity. If you feel secure you are vigorous, cheerful, happy, enthusiastic, enterprising, self-confident. All of this can be summed up in the word "joy" or its finer shades of satisfaction, contentment, serenity. The reverse of joy is grief. The latter is the result of a feeling of insecurity. If you feel insecure you lose your vigor; you lack your customary enthusiasm, happiness and initiative, and are deficient in courage and self-confidence. Grief may shade off into sorrow, gloom, concern, misgiving. All these feelings affect the *physical and psychological person*. If the affection spreads to the *social personality* we speak of sentiments. Sentiments are exercised in a group, feelings can be experienced apart from the group. Animals and babies can feel happy or grieved. But the sentiments of sympathy, companionship and fellowship, of duty accomplished and responsibility discharged can be operative in adult or adolescent members of the group only. If a person is commonly affected by these sentiments, practicing them systematically, he lives up to the standards set down by the group and by this token acquires the title of a mature personality.

Feelings of security give the person a sense of efficiency and adequacy. They are exciting, stirring, stimulating. They make the person feel vital and dynamic. The converse is true of the feelings of insecurity. They produce a sense of weakness, help-lessness and inadequacy. If they predominate the person lacks a sense of vitality and dynamism. This is different with senti-ments. If you are moved or affected by sympathy or by the spirit of fellowship you will hardly experience the flush of vitality or the push of dynamism. You will merely acknowledge that you did a good turn or that you conformed to the group standards of duty and responsibility, that you did the right thing and lived up to your principles. This will give you the sense of right-thinking and right-acting. Your behavior was in accord with established values; it was valid but not necessarily vital. Feelings express *vitality* or the lack of it; sentiments stand for *validity* or the lack of it. A person driven on by his feelings is vital, perhaps also colorful and forceful; a personality guided by group-approved sentiments is valid, perhaps also colorless and dull.

The daily life of the average man is so arranged that his feelings and sentiments are held in a fair state of equilibrium. You feel distressed at a rebuff suffered in your place of employ-ment but returning home in the evening you enjoy the comfort and peace of your home, the loyalty of your wife and the loveliness of your children. The grief experienced on the job is neatly balanced and perhaps cancelled out by the joy accorded you in the domestic sphere. Or, you are worried by the thought of having defaulted on some duty but your sense of failure is soon counter-balanced by the evidence of an accomplishment that raises your morale. Today you have misgivings about your standing among neighbors and friends; tomorrow you will have proof positive that you are well thought of. Grief is balanced by joy, failure by accomplishment. In this manner, both your vitality and your validity are kept in a satisfactory state of adjustment. This serene, happy and complacent life may be interrupted suddenly by a blow dealt you by fate. Your child is stricken with an incurable disease. He is or may be crippled for life. Now you are seized with a grief which is deeper and far more intense than that caused by the pinpricks, failures and rebuffs encountered in the daily round. The mild feelings of routine existence, coming and going, causing only transient disequilibrium, have now been replaced by a feeling of extraordi-nary depth and duration. This is still a feeling, deeper and more intense than the average variety but a feeling, nevertheless. The question is: Will you "process" or "work-up" this deep *feeling* into a fierce, turbulent *emotion*? Will you, for instance, permit yourself to think and exclaim that life is now unbearable, that all is lost, that no joy can henceforth enter your existence? Will you rave against fate that has betrayed you? Against medical science that has failed you? Against Divinity that has forsaken you? Will you go into rages and explosions against yourself and others? If so, your deep feeling has changed into an emotion that is loud, boisterous and furious but lacks the depth of genuine inner experiences. You are now the victim of *emotionalism*, and your affect is one of *emotional hysteria*.

There is another possibility. Instead of venting your wrath on fate, humanity and Divinity you may turn it against yourself mainly or solely. You will then embark on a wild crusade against your own deficiencies. Why did you wait before you called the physician? If you had summoned him immediately the calamity might have been averted. What kind of a father are you? How depraved, how devoid of the most primitive sense of duty and responsibility? If your child is doomed to life-long suffering it is you who wrought his doom. You charge yourself with carelessness, neglect and indifference to the welfare of your family and set yourself down as a man without morals, without character, without judgment. You doubt whether you are possessed of the ordinary sentiments expected of a father. You give yourself over to a paroxysm of self-accusations and self-torture. If that happens your ordinarily deep or average sentiments have degenerated into a disordered, unbalanced, frenzied *sentimentalism*. Your affect is now one of *sentimental hysteria*.

In the instance of the child stricken with an incurable disease the father had ample opportunity to display genuine feelings of grief and pertinent sentiments of devotion. A combination of this kind would have led to plans and actions meant to remedy or mitigate the affliction. The grief would have inspired a mood of resignation and might have prompted a reappraisal of previous valuations and ambitions. The father might have realized that in the past he spent too much time and energy on vocational and social pursuits, that as a consequence home life was neglected, that the domestic scene suffered from a deficiency of affection and intimacy. Considerations of this kind would have suggested settled plans to rearrange time schedules and work habits. As a result, the needs of the family would henceforth have taken their rightful place side by side with the demands of social and business obligations. The genuine feelings would have produced a reorientation of goals and aims. In a similar fashion, the sentiments of sympathy and parental devotion would have led to decisions to do everything to shape and prepare the future of the handicapped child. There was the issue of how to substitute home training for school education, how to implement projects for medical supervision, recreation, group life, play, travel. The father might have given thought to a suitable though limited career for the boy, perhaps even to the possibility of married life in spite of the handicap. In all of this, the father would have thought of the boy and the family first and of himself last. Instead, he gave himself up to a burst of emotionalism and sentimentalism, and now he thought of himself first and the boy last. He lamented *his* own fate, the frightful loss which *he* suffered. His wails and moans centered on the sorrowful reflection how *he* would be able to bear up under the strain of anguish and despair. His feelings and sentiments were primarily focused on *his* own self, on *his* poor ego, secondarily only on son and family. The difference is clear; genuine feelings and sentiments tend to produce plans and actions designed to manipulate or remedy a situation *outside* the person who experiences the affects. Emotionalism and sentimentalism have the opposite effect. They turn the attention of the affected person *inside*, to his own inner experiences, to his own woes, anxieties and anticipations. The difference is one between fellowship and individualism. Genuine affects make for fellowship and group-centered interests; emotionalism and sentimentalism produce stark individualism and self-centered egotism.

The tendency today, in daily life, literature, art and popular scientific pursuits, is to emphasize emotions (fear and anger) to the neglect of genuine feelings and sentiments. Unfortunately, this trend has served to put the stamp of approval on the emotional and sentimental hysteria practiced by the nervous patient. Experiencing disturbing sensations or thoughts the patient's first impulse is to concentrate his attention on his dear self and his poor ego. He expatiates in unending tirades on the nature, quality and intensity of his inner perceptions. He picks them apart, goes into details of analysis and explanation, insists that his feelings and sentiments are real, not imaginary, that his sensations are excruciating and unbearable, that instant relief is imperative. Otherwise how is he going to "stand them?" He appeals for sympathy and attention, demands understanding and above all a "friendly hearing," an opportunity to pour forth a stream of complaints, an occasion for "processing" his feelings and sentiments into wild orgies of hysteria. This patient is interested first and foremost in coddling and pampering his inner experiences. He "works them up" or "processes" them into excitements, frenzies and panics. The preoccupation with his experiences *inside* him keeps him from taking adequate courses of action *outside* him for the purpose of remedying the situation. Moreover, if such a course of action is suggested by his physician he counters with reactions of sabotage sensing keenly that outside action is bound to divert his attention from the painful delights of inside analysis and self-observation. This patient is a confirmed individualist, self-centered and thoroughly egotistical with reference to his symptoms, oblivious to his own realistic needs and indifferent to the demands of fellowship. His endless complaints disrupt group life and aggravate his own hysteria and suffering. If this deplorable situation is to be rectified the nervous patient will have to learn that emotionalism and senti- mentalism are the enemies of his own welfare and a blight on the group he lives in. In order to do that efficiently he will have to train himself to spot his inner experiences and to prevent his originally mild and innocent feelings and sentiments from being processed into emotional and sentimental hysterias by means of the "working-oneself-up" procedures. The technique for spot- ting emotionalism was described in the preceding chapter. In- structions for spotting sentimentalism are offered in the following examples.

Examples: A woman who had been suffering from numerous disturbing sensations, obsessions and compulsions released a veritable torrent of moans, sobs and complaints whenever she found somebody willing to listen to her. She had been given instructions in classes and in private conferences to the effect that moaning, sobbing and complaining are done through the medium of speech muscles and that muscles can be controlled at will. The precise technique of practicing this type of muscle control had been discussed with her repeatedly. There was no doubt but she understood the procedure. She also understood that restraining muscles meant to produce increased tenseness in the restrained muscles but the tenseness disappears in a few minutes or seconds if the "command to the muscles" is main- tained resolutely. She understood but failed to practice control. Instead she bewailed her fate. "I know I am a drag on my family.

I hate to torture them but I cannot help it. Honestly, I don't understand how they stand up under the strain. I know I'll be their ruin." She loved to pamper her inner sentimentalisms and refused to control her muscles for purposes of inner control or for proper outer action.

Another patient with a similar bent for incessant complaining exclaimed, "I am afraid I ruin my family." The following conversation developed between patient and physician: Physician: "The best way to stop ruining your family is to stop working yourself up. You can do that easily if you control your speech muscles." Patient: "I try but I can't. Maybe I don't understand you." Physician: "Don't work yourself up over your inability to understand. Stop making an issue of it." Patient: "How can I avoid making an issue of the health of my family. I certainly can't stop worrying about that." Physician: "Don't make an issue of your worries." Patient: "And I can't stop this daydreaming." Physician: "Daydream but make no issue of it. Don't work yourself up over it." Patient: "And why can't I shake off these ugly thoughts?" Physician: "Have the thoughts and wait till they disappear. But above all, make no issue of your having thoughts." Patient: "But, doctor, you don't listen to me." Physician: "The most important thing is that you listen to what I tell you. You told me of your inner experiences and your sentimentalisms so many times that I know them by heart. You should stop talking about your worries and issues and start controlling them by using your muscles."

A male patient had difficulty controlling his temper. But instead of making an honest effort to "command his muscles" he relished indulging in sentimental self-accusations. "I strike my children," he exclaimed, "Is that human?" He was told, "Control the muscles of your arms and command them not to strike. But above all, don't become emotional and sentimental after you have struck your children. Avoid working yourself up." The patient replied, "Maybe I haven't got the mental capacity to do that." Physician: "I asked you to use your muscles for control, not your brain." Patient: "But how can I carry out your orders if I don't think?" Physician: "You do an excellent piece of thinking right now arguing with me. The trouble is you think too much and too well when it is a matter of convincing yourself that you cannot do what I ask you to do." Like so many other patients, this man made use of sentimental self-condemnations in order to prove to himself and the physician that he is desirous but incapable of improving.

One articulate patient expressed the relationship between sentimentalism and the will to sabotage in the following words: "I like to think of myself as a lost soul. I feel I am irretrievable. If I went with as much enthusiasm about the job of getting well as I go about moping and feeling sorry for myself I'd be well in no time." Another patient expressed a similar thought when she said, "I am getting more tired in the morning thinking about what is to be done than doing it." These patients love to pamper their sentiments but hate to control their muscles.

10

SABOTAGE METHOD NO. 9

Failure to Practice Muscle Control

Recovery stands for simplicity. Its systems of instruction and training are meant to enable the plain, humble and untutored patient to practice self-help. An objective of this kind cannot be achieved by means of involved explanations and complex techniques. Self-help in psychiatric after-care calls for simple methods of interpreting and manipulating symptoms. It is for this reason that Recovery offers to its members plain common sense instead of intricate philosophies and artless techniques of training in place of elaborate procedures.

Whatever else a disturbing nervous symptom may mean, its main effect is that it interferes with the adjustment of the patient. And adjustment is effected through action, and action is carried on through muscles, including the muscles of speech. The patient says he suffers from fatigue. The fact is, however, that he thinks his muscles are exhausted and fears or neglects to use them for the purposes of walking or working. "Fatigue," then, thwarts proper muscular behavior. With the thought of exhaustion in his brain the patient is doomed to inactivity and incapacity. The conclusion is plain: convince the patient that his muscles are neither weak nor damaged, and he will regain the courage and determination to use them for his daily activities. Adjustment will be restored and action reinstated.

Nothing is more convincing than muscular performance. A letter is waiting to be written. The message which you are to deliver is embarrassing or difficult to present in proper language. You doubt whether you can choose the right phrasing to express it without being too sharp or overcourteous, or too dull. Finally you decide to proceed with the irksome task and find to your surprise that in the end your communication is little short of a fine accomplishment in wording, style and composition. You are proud of your product and have gained considerably in self-confidence. The action of your muscles conquered and convinced the anxieties of your brain. Instances of this kind are too common to need amplification. The underlying principle is of universal application and finds its pertinent formulation in the proper prescription: try and you will find out. To a mind reared in the tradition of intellectual pomposity such a naive method may appear to be too simple to deserve the name of a technique. But self-help is based and predicated on simplicity, and simple rules only will serve the mass of nervous and former mental patients who, in the mass, are composed of simple folk.

Nobody will doubt that a patient can convince his brain through the muscles that he can walk on in spite of his "exhaustion" without incurring the danger of collapse. All he has to do is to step out in forceful movement and if he fails to "keel over" or to "cave in" he has given incontrovertible evidence that his muscles are anything but exhausted and that the menace of collapsing is a myth. Nor will anybody dispute the fact that a temperamental person can cut short his emotionalism by commanding his speech muscles to stop arguing or his skeletal muscles to stop fighting. Temper of this kind creates an impulse to strike or shout, and since the shouting or striking must be done by the muscles they can be stopped by an order to the same muscles to refrain from striking or shouting. The same transparent relationship obtains in the case of many disturbing sensations. An itch mobilizes the impulse to scratch and it is well known how difficult it is for most people to resist the temptation. Nevertheless, in company or on the street, intuitively or reflectively, the itch is successfully controlled, that is, the muscles have been commanded to refrain from scratching. Similar examples of effective blocking of symptomatic reactions through control of muscles could be quoted from experiences with other disturbances, for instance, the control of restlessness and agitation through determined motionless sitting, the conquest of "sleeplessness" through persistent lying in bed without turning and twisting. But these illustrations refer to sensations that have or seem to have their seat in the skin or the muscles of trunk and extremities. How about sensations which are produced in inner organs? How about experiences other than sensations, for instance, fears, obsessions, preoccupations? Can muscle training stop a lump in the throat, pressure in the head and churning in the abdomen? Can muscles do away with the thought that the body is expanding or that people are looking at you?

An intelligent approach to these questions will have to consider the nature and character of both sensations and obsessions. Sensations are notorious for their transient and ephemeral existence. They come and go. All you have to do is to observe yourself for a few minutes' time and you will have no difficulty spotting numerous mild sensations rising to consciousness and instantly falling back into unawareness. You can then notice in quick succession a warm feeling in the lobe of the ear, some tenseness in the neck, a tickle in the throat, a momentary heartburn in the region of the sternum, a pulling in the shoulder, an itch somewhere and a pressure somewhere else. Some sensations, if mild, are pleasing, like the warmth, the tickle and the itch; others are displeasing, like the heart-burn, the pulling and the pressure. In this manner, stimulation and irritation alternate. The one set of sensations are relaxing; the others are tensing. This continuous ebbing and flowing, appearing and disappearing has been likened to the systolic and diastolic phases of the action of the heart and has been called the "sensation pulse." How is it, one may ask, that the sensations felt by nervous patients come but do not go? What causes them to lose their transient character and to acquire the quality of sustained duration? To express it differently, why do the sensations experienced by nervous patients tend to lose their pulse?

The same consideration may be applied to the obsessions which plague nervous patients. An obsession is a thought, usually a suspicion. The suspicion may be directed at others as in jealousy, or at one's self as in the case of the obsessive thought that one's body is changing or that people stare at you. Of thoughts it is just an axiomatic as of sensations (and feelings) that they are of transient duration, flitting through the brain, coming and going, unless they are concentrated on. Just give yourself over to a few moments of revery or day-dreaming and you will realize how your thoughts wander across the field of experience, now reaching out into the future, then roaming through the past with a motley assortment of ideas, opinions, plans and dreams crowding in on one another, the ones just entering your brain, the others leaving. This ceaseless hustle and bustle of an up and down flowing mentation has been called the "stream of thought." The question is again permitted: How is it that with nervous patients the ordinarily fading and floating thought elements harden and crystallize into perennial and unending suspicions and obsessions? Why does their stream of thought cease streaming? Obviously, some factor operating in nervous patients upsets the pulse of their sensations and interrupts the stream of their thoughts. That factor is an abiding sense of insecurity producing, through concentrated preoccupation, sustained tenseness and preventing the nervous system from relaxing.

If the patient could gain the unquestioned assurance that his condition is "just nerves," distressing but not dangerous, he would have no difficulty relaxing his organs and reinstating the pulse of sensations and the stream of thought. Unfortunately, the assurance given the patient by his physician is verbal, mainly or exclusively, and words do not necessarily carry conviction. Usually the patient is an "experienced complainer," has made the round of physicians and clinics, and numerous past attempts at reassuring him met with failure. He is now skeptical, listens but is not convinced. The physician's "sales talk" strikes against the patient's "sales resistance." Verbal explanations, no matter how skillful, usually fail to reach the "expert sufferer." The thing that will convince him is his own performance. Make him walk ten blocks and the action of his own muscles will demonstrate to him that he *did not* collapse in spite of his feeling of exhaustion. The myth of exhaustion is then reduced to absurdity by the patient's own muscular movements. Or, to give another illustration: the patient is tense, restless, in constant motion. He is unable to sit through a theatre performance. Hence, in a show, he chooses a seat near the aisle so he can make a hasty escape if the tenseness becomes "unendurable." Patients of this sort are gripped with fear that unless they rush instantly out of the door into the fresh air they will faint or burst. Train them to force the muscles to sit through the ordeal of tenseness which is "extremely distressing but utterly harmless," and the first trial, as a rule, will convince them that the "intolerable" tenseness can be tolerated and that the burst or faint do not materialize. If the patients have been exposed to group psychotherapy classes and Recovery meetings, the example of other patients who "have done it" prepares the new practitioner for the first trial. In classes and meetings he has obtained the conviction that others have conquered fears by the muscular route. Later his own practice reinforces the assurance gained from the reports of the others. After a few more trials the fears disappear, the tenseness recedes and relaxation re-establishes itself. And under conditions of relaxation, the suspended pulse of sensations regains its balance, and the disordered stream of thought restores the regularity of its flow. The following illustrations will demonstrate the details of technique which patients are taught to employ in order to conquer disturbing sensations and obsessive thoughts by the simple means of "commanding the muscles to do what you fear to do." That most patients bungle the method in the beginning ought to be understood. Many patients not only bungle but also sabotage the method.

Example 1. A woman patient had been suffering from numerous anxieties, obsessions and compulsions for upward of three years before she was assigned to classes and Recovery membership. She feared going out unaccompanied, anticipating fainting spells although she had never experienced any. Her most distressing difficulty was the compulsion to "repeat." Whatever she did had to be done over numbers of times, sometimes for hours on end. Making beds was a never ending procession. After the sheet was tucked in it had to be pulled out and smoothed and stretched and tucked in again. Then the pulling out and smoothing and stretching had to be done again, undone, redone. In this manner, every task took hours to perform and seemed never finished. Washing the hands, cleaning the bathtub, locking the door required the same protracted ceremonial. No matter how well the original act was performed it had to be done over in interminable repetitions. Particularly agonizing was the compulsion to repeat sentences and questions. It was hazardous for the patient to engage in any kind of conversation because each statement made by her had to be reiterated until it finally "sounded just right." If a statement was made by another person the patient had to ask question after question to make sure that she had actually understood what was meant. If the ritual of repeating was interrupted because a visitor appeared on the scene or the door bell rang the patient experienced an "unbearable" tenseness, tremors and tightening of the throat. The repetitions had to be resumed instantly after the visitor was disposed of or the telephone message was received. The patient learned soon that what she feared was not rumpled bedsheets and dirty bathtubs, misphrased sentences and misunderstood questions but rather the "intolerable" tenseness, tremor and tightness which resulted from the fears. "I know that, doctor," she replied, "but the knowledge doesn't help me." She was then trained to do with the muscles what her brain feared to do; to command her speech muscles not to repeat statements and questions; to order the muscles of the arms to interrupt the movements of washing, scrubbing and straightening after a reasonable amount of time had been spent on these activities. Above all she was asked to be prepared to stand the tenseness resulting from a frustrated impulse and to know that it was "distressing but not dangerous." With the example and encouragement of other patients she practiced but with partial success only. One day she remarked, "I can now stop the repeating with regard to bedmaking, dusting, locking the door, and I no longer repeat statements and questions as much as I used to do. But with washing the hands and cleaning the tub I have had no luck." It was not easy to persuade her that the tenseness was the same in both series of tasks and that if she was able to brave it in one type of activity and not in the other the reason for this senseless discrimination was her tendency to sabotage. Prior to joining classes and Recovery she had been treated with methods of verbal assurance and found the technique of muscle training tedious, absurd and "not suited to my case." Many patients offer this negative reaction. They resent simple methods of this kind as an insult to their intelligence. The procedure is likely to appear insulting and, indeed, humiliating because if excruciating tortures of years' duration can be disposed of with such simple means why were the pains and pressures and dizziness made the object of years of wailing, temper tantrums, neglect of duty and financial sacrifice? The question is unanswerable but is rated as sabotage in Recovery and countered with the alternative question: Is the fact that you suffered needlessly in the past sufficient excuse to continue the suffering into the future just because the mode of treatment fails to impress you as intricate or dignified? In the present case, the sabotage against the "indignity" of being treated with a too simple method was overcome after months of therapeutic effort and the patient has done well for the past seven years. When her husband was called into service in 1944 the wife had no difficulty taking over his business and conducting it till months after Armistice day.

Example 2. A young woman had been afflicted with a most distressing condition for upward of four years prior to being assigned to classes. On walking along the street the sidewalks seemed to heave up against her and the buildings appeared to bend toward her. This caused dizziness, tightening of the abdomen and, or course, panicky fear. After due explanations concerning the utter absence of any danger that she might be caught and crushed by the collapsing buildings or by the uprising pavement she was trained to walk on in spite of the threat of the sensations. She soon learned to step out fearlessly into the street and acquired mastery in ignoring the "symptomatic idiom" of her sensations. But after a while she complained that although she had conquered successfully the fear of being swallowed up by pavement and buildings she still had the tightening of the abdomen, the dizziness and tenseness. "How can I get rid of this by practicing muscle control?" she asked. She was told: "When the abdomen tightens up command your muscles to continue the meal regardless of the pains and spasms in your stomach. Discipline your body by means of your muscles, always keeping in mind that no danger whatever is involved. If sensing the tightness of the stomach you refrain from eating you incidentally tell yourself that the condition of your stomach is one of a crippling disease. This intensifies your tenseness, and the tenseness keeps your stomach from relaxing. The abdominal spasms and pains are thus perpetuated. They will disappear only if you relax, and you will relax only if you are fully convinced that no danger threatens. This conviction you can gain if you continue to eat, demonstrating to yourself that nothing happens if you do continue. After a few performances of this kind your confidence will return, and your conviction will be established. Then your body will relax and the stomach will follow suit and the dizziness will subside because there will be little tenseness left to sustain it." After a short period of bungling trials and attendant sabotaging thoughts she manipulated walking and eating with the aid of muscle control and has been comfortable for the past six years.

Example 3. A woman patient complained of an itch in the rectum. The itch had been with her off and on for over twenty years. It was experienced for weeks and months uninterruptedly during the day, never at night. At times it disappeared for a few days or weeks spontaneously. She had done well with regard to a number of other nervous symptoms but was unable to get rid of the itch. "It just drives me crazy," the patient said, "How can I control that?" She was asked, "Do you scratch when you are in the street car?" "Isn't that strange," she replied, "Now that you ask me I remember I never scratch when I am in the street car. I don't even have the itch there. I don't have it anywhere riding or driving." She was then told, "You sat in my waiting room for over an hour today. Did you scratch there?" "Why," she said, "I didn't have to scratch. I didn't itch. Isn't that funny?" "That is not at all funny," the physician remarked, "When you are among people you give the order to your muscles intuitively and instinctively not to scratch and muscles always carry out orders that are "meant"—orders which are resolutely passed on to them. After you have given that order you know by experience that it will be obeyed implicitly and don't give a thought to the itch any more. Removing your thought from the itch you are without preoccupation, and there is neither itch nor scratch. But once you approach your home you know that there scratching is permitted or at least possible. Now your mind is preoccupied with the itch which is trouble and pleasure at the same time. Again intuitively and instinctively you decide that now at last you will be able to indulge the pastime of scratching." The patient, a member of Recovery, soon learned to command the muscles discursively and reflectively and got rid of the itch in a short time.

Brief examples: A patient was obsessed with the fear of dying. As a consequence, he dreaded reading the word "death," shied away from funeral parlors and gave up reading newspapers from fear of encountering reports of killings or sudden deaths. After proper explanations in classes and during office interviews he was trained to command his muscles to stand in front of funeral parlors and to practice reading newspapers deliberately and assiduously. He had little difficulty shedding his fears.

Patients with fears of crossing streets, riding in elevators, looking down from high places are currently treated by the method of "commanding the muscles to do what you fear to do." Success is almost always prompt and lasting.

Of particular interest are patients who suffer from outright delusions subsequent to discharge from the hospital as improved but not fully recovered. One patient still complained that the neighbors were knocking at the walls, another that automobile lights were again flashing their headlights signalling threatening messages. In these and other instances, it is sufficient to train the patients to first spot the experience as a "nervous symptom, distressing and annoying but not at all dangerous," second, to exhort them to ignore the symptom and not to act on it. If the patient commands his muscles not to shout at the neighbors who "knock at the wall" and not to knock back at them, or to ignore the flashing of lights, not to draw the curtains or retire to another room, then he avoids the process of "working himself up." And with no hysteria engendered the symptom disappears. It "comes and goes." The sensation and thought pulses reestablish themselves even with such pathological experiences.

An experience reported by an observant relative of a patient threw light on the mode of operation of some delusions. The patient complained of being stared at by people. Her cousin stated that when she was in a restaurant with her, nobody did any staring during the first few minutes. But then the patient, suspicious that she may be stared at, began looking at people, turning her gaze in all directions, staring at everybody and anybody, thus attracting the attention of the diners at various tables who actually began staring at her. In this manner, the suspicion of being stared at had produced the staring.

PART IV

GROUP PSYCHOTHERAPY INTERVIEWS

1

THE MYTH OF "NERVOUS FATIGUE"

Evelyn had been irritable, restless and tense for the past ten years. Sleep was poor. Appetite had declined to the point of making a meal an ordeal. There was a constant tightness of the throat, pressure in the head, palpitations and gastric discomfort. Overshadowing all complaints in importance and intensity was "an awful fatigue, an exhaustion that starts right when I get up in the morning and continues without letup till late afternoon. Then it eases up and in the evening I feel almost well."

In spite of this sustained suffering, "without letup," Evelyn managed to keep her job for years, supplementing her husband's income. It was only in the past two years that the fatigue and exhaustion became "unbearable." She resigned her position and tended to her household and her young son. "But in taking care of my home I have to drag myself all morning and the greater part of the afternoon. I am exhausted most of the day."

E—Examiner
P—Patient

E: You have attended classes for several months. Has your condition improved during these months?

P: It has. I sleep well, and my appetite is much better. The pressure in the head has hardly bothered me lately, and the pain in the abdomen is getting less and less. But I am still fatigued. In the morning I have to drag myself and can hardly keep on my feet. Then I take lunch, and right after I have finished eating I am all exhausted, my eyes droop and I have to lie down for an hour or so.

E: You say that you are "all exhausted." May I ask you what precisely you mean when you use the word "exhaustion?"

P: Why, I am all in. I have no pep and must force myself to do the simplest thing.

E: Look here, Evelyn, an exhaustion that has lasted for years, day after day, even hour after hour, ought to have finally reduced you to a physical wreck. Your muscles should have shrunk, your face should by now look gaunt and haggard. Instead, you maintained your weight, your complexion is blooming, and your capacity for working is equal to the task of taking care of house, family and social activities. Several months ago when sleep was poor and appetite scant your claim to be exhausted might have been logical. But with a good appetite and sound sleep it is difficult to think that you are suffering from a state of exhaustion.

P: I don't understand it myself, but it is a fact that I feel tired and weary all the time, except in late afternoon and evening.

E: You say you "feel tired and weary all time time." I do not deny that. You alone are competent to state how you feel. What interests me is whether your so-called fatigue is a mere subjective feeling or an actual and objective condition, whether you merely feel tired or actually are tired. You seem to be puzzled by the sharp distinction and I shall try to be more specific. You understand that if somebody says he feels guilty that does not necessarily mean he is guilty. And if somebody feels feverish that does by no means establish the objective fact that he has fever. These examples will prove to you that a subjective feeling does not necessarily point to an objective condition. And if you say you "feel tired and wearly all the time," I shall ask you whether you consider your tiredness a subjective feeling or an objective condition?

P: All I know is I am miserable all day. I wake up in the morning, and the fatigue is there the moment I open my eyes.

E: You told me, Evelyn, that for the past few months your sleep has been good. Suppose you awoke this morning after a good night's rest. Would you nevertheless have felt fatigued immediately after awakening?

P: I feel fatigued immediately after I wake up in the morning regardless of whether sleep was good or poor.

E: If this is true then it is established that you suffer from the subjective feeling of tiredness and weariness, and not from the objective condition of fatigue. I shall tell you why I can afford to be so positive about my statement. You see, Evelyn, soldiers after a long march, athletes after an exhausting race, laborers after a strenuous effort, may sometimes be too tired to fall asleep. But once they lapse into a sound sleep they invariably and inevitably feel refreshed after awakening. These are examples of extreme fatigue. Even in these utmost exertions sleep eliminates fatigue with unquestioned certainty. In minor exertions, mere rest without sleep will have the same effect. The only exception to this rule is physical ailment, like an anemia or tuberculosis. In these conditions, even a sound sleep may not do away with fatigue. But with physically healthy persons, sleep never fails to remove fatigue. If it is true that for several months past you have enjoyed good sleep you have no reason for being tired in the morning. To sleep means to rest the muscles. How can your muscles be fatigued if they are rested?

P: I don't know what to say. The fact is that I am all in no matter how well I slept. If you call that a subjective feeling you must think it is mental. But I don't even have time to think about it. It is there the moment I wake up.

E: I do not know what precisely you mean when you use the word "mental." Presumably you refer to the possibility that you may have the thought of fatigue in your mind and instantly feel the fatigue in your muscles. This instantaneous response of the muscles to a thought seems to puzzle you. I do not see why it should. You have certainly gone through similar experiences hundreds of times. Remember the occasion, for instance, when you were at a meeting and were called upon to make a speech. Instantly, your heart began to palpitate, your face reddened, your abdomen trembled and the knees shook. To use your own words, you "didn't even have time to think" of the speech; you merely heard your name called, and the muscles of your heart, abdomen and legs were thrown into violent tremors "in no time." In the instance which I quoted the thought in your mind which caused your muscles to shake was the fear of not being able to deliver a well constructed address. It was a fear, or you may call it a fear idea, or the idea of danger. Do you understand now that if an idea strikes or occupies your mind the muscles may respond with a violent reaction in a fraction of a second?

P: I understand that. But when I get up in the morning there is no idea of danger in my head.

E: The question is what you mean by danger. If you wish to indicate that, in the morning, you are not trembling with the fear of being killed or trapped or burned I shall fully agree with you that no such idea may occupy your brain immediately after awakening. But there are subtler forms of fears and dangers. These subtle anxieties and apprehensions go by the name of preoccupations. I happen to know from your own account how readily you fall victim to such preoccupations. Let me remind you, for instance, of the anguish you experience whenever you expect visitors for the afternoon or the evening. You fret and worry days in advance, anticipating some bungling or clumsiness while performing the part of the hostess. You know that when finally the much dreaded day arrives you feel troubled and helpless "the very minute" you awaken. The day stares you in the face as a threat, as an event fraught with heavy responsibilities. You are without pep or zest. Your vitality is at a low ebb. A heaviness seems to descend on your limbs. Everything is done with effort. You have to drag yourself, feel "all in," exhausted, lifeless, fatigued. Do you understand that all of this is caused by your preoccupation, and that the preoccupation is based on the idea of danger?

P: It is true I am worrying my head off when I expect guests. People are critical, and it is not easy to please them and make them feel at home. But we don't have visitors every day, and there is not a day when I feel relaxed. I am always tired.

E: I mentioned your preoccupation with your guests as an example only. The example will demonstrate to you that a preoccupation of this kind is apt to produce, in a split second, a condition in which you feel "all in," dragging, exhausted and listless. Being a nervous patient you are always preoccupied with your disability. This preoccupation is a kind of worry which hardly ever leaves you. You are always on guard against something untoward happening in some part of your body. Looking back on your unhappy experiences of the past ten years you can recall numerous instances in which you planned a social engagement, a card game, a show, a trip and were stricken with a severe head pressure or palpitations or abdominal pain or numbness. The card game had to be interrupted, or you managed painfully to go through with it in wretched agony. You remember the frequent occasions when dinner parties had to be cancelled because your throat suddenly "locked," and you were afraid you might not be able to swallow or speak; or the dances that had to be called off because a heaviness settled on your legs so that you could hardly walk. It was observations of this character that in time suggested to you that it was no use planning. The unpredictable suddenness with which your symptoms could make their appearance gave you no guarantee that if you made a plan you could go through with it. Gradually the inability to plan spread to the trivial chores of everyday life. You set out to prepare a meal, and your eyes blurred. Or you decided to darn your husband's socks, and the hands trembled. The symptoms came without warning. They shot through your body without cause, without provocation. To use your own words,

you "didn't even have time to think about them." I may tell you
that symptoms which shoot up so unexpectedly, in a mere fraction of a second, are called "trigger symptoms." They shoot
forth with the rapidity of a bullet after the trigger has been
pulled. Their trigger character makes them appear weird,
mysterious, threatening. In essence, they suggest to you that you
have utterly lost control of your primitive bodily functions.
Having noticed time and again that your organs may go on a
rampage without warning you feel you cannot trust your body.
You must always be on the alert for some sudden disturbance.
You cannot plan with any assurance of carrying out your decisions. But if you are deprived of the power to plan, your day is
carried on without accomplishment. Moreover, without planning, you miss that singular joy of looking ahead to accomplishments. The joyous trembling of watchful anticipation is taken
from your daily routine. Life becomes a never-ending drabness
and drudgery. It is this type of life that you look forward to
when you awaken in the morning. In a flash, before you had
"time to think about it," the dismal dreariness of your existence
stares at you. Again one of those empty days with no plans, no
decisions, no accomplishments. You become discouraged, disgusted with the dead monotony that is in store for you, and it is
the self-disgust that robs your tissues of their vitality. There is
no vigor, zest or incentive with which to start out on the daily
routine. Your body is devoid of stimulation; it feels uninspired,
flabby, limp. This feeling of limpness you call "fatigue." You
will now understand why towards evening your vitality returns
and why, after supper, you "feel almost well." There is nothing
left for planning after supper, no drabness to be anticipated, no
drudgery to be performed in self-disgust. The dreadful day is
gone or going. Nothing is expected of you any more. You
breathe freely now, and your vitality returns. Do you realize
now that what you call "fatigue" is nothing but a psychological
reaction to the anticipated and dreaded boredom of daily existence? Do you understand that the tiredness of which you
complain is not in your muscles but in your mind?

P: You are right, doctor. I realize now that everything you say
is exactly as I feel it. My mornings are dreadful. I have nothing
to look forward to. I can't plan; I am afraid to plan. You are
right, doctor, but why was I never told what is wrong with me? I
have seen all kinds of physicians, and the one told me I was
suffering from nervous exhaustion, another said my energy was

running down, and I should take it easy. One blamed it on my thyroid gland; another told me I had a poor constitution and he couldn't do anything about it. I was warned not to overwork, was told to take long periods of rest, to go on trips and vacations. If you say that my trouble is nothing but boredom and disgust why did nobody tell me that before? It would have spared me ten years suffering, and I could have saved thousands of dollars spent on cures, sanitariums and trips.

E: It is painful for me to answer this question. I do not like to be critical of what other men think or believe. Unfortunately, there are superstitions that refuse to die. One of them, very preposterous and pernicious, is the myth of nervous fatigue or nervous exhaustion. All I can tell you is that, in 1880, a New York physician formulated the absurd theory that a group of patients whom he called "neurasthenics" suffered from a state of nervous exhaustion.* How uncritical this man was is evident from the fact that he did not hesitate to make unwarranted and extravagant claims, for instance, that the "disease runs in families," that it is due to inheritance, that it has its origin in the spine, that it is typically American and, hence, proposed to call it "American Nervousness." Somehow this fanciful idea spread all over the globe and is still widely accepted today as a message of scientific truth. I cannot tell why a theory of this kind has been permitted to figure in textbooks and to be practiced on hapless sufferers. All I can state is that superstitions are born easily but die with difficulty. I do not blame you for feeling resentful of the unnecessary hardship that was imposed on you during ten long years of anguish. But resentment will not help you. It will only serve to whip up your emotions and throw an additional load on your nervous system. What you need is re-education. You must learn to reject as untrue all the silly notions that were crammed into your head and to accept the explanation which I gave you. Up to now, with the thought of exhaustion in your brain, you were afraid to move, to work, to tax your "weak" muscles. I take it for granted that henceforth you will throw to the winds all this drivel about nerve exhaustion and will not hesitate to tax your muscles to your heart's delight.

P: You told me that before, and I made every effort to accept your view. On many mornings I jumped out of bed without

---

*George M. Beard, A Practical Treatise on Nervous Exhaustion (Neurasthenia), New York, 1880, William Wood.

paying attention to my fears. I ignored the heaviness in my
muscles and did my work, but it was certainly difficult. Your
assurance that the fatigue is in the brain and not in the muscles
helps me at times. But after I continue with my work for awhile
the thought strikes me that maybe the other doctors were right
when they warned me not to strain my muscles. After ten years
it seems not easy to shake off the fears.

E: You said you made every effort to accept my views about
fatigue. This is, of course, an exaggerated claim. I do not expect
anybody to make "every" effort in any endeavor. What you
mean is that you tried hard but did not succeed. But remember,
Evelyn, I never asked you to "accept my views." I asked you to
practice them. My view with regard to "nervous fatigue" is that
you can safely ignore it, that it is a bugaboo and not a real
danger. This view cannot be "accepted" and, as it were, placed
in your brain there to preside over your actions. In order to
make a view direct your action it must be acquired, digested and
absorbed through patient practice. This is true of every sphere
of life in which you wish to plant views into the thoughts and
brains of a person. In bringing up your children you did not
merely present them with lovely notions and lofty principles,
asking them to accept them. These views had to be practiced,
again and again, till finally they were incorporated and lived and
experienced and acted out spontaneously. When you intended to
make your boy adopt the view of group responsibility you did not
tell him to accept your principle of group behavior. Instead, you
told him not to make noise in the presence of people. You urged
him to say "thank you" and "please." This you did for months
and years until finally the new habits took root. After ceaseless
practice your boy finally incorporated the view in his system,
made it part of his organism. The practice made the view "sink
in" and take its firm place in the brain from where it then
directed action. In this process of child training you influenced
your boy's muscles and through them established a firm structure
of habits. It was these good habits that represented your view.
You understand now that I asked you to practice my view, not
merely to accept it. The continued practice would have brought
acceptance in its train. You will perhaps remember what precisely I asked you to do. I told you to jump out of bed and to go
about your work, fatigue or no fatigue. But I also warned you to
avoid all actions that embody the view of danger. I specifically
instructed you not to look in the mirror to watch your so-called

fatigue in your anxious features. I asked you to avoid the practice of touching the muscles of your arms and legs to investigate the degree of their flabbiness. I cautioned you not to sit down after a few steps or a few manipulations. Most important, I enjoined you not to complain about your fatigue, not to moan or sob, not to ask for help or sympathy. If you had complied with these instructions you would have established a new set of habits of how to deal with this legendary thought of nervous fatigue. The old habits of fear would have been crowded out of your mind, and a new set of constructive trends would have settled down or sunk into your brain. My view would then have occupied and taken possession of your brain without any effort on your part to accept or adopt it. If you say that "after ten years it is not easy to shake off the fears" I shall advise you that you had no business assuming that it might be easy. Mere acceptance of a view is easy, but practicing it means sustained application with endless trials and endless failures till finally you score the ultimate success. You thought of merely accepting a view. That would have been easy but ineffectual. What I wanted you to do was to practice, i.e., to direct your muscles to carry out my view. I presume that after tonight's interview you will no longer entertain the unrealistic notion that mere lip-service to a principle will reestablish a new set of habits. Practice alone will do that.

2

SABOTAGING SLEEP

Bill complained of episodes occurring every few weeks in which he experienced intense fatigue and numbness in both legs from the knees down. On these days he felt choked and had difficulty breathing. The condition lasted upward of eighteen years but improved greatly after he attended classes. The spells no longer interfered with his work. "In the past," he said, "I was out of circulation because of these spells. The choked feeling and numbness and weakness were with me for several days on a stretch. Then they became milder but would start again after another few days. I was in bad shape even on good days. On a Wednesday I might want to buy tickets for the coming Saturday. But I was afraid I might go through a spell on Saturday and dropped the plan. Gradually I stopped going out with people, except that I kept associating with one boyhood friend."

When questioned concerning the degree of improvement since attending classes he stated that the spells were milder now and the intervals between them longer. "But I am still having trouble with sleeping. It takes me a long time to fall asleep, and the slightest noise gets me awake again. The other night I couldn't get to sleep till after 4 A.M., and when I got up in the morning I was worn out and felt I hadn't slept a wink."

E—Examiner
P—Patient

E: You say you could not fall asleep till after 4 A.M. Suppose you retired at 11 P.M. What did you do while you lay in bed between 11 P.M. and 4 A.M.?

P: (Bill)—I retire late, usually after midnight. I hate to go to bed early and lie there fighting for sleep.

E: If you retire at 1 A.M. and fall asleep at 4 A.M., what do you do between 1 and 4? Do you lie in bed? Or do you get up walking, smoking, reading?

P: I may lie in bed for a while. Then I become tense and feel I have to get up. I take a book and read, or I go to the kitchen for a drink of water, or get myself a bite from the ice box. After that I may return to bed and lie down for a while, but the trouble starts all over and I get up again.

Ethel Is Asked to Join the Interview

E: Ethel, several months ago, when I first saw you, you also complained you were unable to fall asleep. Is that still the case?

P: (Ethel) I have no trouble now. I sleep like a rock.

E: How do you do that?

P: I used to go to bed fearing that another one of those dreadful sleepless nights was in store for me. Now I know it was this fear that kept me awake. Ever since I stopped fearing the sleepless nights I don't have any.

E: To put it differently, the fear of not sleeping made you tense, and the tenseness kept you awake. After you eliminated the fear you were no longer tense and had no difficulty sleeping. But tell me, Ethel, how did you manage to eliminate the fear of not sleeping?

P: I did what you told me to do.

E: What was it I told you?

P: You said there is no such thing as lack of sleep except in acute diseases. If a person is not suffering from an acute ailment he may have trouble falling asleep, or his sleep may be broken and interrupted. But he will get a good deal of sleep if he keeps lying in bed. You also said a person may not get sufficient sleep in one particular night but will get enough of it the next following night to compensate for what he missed the night before. I remember you saying that difficulty of sleeping deprives one of comfort but does not interfere with health.* After I grasped that, I no longer worried about sleep.

Bill Rejoins the Interview

E: Bill, having attended classes for many months, you certainly know the rules mentioned by Ethel. How is it you do not practice them?

P: (Bill) I know the rules and practice them night after night. But I can't sleep. I know you will call that sabotage. If it is I am not aware of sabotaging. I go to bed keeping in mind that sleep is nothing to worry about; nevertheless, I feel tense the minute I stretch out. Is this sabotage?

E: It could hardly be anything else. You say you practice the rules for sleeping but cannot sleep. How is it that Ethel, practicing the same rules, applies them successfully? Obviously, Ethel's practicing is done with determination, yours without.

---

*This does not, of course, apply to growing children whose health may suffer from insufficient sleep.

She carries out my orders resolutely, you half-heartedly. The half-hearted practice is sabotage. If you were determined to carry out my instructions you would not wait till after midnight before you retire. You say you are without worry or fear about sleep. Why, then, do you wait for hours hesitating to retire? Hesitation is fear and the reverse of determination. Do you understand now why I call your effort undetermined and half-hearted?

P: I admit it must be fear that keeps me from going to bed in time. But I don't see why it is sabotage if I can't get rid of my fears. I certainly try my best.

E: That is all you do. You try your best which is the half-hearted practice I mentioned. Every sabotaging patient offers the excuse that he tries his best. What you try is a method, the method of initiating and maintaining sleep. You described your method. It may be your best. However, my instructions do not call for your method, poor, good or best. They demand that you employ that method which I have outlined here repeatedly. You sabotaged that method first when you delayed the process of retiring by hours, second when after retiring at a late hour you failed to lie quietly, but instead kept jumping out of bed, reading, walking, or rummaging for a drink and food. Both sequences of sabotaging acts were carried out through the medium of your muscles. You may have difficulty controlling fears and worries. But muscles can be controlled "at will." Everybody has it within his power to command his muscles to effect an act or to refrain from effecting it. That is all my instructions require you to do. They direct you to order your muscles to walk toward your bed at a given early hour, to lie down and to maintain the recumbent position until you fall asleep. If you permitted your muscles to do otherwise you may have tried your best, but you failed to carry out my instructions. Of course, it is difficult to forbid the muscles to stir when you are tense and feel the imperative urge to move. The muscles become more tense and press with greater vehemence for relief through motion. But you heard me state repeatedly that no matter how agonizing muscular tenseness may be it disappears after a few minutes if you refuse resolutely to move the muscles. A resoluteness of this sort requires that you are ready to pass for a few minutes through the torture of lying quietly when every fiber of yours is aching for motion.

P: In the beginning I frequently did what you asked me to do. I went to bed early and stayed in bed without leaving it. At times I kept that up for hours. Finally I got so tense I couldn't stand it. I don't think you can call that sabotage or half-hearted practice.

E: I must challenge your statement that you couldn't sleep although you stayed in bed for hours. That may happen occasionally and does happen with great regularity in the instance of persons suffering from acute distressing ailments. Otherwise, *to lie in bed for hours means to sleep part of the hours.* The sleep may be of poor quality and may proceed in fitful snatches. After each snatch you awaken having the feeling that you "did not sleep a wink." Nevertheless, you slept a considerable portion of the time which you spent in bed.

P: I know I don't sleep. I am aware all the time of everything that goes on. I hear every little noise and am wide awake all the time.

E: What you said right now is nothing but an act of sabotage. After I explained that everybody who lies in bed for hours sleeps part of these hours you exclaim, "I know I don't sleep." With this, you contradict my statement. Apparently, you intend to engage me in an argument. After months of attending classes you ought to know that I do not permit patients to question my statements. If you do that you set your own immature knowledge against my seasoned experience. Indeed, you challenge my authority. You know that this is one form of sabotage, perhaps its worst form.

P: I don't understand why you speak of arguing. Am I not supposed to tell my side of the story?

E: The trouble is that you consider this a story of which you take one side, and I the other. Why should we take sides? If you think we should, you conceive of an interview as an argument or debate with "two sides to the story." While interviewing a patient I do not engage in story telling, not even in story listening. An interview deals with an account of symptoms, not with the telling of a story. Your sleeplessness is a symptom, not a topic of conversation. In a conversation you are permitted, even desired, to state "your side of the story" which is based on your common knowledge. But in a discussion of symptoms you cannot rely on common knowledge. In order to understand the nature and action of symptoms you are required to possess special and authoritative knowledge. Where and when did you acquire authoritative knowledge about sleep and sleep disturbances? All you were ever able to observe were your own difficulties of sleeping. What you observed was one single case which is a slender basis for any kind of knowledge. I shall ignore the fact that your manner of observing was naive and amateurish. You are of course not trained in making valid and expert observations. This I will ignore. But tell me, Bill, would you apply to me for help if you knew that I had experience with only one case like yours? You would not consider me an expert with authoritative knowledge unless you were certain I observed and studied hundreds and perhaps thousands of cases. You see, Bill, when you said, "I know I don't sleep" you referred to your own haphazard and hazy knowledge which you obtained by means of untrained observation and inexpert interpretation. In relying on your own irrelevant knowledge you rejected my authoritative opinion. You told "your side of the story" and "took sides" against me. Do you realize that this is sabotage?

P: I cannot get it into my head that I should not be able to know whether I am awake or asleep. That doesn't seem to require expert knowledge.

E: I grant that you know when you are awake. But after you awaken from a brief snatch of sleep you do not have to know at all that you have slept. I have heard it stated a hundred and perhaps a thousand times from patients and non-patients that last night they "didn't sleep a wink." Some people go to absurd extremes claiming they "did not sleep a wink" for solid weeks or months. I told you that to lie in bed for hours means to sleep part of those hours. I added that the quality of this kind of sleep may be poor, proceeding in snatches. The snatches may last ten minutes or half an hour or an hour or longer. The sleep being light and superficial it is easily interrupted by every sound, by a mild muscular pain, by a moderate irritation of one's bladder or a slight spasm of the intestines. Awakening from this superficial slumber the sleeper is not aware of having slept. Added together the successive snatches may have amounted to a sizeable total, let me say, five or six hours in the aggregate. During these five or six hours the muscles rested, and the conscious attention was relaxed. This is all that sleep is required to do for purposes of health. For purposes of comfort it is desirable to enjoy deep sleep from which one awakens refreshed with new vigor. But I do not cater to your comfort; I tend to your health. And health is adequately served by the brief snatches of light and superficial sleep. You will now realize that you have a fitful, broken and superficial sleep. It serves your health but does not give you the subjective feeling of having slept. Lacking this subjective feeling you think you have been awake and express this conclusion in the wholly unwarranted exclamation, "I know I did not sleep." By making this statement or thinking this thought you oppose your common sense observation to my expert knowledge, and this is sabotage.

Lester Joins the Interview

P: (Lester) Doctor, is a question in order?
E: If it is to the point.
P: I think it is. I frequently read health articles and listen to health broadcasts in which sleep is said to be essential to health. I know you are our only authority in matters of health, and I know it is sabotage to accept other opinions. And if you say that sleep has little to do with health that settles it for me. But I hear plenty about the importance of sleep from friends and relatives, and I should like to know how to answer their arguments.

E: Your point is well taken, and I shall be glad to oblige you. Since I am supposed to be your only authority on health, as every physician ought to be to his patients, you are entitled to know the sources of my authoritative knowledge. They are, first, my own experiences; second, the studies of leading men of science who are unquestioned authorities in this field.

I shall first tell you of my own experiences. They are manifold and concern observations on patients mainly, but also observations on my own sleep performance. I am of course not immune to "sleepless nights," which means that I pass occasionally through nights in which my sleep is fitful and superficial. When this happens I also awake in the morning with the subjective feeling that I "did not sleep a wink." On one such night, years ago, I noticed that precisely at a moment when I felt distressed at my wakefulness I still had in mind the tail-end of a dream that had just occupied my brain. At that moment there was no doubt that I had slept. Otherwise, how could I have dreamt? I then decided to look out for these dream fragments, and the method seldom fails me. Whenever I feel wretched because I seem to waste futile hours trying to fall asleep I instantly recall the last dream fragment that I can bring to consciousness. Then I know I have been sleeping and dismiss anxiety and apprehensiveness. You will be well advised to hunt for these dream portions of the past few seconds or minutes whenever you are obsessed with the idea that you have "not slept a wink." Do you understand, Bill, that if you know you had a dream you must have been sleeping?

Bill Rejoins the Interview

P: (Bill) I shall certainly look out for these dreams when I can't fall asleep. I hope I'll catch them.

E: If you say, "I hope I'll catch them" you indicate that you are by no means certain about succeeding. With this you express doubt whether you will be able to convince yourself that lying in bed for hours means sleeping part of the hours. Perhaps I shall be able to furnish you with more conclusive evidence. Since you have not gone through a mental disease but suffer from a so-called psychoneurosis I shall quote observations from psychoneurotic patients first. On numerous occasions I witnessed patients of this description sleeping and snoring but when awakened they protested they "didn't sleep a wink." Other patients of this kind were observed by my nurses, interns and resident physicians who reported that the patients who complained of utter inability to fall asleep either snored or failed to respond when their names were called, when they were sprinkled with water or pricked with a pin. Does that prove to you that to lie in bed means to sleep?

P: I am making every effort to take in what you say. Nevertheless, it seems to me I don't sleep. Couldn't there be an exception to the rule?

E: I am sure you are not the exception. But I agree there are exceptions. I told you that patients with acute physical distress may actually fail to sleep although they lie in bed all night. This is true also of acutely suffering mental (psychotic) patients. It is well known that so-called depressed patients may go without sleep or with a minimum of it for nights and even weeks in succession. Nevertheless, after they get well, not a trace of evidence can be found that the prolonged vigils have caused any damage to their health. If any proof is needed that sleep has little bearing on health these patients provide it. More convincing evidence yet is furnished by the so-called manic patients. In the days when we had no shock treatment many of these wretches spent weeks and months on the wards raving day and night with scarcely any interruption. They hardly slept or rested. Day after day and night after night they were in almost continuous motion, talking incessantly, jumping, running, fighting. In this manner, their well nigh complete sleeplessness was combined with a terrific expenditure of energy. If prolonged wakefulness is supposed to drain a person's strength and to undermine his health these manic patients should have emerged from their spells as irreparable physical wrecks. Nothing of this kind, however, was observed. After they recovered their state of health they gave no indication of having suffered as a result of the ordeal. Do you think, Bill, I have finally demonstrated to you that lack of sleep (1) is a myth as concerns persons not afflicted with acute physical or mental illness, (2) leaves no permanent damage if it actually does occur as, for instance, in the mental ailments which I mentioned?

P: You certainly proved your point. I am now convinced that to lie in bed means to sleep. But will I be convinced tonight when I lie down and my brain begins to rattle?

E: When your brain rattles you must let it go on rattling, but you must remain calm. Your look of surprise indicates that you do not think it possible for anyone to be calm when his brain is in uproar. Many patients have told me about this rattling. They call it variously "brainstorm," "chasing of thought," "racing." What it actually means is that the brain has difficulty relaxing. The thoughts are in a welter of confusion. The "stream of thought," ordinarily calm and well ordered, becomes stormy and feverish. Such disorder is frequently found in other organs. The heart may be thrown into sudden palpitations, the muscles into tenseness, rigidity and tremors. Every organ may begin to "rattle" at any time, to use your expression. This "rattling" is nothing but our old standby—tenseness. After attending classes for months you ought to know how to deal with tenseness. An organ that becomes tense is thrown into a storm of activity. A storm rises, but it also subsides after it has run its course. How is it that your storm of tenseness keeps up its fury for hours without subsiding? Tenseness is a sensation ordinarily produced by fear. I told you repeatedly that sensations and feelings rise and fall provided you do not attach the idea of danger at the moment the curve reaches its peak. How is it that your fearful feelings and sensations rise but do not fall?

P: I know what you are driving at. I create a vicious cycle.

E: Correct. And I shall describe the precise manner in which your vicious cycle operates. When you merely think of going to bed you are seized with an apprehensiveness, a not yet marked fear that you are again headed for one of these dreadful sleepless nights. Now you postpone the ordeal. You wait and hesitate and keep yourself busy with chores. Soon you notice that you have difficulty concentrating on the chores with which you busy yourself. The less you are able to concentrate the stronger grows your tenseness; the greater the tenseness the worse the concentration. You are already in the throes of a minor vicious cycle. After hours of tinkering you finally retire, apprehensive, anxious, disheartened. You said, "I feel tense the very minute I stretch out." I presume you meant to suggest that the very act of contacting the bed makes you tense. Fear, you mean to say, has nothing to do with it. Rather it is some mysterious habit which makes the muscles tense when they merely touch the bedsheet. But from what I just told you it ought to be clear to you that you are choked with fear long before you "stretch out." The vicious cycle was set going hours before you touched the bed. Feeling tense you have difficulty lying still. You twist, turn, throw yourself from side to side, thereby increasing your tenseness many times its original intensity. You say you "hate to lie there fighting for sleep." There is nobody and nothing to fight, and be certain you do nothing of the kind. What you do is to work yourself up to a paroxysm of rage and fury. Against whom do you rage? Presumably against yourself. Or, it is nothing but a blind anger directed against nobody in particular. At any rate, to the original fear of not sleeping is now added this senseless anger that merely serves to accelerate the vicious cycle and to fan the tenseness to an intolerable pitch. Then the brain begins to "rattle." Do you understand that all of this is the result of fear? Fear can be remedied only by the certain knowledge that no danger threatens. You cannot gain this knowledge from your own experience which is amateurish and limited to the acquaintance with one single case. What must guide you is my authoritative knowledge which is based on solid study and expert observation. This alone can give you the conviction that no danger whatever attends a night spent in bed even if you feel you "haven't slept a wink."*

---

*The reader will notice that the author who set out originally to buttress his argument both with his own experience and "the studies of leading men of science who are unquestioned authorities in this field" failed to quote scientific evidence. Omissions of this kind are unavoidable in interviews. They are due either to oversight or pressure of time. For the benefit of those interested in the subject it may be pointed out that the experimental evidence that prolonged periods of sleeplessness cause little or no harm is fully dealt with in a study by Nathaniel Kleitman, entitled "Sleep and Sleeplessness," University of Chicago Press, 1939.

3

SIMPLICITY VERSUS COMPLEXITY IN COMBATING FEARS

Nancy had been apprehensive and self-conscious all her life. After she married and had children the responsibilities of caring for the family weighed heavily on her tender conscience. One day, about twelve years ago, she became panicky, with palpitations, dizziness, dry throat, and body tremor dominating the picture. She was so scared that she feared she was losing her mind. She recovered from the first scare but the fear of mental collapse persisted. Her sleep was poor. She watched herself continuously magnifying minor observations. When she discovered that her memory or concentration failed her on some occasion she considered this as incontrovertible evidence that her mind was slipping. In time she developed other well defined fears. The main fear was to be confined in a closed space. She suffered agonies of dizziness, sweats, churning of the stomach, sinking feelings, faints and palpitations whenever she ventured to take a ride in an automobile, street car, elevated or railroad train. Rides in an elevator were less disturbing if they were short stops but if the point of destination was a high upper floor the performance was a nightmare. Since the physician's suite was situated on the 17th floor of a downtown building a visit to his office was looked forward to with great apprehension and required a companion to reassure her. As the years passed Nancy's fears expanded. She grew to fear her impulses. She dreaded the thought of being alone with her daughters or with her husband for fear she might do harm to those she loved. "My impulses," she said, "become confused. I feel the urge to be helpful, but once I have done a good turn I instantly resent it and feel a hatred against the person to whom I was friendly a minute ago. Isn't that proof that I am going insane?" She attended classes and Recovery meetings and begged to be interviewed after merely four weeks of participation in the self-help program before she had a reasonable opportunity to stage an initial improvement. Such early requests for class interviews are generally considered a good sign of cooperation.

E—Examiner
P—Patient

E: You have been in classes for only four weeks and I do not expect you to have improved a great deal. Are you still afraid of closed rooms and high places?

P: Right now I feel awfully weak and exhausted after a thirty minute ride on the I. C. (Illinois Central).

E: If that is so I presume that your other fears have not improved, either, and that you are still obsessed with the thought that you will lose your mind and that you might do harm to the members of your family.

P: I have not noticed any change, except that I am now more hopeful.

E: Let me ask you, Nancy, what precisely do you fear when you enter an automobile or train coach or an elevator? Are you afraid of an accident?

P: I was in three major accidents and was not a bit scared. As a matter of fact, I was the calmest person in the crowd, perhaps because I don't care if I die. Another thing: I am afraid to be in an automobile even if it stands in the garage.

E: I understand, Nancy, that if you notice a weakness of memory and attention you think of a possible mental ailment. I also understand that if you have frightening impulses you fear you might some day carry them out. These fears are exaggerated but they are not absurd or ridiculous. But if you state that you fear being in an automobile even when it is not moving, well, that is absurd. You cannot possibly think of danger under these circumstances, and your fear is without rhyme or reason. Can't you tell me what makes you quiver with fear in situations that neither you nor anybody else considers dangerous?

P: I get so worked up when I step into a car or an elevator that I fear I am going to collapse the next minute.

E: People get "worked up" on many occasions but do not fear they will collapse. Why do you?

P: I get those awful palpitations and the sinking feeling in my stomach, and I go into a cold sweat and I feel so faint that I think that's my last moment. Right now when I merely speak of these things I have my palpitations.

E: Now I know what you are afraid of. You don't fear cars and elevators or closed spaces and high places. What you fear is your sensations that are called forth by these closed or high localities.

P: You may be right but it does not matter to me whether it is the sensations or the places that frighten me. I simply feel that I am going to pass out.

E: The distinction which I made may matter little to you. But to me it is a fundamental difference whether your fears are caused by sensations within you or by objects without. If your fears are the result of frightening sensations and overpowering impulses I ought to be able to teach you how to control them, but I am unable to give you directions how to exercise control over automobiles and elevators. I do not mean to be facetious if I mention in the same breath such disparate things as automobiles and sensations, elevators and impulses. But it is about time that patients should know that the only things they are afraid of are their own inner experiences, their thoughts, feelings, sensations and impulses. I do not deny, of course, that some fears stem from objects outside you. There are holdups and burglaries and drownings and killings. But these objective dangers, as a general rule, hold little terror for nervous patients. What they are mostly afraid of are terrifying sensations, threatening impulses, obsessing thoughts and depressing feelings, that is, their own inner experiences. You gave an excellent example of your indifference to realistic, objective dangers when you stated that in three separate automobile accidents you were "the calmest person in the crowd." This is a common rule with nervous patients. In situations of grave realistic and objective danger they may be calm and fearless. But let them be confronted with disturbing inner experiences and they become panicky and hysterical. Do you realize now that what you fear is not automobiles, street cars and elevators but your own inner storms and excitements that are aroused when you approach or enter these objects?

P: I understand. But will that stop my palpitations and sinking feelings?

E: Why do you question that? Common sense ought to tell you that you cannot conquer a fear unless you first know what it is that you are afraid of. And if I succeeded in demonstrating to you the true object of your fears you ought to have gained some relief already. You ought to feel more confident now because at last you know what it is that scares you. The fact that you do not feel relief proves that you did not accept my explanation. You still doubt and question it. If this is so I shall have to give you other and perhaps more convincing examples. You know, Nancy, that many people hesitate to admit trivial misdemeanors, for instance, children to their parents. They hesitate even if the parents have seldom inflicted bodily punishment on them. What they are afraid of is that after confessing they will have the tortured feelings of shame, embarrassment and loss of face. They do not fear anything realistic like being spanked; what they fear is their own inner feelings. You have also heard of mature men who fear asking their employer for an increase in salary. They fear to advance their request even if they know for certain that the boss is a kindly person and by no means bossy. In most instances, this fear of approaching another person with an otherwise well justified request is due to the fact that on previous occasions the making of requests was followed by a sense of embarrassment and sensations of tenseness, stammering, flushing and perhaps palpitations and faintness. That man who trembles at the thought of approaching his superior may try to analyze the nature of his fear. In all likelihood, he will then advance inconsequential reasons. He will say that what he fears is that his "boldness" may cost him the job or that, after all, his services are not worth more than he earns. In all of this he will ignore or evade the real explanation that what he fears is the possibility of arousing unpleasant inner experiences. Do you think you understand better now what I am driving at?

P: You mean to say that I am afraid of my sensations when I fear rides in automobiles and elevators. I think I know that now. But will the knowledge help me get rid of the fears?

E: Knowledge alone will not help. But once you know what you are afraid of you can devise plans for eliminating fear. You will agree that if you fear something you think of that something as a danger. You will also admit that in order to fear a danger you must believe it is real and not imaginary. In other words, you must take the danger seriously and be convinced of its reality. All you have to do to dispose of a fear is to refuse to believe that there is danger. Then you will ignore it or laugh it out of existence. If you laugh at a thing and ridicule it you cannot possibly fear it. That is the reason why a sense of humor is such a strong antidote against fear. You see, Nancy, if at the moment you are gripped with the fear of your sensations, if at that moment you could reach the conviction that the danger is unreal, imaginary or not serious you could laugh at it and make it disappear in an instant. Unfortunately the many scares you have gone through in the past ten or twelve years have cowed you into such an abysmal fright that you have lost every trace of a sense of humor with reference to that fear. Your only salvation is to gain the unquestioned conviction that the danger you think of is not existent. I have tried to convince you of that; I pointed out to you the reasons why a fear of this kind cannot possibly be based on a realistic danger. But it seems you are not convinced yet. Why do you still listen to the language of your body instead of accepting what your physician tells you?

P: I have tried my best to accept what you told me. I have read many times what you said about the symptomatic idiom and the temperamental lingo. I have listened to what the patients told me and I have studied the interview with Ruth on the "Vicious Cycle of Panic."* I am convinced that you are right. And if I do not happen to be cooped up in a street car or in an elevator I can reason with myself and realize that your authoritative knowledge is superior to my personal experience. I know all of that. But when I enter an automobile my knowledge is gone. What can I do about that?

E: What you can do is to gain conviction. You have acquired knowledge but you do not possess conviction. You say that your conviction fades the moment you enter an automobile. What happens is that the moment you reach the car your heart begins to palpitate, your stomach churns, your throat contracts. To put it otherwise, your inner organs are "scared." That scare communicates itself to the muscles of your arms and legs. They feel tense and heavy and refuse to move. In a sense, they feel paralyzed. Having read the interview with Ruth you will know that this is the proper setting for a vicious cycle. The panic "marches," as it were, from the inner organs to the outer muscles and to the brain. The greater the commotion of the organs the more intense is the "paralysis" of the muscles, and the more threatening the paralysis of the muscles the more terrifying is the fear in the brain. You ask what you can do. Well, you cannot dictate to the heart to stop the palpitations, or to the stomach to cease churning. But you can command your muscles to move, paralysis or no paralysis. And once you make the muscles move in spite of their apparent paralysis the brain will instantly be convinced that at least one of the dread dangers it feared is without foundation and nothing to be taken seriously. That may not do away with the commotion of the inner organs. The

---

*The interview with Ruth on the "Vicious Cycle of Panic" was published in volume 2 of the "Techniques of Self-Help," page 31.

palpitations and other sensations may continue. But a breach has been made in the solid rampart of the panic, and the implicit belief in the reality of the danger is shaken. When on the next occasion you enter the car the organs may again be thrown into a violent turmoil but you will no longer be scared by the "paralysis" of the muscles. Assurance and conviction will now be more assuring and more convincing with the result that the brain will be more calm, and with a calm brain there is no possibility of a sustained panic. With the panic petering out in consequence of reassurance the organs will soon quiet down, and this time conviction will be strengthened. On the occason of a third or fourth or a dozen other trials you are certain to cut short the panic in its very beginning. Then conviction will score the final triumph and you will be cured of your fear and incapacity. Do you realize that the way to shed your fears is to give the proper directions to your muscles?

P: Frankly, that sounds a bit too easy. It doesn't just seem possible that I should cure my fears by moving my muscles. It should take more than that.

E: It will be difficult for you to convince me that it is "a bit too easy" for persons to command their muscles to move if they feel paralyzed by the fear of making another step. You did not mean to say that my suggestion sounds too easy; you thought it sounds too simple. I shall not enter into a detailed discussion of this very important distinction. I shall merely tell you that I do not want my patients to believe that cures and remedies must necessarily be complex, involved and time-consuming. It is easy to sit in a chair and to be given lengthy and interesting explanations about how fears arise and develop. That is complex but easy. But if a boy is afraid of swimming or diving it is not at all easy to make him move his muscles for the purpose of a resolute jump. That jump is simple but difficult. Do you realize that you expect to be cured of your fears by means of complex but easy and sometimes glib explanations instead of by means of simple but exacting directions? You want to be studied and analyzed and discussed but you do not want to be told what to do and how to act. What will the most lucid explanations profit you if you are seized with a deep anxiety or a paralyzing panic? In a condition of this kind you are utterly unable to make use of the ingenious and fascinating explanations you may have been given. If in a panic you try to remember what you learned and to reason out what is the sensible thing to do your mind will fail you disastrously. The panic weakens your memory and blots out your reasoning power.

INDEX

"MENTAL HEALTH THROUGH WILL TRAINING" by Abraham A. Low, M.D.
(and also "Selections From Dr. Low's Works")

Recovery, Inc., 802 N. Dearborn St., Chicago, IL 60610

All you will be able to do in a commotion of this sort is to apply simple rules. Their very simplicity renders them capable of being employed in a situation in which complex thought is impossible.

P: I do not mean to be contrary, doctor. But it seems to me that when I get into a panic I will not be able to carry out even simple rules.

E: That may be correct for the first and second trial. But if you continue to practice you become ever more proficient in the application of these simple rules. Moreover, you have ample opportunity to practice in situations that are less disturbing or threatening. You mentioned that you are obsessed by the fear of doing harm to your husband and your daughters. This fear does not throw you into a panic. It is with you all the time and being strung out over endless hours and days it is milder, less vehement, less acute. This fear can be handled with a method that is not only simple but also easy. You know that in consequence of the fear you avoid touching knives or any sharp objects. Well, should you practice the simple method of deliberately touching sharp objects in the presence of those that you fear to harm you would have no difficulty convincing yourself that your impulse to do harm is not dangerous. You would soon refuse to take that impulse seriously and would learn thereby that at least some of your fears are ridiculous and can be laughed at. Once you have succeeded in discarding one of your fears by the simple method of commanding your muscles to act against them you will have learned the general principle that fears can be checked by a command to the muscles to counteract the suggestions of danger. The lesson that you have learned with minor fears will then carry over to the region of the major fears. As with most patients, your fears are many in numbers. Some of them are strong, some are mild. You may say that the fears form a chain with strong and weak links. If you wish to break a chain you must attempt to pry it open at its weakest spot, not where the links are strongest. This is the Method of Attack on the Weakest Point which I have mentioned in interviews repeatedly.

P: I have tried so often to touch knives. I wish I could, but I can't.

E: What happened when you stretched out your arm toward the knife?

P: Well, I felt I couldn't do it.

E: Don't tell me that you couldn't do it. Tell me what

happened. Tell me whether you had a panic when you advanced your arm in the direction of the knife. Did you feel like fainting? Did you have violent palpitations, sweats and weakness and churning?

P: No, I simply couldn't move my arm.

E: Do you see the difference between entering the car and picking up a knife? In both instances you are afraid, that means, you have the idea of danger in your brain. But in the case of the automobile the idea of danger is attended by threatening sensations, while in the case of the knife it is nothing but a thought. You will now understand why I call this fear of touching a knife a weak link in the chain of your fears. All you have to do to get rid of your fear of the knife is to convince yourself that your thought of danger is absurd. And the best means of reducing an idea of danger to its absurdity is to act against it. The moment you touch the knife and notice that nothing happens, not even a palpitation, certainly no fainting or any other sign of a panic, once you notice that the thought of danger is immediately proved absurd. Although you are a newcomer to this group, nevertheless, I am certain you heard the members of Recovery mention in their panel discussions how they learned to conquer their fears through their muscles. Many of my patients were afraid to be on their feet because they thought their muscles were exhausted by nervous fatigue. When they decided to walk on in defiance of their fears they became convinced in an instant that their idea of danger was absurd. With some, success came on the first or second trial, with others after a period of extended trials. But whether success comes quickly or slowly the underlying principle is the same: attack the chain of your fears at their weakest point and convince your brain through your muscles that its ideas of danger are absurd.

4

VICIOUS CYCLE AND VITALIZING CYCLE

Virginia's health broke when she was 20. Her previous history was that of an average girl with a good record of school, job and social adjustment. But after she passed her twentieth year she suffered an attack of depression. She lost weight, ate and slept poorly. Her interests weakened. She neglected her job and her appearance. She felt tired all the time and had to make an extreme effort to perform the trifling tasks of her daily routine. Dressing, speaking, walking required an excessive amount of energy. Her mood was down. She experienced the desire "to make an end of it" but lacked the courage to do so. Due to her dejected spirit she blamed herself for past mistakes and petty misdemeanors. Finally she had to be taken to the hospital. She returned after six months and felt well for four years. Then she drifted again into a mood of depression. This time she received a course of electro-shock treatment and regained her health after only five weeks of hospitalization. She resumed her activities, secured a position with a real estate firm but continued to be tired, restless and irritable. It was at this point that her mother heard of Recovery. Virginia joined the organization practicing the system of self-help and conquering fatigue, irritability and restlessness. But in spite of her patient application she was unable to shake off a sense of shyness which made her feel miserable and helpless when she was to meet people singly or in social groups. She volunteered for a class interview in the spring of 1947 stating that a previous interview two years ago had given her much relief.

E—Examiner
P—Patient

E: How are you, Virginia?
P: I feel all right. But I am so self-conscious. I shut up like a clam when I am among people. When I want to say something I can't find a thought. It seems my brain freezes and I can't think. It is all a fog and blank. If somebody asks a question my throat tightens and I can't speak a word.
E: Have you been working all the time?

P: I have worked continuously since shortly after I left the hospital.

E: That makes it close to four years of continuous work. Did you change jobs during this time?

P: No, I am still holding the same job that I got four years ago.

E: Do you think your employer is satisfied with your work?

P: I got three raises and my boss leaves the running of the office practically to me.

E: I consider this a neat accomplishment and a very creditable comeback after what you went through. You ought to be proud of yourself. Instead, you shrink and almost swoon when you are asked to do nothing more than open your mouth and formulate a simple sentence. You say your brain freezes and you cannot think, your throat tightens and you cannot speak. How is it you do a good piece of speaking and thinking right now? How is it your brain thaws up and your throat unlocks during this interview? You are certainly among people here. More than that, this is an audience and you the star performer tonight. You are in the limelight, watched by everybody in this hall. Many people with strong nerves and no record of a past breakdown wilt when they are asked to make a speech before a public gathering of this size. And, remember, what you say here is a tale of weakness, a recital of your shortcomings, a confession of personal inadequacy, while in a social group the conversation turns around more or less impersonal and indifferent topics. You show courage here in a highly embarrassing situation in which your failures and inefficiencies are laid bare, and exhibit fear in a social setting where courtesy and etiquette banish all possibility of being exposed. Can you explain this strange behavior?

P: I am relaxed here. But when I meet people on the outside I am tense.

E: I am frequently tense myself. But that does not cause my brain to freeze and my throat to tighten. No matter how tense I sometimes am I get my brain to think and my speech muscles to produce words and sentences. How is it you cannot think and speak when you are tense?

P: I don't know how to explain it. I simply don't get thoughts and the words don't come.

E: I shall try to give the explanation. You will grant, Virginia, that to speak means to produce movements of the muscles of speech. To put it differently: speaking is a muscular act. I take it you know that muscles will act only if they are stimulated and will refuse action if they are frustrated. From this you may conclude that your muscles of speech are stimulated here tonight but would be frustrated if you were to repeat this performance elsewhere. What stimulates muscles is courage and self-confidence, that means, the sense of security. What frustrates them is fear and self-distrust, that is, the sense of insecurity. Do you understand now, Virginia, that when you have the thought of insecurity in your brain it will frustrate and tighten your muscles and keep them from acting and speaking?

P: It seems to me I have no views or thoughts in my brain when my speech stops. My head feels like a blank and no thoughts come, not even the thought of insecurity.

E: If you say you have no thoughts in your brain you seem to believe you know how your brain works. In this, you presume a trifle too much. Right now you sit on this chair. Moreover, you keep sitting. You do not jump up or run away. How could you maintain your seat unless you were certain that the chair is solid and you are in no danger of falling? Yet, you may insist the thought of security was not in your brain while you kept up your sitting activity. Do you realize that you could never sit down or continue sitting unless your brain told you that the act of sitting is safe and secure? The same consideration holds good for every variety of acting, for eating, standing, walking, speaking. You would never dare voice a sentence unless your brain told you that the statement you are about to release will not endanger your social, moral or ethical security; that the remark you intend to make is neither offensive nor compromising. This rule applies to every act, no matter how simple or how insignificant. You could never make a step unless you were sure you would not fall and fracture your leg. You could never ask even the most innocent question unless you were reasonably certain it would not be resented. These examples which could be multiplied indefinitely will tell you that ordinarily no act of yours will be released unless the brain first takes the view that no danger is involved. After the brain has, in the flash of a momentary decision, reached the conclusion that the situation is one of security it stimulates the muscles to release the appropriate act. The conclusion that the planned act is safe is formed without your conscious knowledge. We say it is arrived at intuitively and not discursively. When you came here tonight you had already formed the conclusion in your brain that the situation of this interview is one of security. Hence, your thoughts did not freeze and your throat did not lock. Why is there freezing and locking when you attend a social gathering?

P: I guess because there my brain forms the conclusion of insecurity.

E: Correct. But how is it that this conclusion of insecurity keeps occupying your brain all the time you attend the gathering? Why is there no letup, no change of conclusions?

P: I think I know what you have in mind. I produce a vicious cycle.

E: That is correct if you specify what kind of vicious cycle you have in mind. The most common varieties of vicious cycles are those of fear and anger. But fear and anger are part of life, indeed, a most significant part of life; and if they run in vicious cycles their action represents a very stormy, an almost tempestuous sort of life. However, when your thoughts freeze and go blank they can hardly be said to be stirring with life. In a sense, they are dead. Their life pulse has gone out of them. If you speak of freezing, of fogs and blanks, of shutting up like a clam, that means that you pass into something like a state of lifelessness. Your vicious cycle affects the pulse of your responses and reactions. You know what a pulse means. It means something that rises and falls, something that begins, matures and finally fades away. This is true of muscular movement, of glandular activity, of nerve impulses, of thoughts, sensations and feelings. All of them have their life history of being born, of maturing into full action and of passing out of activity. For the sake of simplicity I shall limit the discussion and consider the pulse cycle of thought only. You know that if you now happen to think of the weather that thought will not occupy your brain for a great length of time. Your attention will soon wander from the topic of the weather to that of your office or home or mother. It will then turn to the book you are just reading, then to the friend who phoned you yesterday, then to the subject of the atomic bomb which was discussed in the morning paper. In order to make the mind hop and skip in this rather careless manner you must be reasonably carefree. That means, you must have a reasonable sense of security. If you feel insecure your thoughts will be focused on the object that threatens and your attention will be riveted on the topic of danger. The one thought of danger will *preoccupy* your brain and will prevent it from *occupying* itself with other thoughts. The thinking pulse will then be interrupted by your preoccupation. The preoccupation will make one single thought dominate the brain with the result that the remaining thoughts will no longer rise and fall, the thought pulse will be suspended and life will seem abolished. The brain will then feel as if in a fog, dense, blank, lifeless, pulseless. How is it, I shall ask, that your thought pulse shows life and vigor during this interview and loses its vitality in other groups?

P: I still think it is the vicious cycle that does that.

E: I told you I am ready to accept the explanation. But it will have to be qualified. There are many types and degrees of vicious cycles. One of them is that of fear, another of anger. These are the most common varieties. If yours were that of fear the vicious cycle would fan it into a panic. If it were that of anger it would be raised to the pitch of rage. I have observed you in the company of other people and you gave no evidence of being rocked by either panic or rage. Your face was smooth, perhaps even blank, and its muscles gave little evidence of lively expression. You sat motionless, staring into space. You give this a different wording when you say that your brain does not think and your speech muscles do not move. They are not lifeless by any means, but you feel that life has gone out of them. The brain feels unable to think, and the muscles unable to act. The more helpless the brain the more limp are the muscles; the more limp the muscles the more helpless is the brain. This is the vicious cycle of helplessness. How is it, I shall ask again, that you are able to shake off this sense of helplessness when you are interviewed here in front of a large crowd?

P: I don't know exactly but the nearest I can think of as an explanation is that I don't feel cramped here as I feel in groups on the outside.

E: That does not explain a great deal. It seems to me I shall have to do the explaining. We spoke of a vicious cycle. That means that some sort of circular movement is set up between the brain cells and the muscles. In this cycle the brain acts on the muscles, and the muscles act on the brain. The two influence one another. The cycle begins its destructive work before you arrive at the particular gathering. For hours and perhaps for days you have anticipated that your brain will be paralyzed and helpless. On the way to the social function which you are to attend the "freezing" process begins and when you reach your destination it has deepened into what you call a blank. The brain feels lifeless and dispatches impulses to the muscles not to stir, not to move. In this manner, the helplessness of the brain communicates itself to the muscles and the vicious cycle is set afoot. I told you that brain and muscles influence one another in this cycle or circular movement. Since they interact or act on one another it ought to be clear to you that if you cause the one to move the other will follow suit. To state it differently: make the one move and the other will perforce join the movement. You may not be able to get the brain moving. But you certainly can do that with muscles. Command your speech muscles to act, and the brain will instantly realize that its theory of helplessness is a myth, a fiction, an untruth. The more vigorously your muscles will move, the less will the brain be able to believe that it is helpless. That this can be done you demonstrated here with your perfect speech performance during the present interview. You remember the first occasion when you were interviewed about two years ago. You stammered, hemmed and hawed and had extreme difficulty squeezing a few words out of your throat. The first sentences leaped out of your mouth explosively. I had to proceed slowly and cautiously, giving you ample time to warm up to the task until finally you took heart and gained courage and gave an excellent account of yourself. At that time you experienced a vicious cycle of helplessness at the beginning of the interview. During this cycle your brain was devitalized and deprived your speech muscles of their vitality. But once you commanded your speech muscles to move the very action of the muscles had a vitalizing effect on the brain. The movement of the muscles convinced the brain that speaking is possible. And when the brain witnessed the living, vital performance of the muscles it acquired a new vitality itself and lost its lifelessness. The more forceful was the action of the muscles the more vitalized became the brain; the more vital the brain the more forceful the muscles. By commanding your muscles to move you had thus transformed the *vicious cycle of helplessness* into the *vitalizing cycle of self-confidence.*

As the interview drew to its close it was explained to Virginia that her energetic performance during the interview could be duplicated and multiplied on numerous other occasions inside Recovery and outside. What she had to do was to practice commanding her speech muscles to initiate the vitalizing cycle of self-confidence whenever she had an opportunity to do so. It developed that Virginia had neglected this practice by refraining from joining the panel discussions at family gatherings. She realized that this was her golden opportunity and felt that having gained revealing information about the nature and operation of the vitalizing cycle she was now in a position to practice with understanding. Reports reaching the writer indicate that Virginia is making a good effort at participating in panel discussions and is ready to transfer to social engagements outside Recovery the experience she is gaining in the family gatherings of the ex-patients.

5

SYMPTOMS MUST BE ATTACKED WHERE THEY ARE WEAKEST

Roy was 35 years of age when he was first seen in the physician's office. He was married, had two children, loved his home and was well liked by friends and neighbors. His employment record was good. He had held his present position for fifteen consecutive years advancing to the rank of a foreman. All in all he had done well until three years ago when suddenly, "out of a blue sky," his right arm and right leg went numb. The numbness had come on at the moment when he entered the plant to start on the afternoon shift. It disappeared as fast as it had come lasting a few minutes only. But Roy was frightened into a senseless fear that he was headed for a stroke. Ordinarily stolid and unemotional, he was now pale, trembling, restless. His fellow workers noticed the change and drove him home. The family physician ordered Roy to stay home for a week and to rest. The following week an electrocardiogram was taken and the doctor was heard to say that something in the graph was "flat instead of round." After that Roy developed violent palpitations, headaches, dizziness, fatigue, air-hunger, difficulty of sleeping, fears of physical collapse and mental breakdown. He saw specks floating in front of his eyes and once "nearly went blind" for a couple of minutes. Some of his sensations were bizarre and intensified his fear of a mental breakdown. Looking at his hands he saw them in a yellow tinge. He felt pains which settled in narrowly confined places, in the left wrist or in the space above the right knee. His teeth began to hurt. There was a pain around the heart. He lifted his little son and instantly felt a pain around his right ear. He lay on the left side and something clicked in the right flank. The fingers of the right hand might hurt and suddenly the pain shifted to the back of the head. He felt pressure of the throat, had night sweats which roused the fear of tuberculosis, pain in the chest, difficulty of sleeping, trouble in concentration and "confusion all the time." A combined course of office and group treatment produced a good improvement. He returned to work and was able to attend to his job in spite of the fact that some of his sensations persisted as weak "reminders." He had learned in Recovery to ignore the threat of symptoms and turned his new knowledge to good account. There were minor setbacks but he handled them well until after about six months of successful self-management a major setback occurred which he was unable to shake off. When he was interviewed in class he stated that the present setback had lasted upward of four weeks already.

E—Examiner
P—Patient

E: What is it that has troubled you most in these past four weeks?

P: My eyes feel blurry, my memory is poor, and I have an awful fatigue and the legs feel heavy and numb. And I have these headaches again and the pain around the heart.

E: You have been ill for three years before I saw you. Is that correct?

P: It was not quite three years but almost that long.

E: And during these three years your trouble got worse and worse?

P: Well, I had some good days.

E: Your symptoms changed. They kept coming and going.

P: I can't say that. Some stayed on.

E: Some of your pains shifted from one part of the body to the other?

P: No, I didn't have that.

E: So far you have denied or corrected or rejected about every statement which I made. When I mentioned that I saw you for three years you set me right by stating that "it was not quite three years but almost that long." You will understand that the difference between "three years" and "almost three years" is so insignificant that you could safely ignore it. Instead you stress and emphasize this trifling distinction, underscore it pointedly and make an issue of things that have no importance. You pick flaws in my argument and turn this interview into an occasion for verbal fencing, sparring and skirmishing. This proves that you came here tonight in a fighting mood which is merely another way of saying that you are in the grip of tenseness. You say that the tenseness has been in evidence for fully four weeks without letup. Does that mean that it was with you all day and every day during these four weeks?

P: It was easier the first few days and the first week. I could relax at a card game or at a show. I guess my mind was taken off my troubles when I had some diversion. But in the past three weeks it got worse and worse. Even a show or a card game didn't help me. I got so tense that everything irritated me, even my little girl and my wife at home. Maybe you are right, I am in a fighting mood. It makes me mad because I like to get along with people. I simply cannot understand it.

E: Perhaps I can make you understand it. Look here, Roy, tenseness is a sensation. Having attended classes for close to a year you heard me state repeatedly that sensations rise and fall. How is it that your tenseness has risen but did not fall?

P: I think I know what you mean. I attached the idea of danger to the sensation.

E: Correct. But what does it mean to attach an idea to a sensation? Can ideas be made to change places, to wander from one spot to another? In other words, can ideas be shifted and shoved and pushed around just as you may please?

P: Yes, you said that a person can choose to think of whatever he wishes. And I think that is right.

E: How about sensations? Can they be manipulated at will? If you have the idea of this table in your mind, can you now "attach tenseness" to the thought of the table?

P: I don't think so.

E: If you deny that, then, you obviously believe that thoughts or ideas can be handled, directed and manipulated at will but sensations cannot. You are right. You cannot say, "I am going to be tense from now on" and actually produce the tenseness by sheer wanting it. But you can say, "I am going to think of this table now" and the thought of the table will be in your mind and stay there as long as you choose to entertain it. If that is so we may state it as a general rule that thoughts and ideas are subject to the action of will but sensations are not. But why speak of sensations only? There are feelings and impulses. You know that when your eyes blur, when your head aches and the legs are numb you do not merely experience these sensations; you also feel alarm about them. They depress your mood, they strike you with despair, with discouragement and the sense of helplessness. Think of the anguish and anxiety that go with the listlessness and fatigue that descends upon you in the morning. Think of the anger and resentment that you feel rising within you when you notice your pains and aches and work yourself up to a pitch of excitement. All of these are feelings added to the sensations. Do you think you can cut them short or bid them to disappear and make place for other more comfortable feelings? Of course, you cannot do that. Feelings cannot be redirected or rearranged at the bidding of your will. Neither can impulses. When you are in agony over your disturbing sensations instantly there is the impulse to call off an engagement or to summon the physician or to turn with fury upon your wife or child because of some innocent remark they may make. These impulses are just as spontaneous and passive as your sensations and feelings. They appear and you know of their presence only after they have emerged. You cannot manage them as you can your thoughts. You cannot command them to come or to go. They come upon the scene spontaneously and passively. If they are to depart the process is again passive and spontaneous. Do you understand now that thoughts are active and deliberate while sensations, feelings and impulses are passive and spontaneous? Do you also understand then that while you cannot drop your sensations, feelings and impulses by a command of will you can do that with your thoughts?

P: I understand that and I know you are right. But somehow I haven't been able to get rid of the thought of danger. I've tried many times to think of what you tell us about sabotage and that we are not permitted to make our own diagnosis. I know that when you say there is no danger there isn't any. But the idea sticks to me and I cannot get rid of it.

E: Several months ago it was just as difficult for you to shake off the idea of danger. But you did it and got well. There is no earthly reason why you should not be able to repeat that performance. But in order to succeed you will have to practice as hard as you did months ago. That practice calls for a method. Do you remember which method you were asked to use at that time?

P: I came to classes and meetings and I accepted your authoritative knowledge.

E: Of course, you have to accept my authority and must attend classes and meetings. But that is not what I meant by method. What you mention is the person who taught you the method and the occasions and places where you were supposed to learn it. You may have some opportunity to practice that method in classes and in my office. But the bulk of practicing will have to be done at home, in the shop, on the street and in all kinds of places and situations where there is no physician and no Recovery to help you along. What you did was to learn theoretically how the method works. But you failed to apply it systematically. You do not even seem to know which method I refer to. What I want you to learn is to throw out of your brain one thought and replace it with another. The thought that I want discarded is the idea of danger, and the thought which I want to take its place is the idea of security. You know that the thought of danger is forced upon you by your sensations. You may, for instance, experience a numbness in the legs. The likelihood is then that the sensation will suggest that you are in danger of a physical collapse or a permanent handicap. I want you instead to think of the numbness as a harmless though distressing bodily feeling. Should you effect this change in thought the sensation would fall soon after it has risen. Similarly, I want you to view your chest pressure and blurred vision as implying no danger to life or to mental and physical health. This requires the proper application of the method I taught you. Now, if somebody wishes to master a method he will have to begin his practice where the application is easiest. Suppose you wish to become an airplane pilot. You will first work on prints and models, then on parts, then on machines of simple design and only in the last stages of your apprenticeship will you venture to manipulate the more powerful engines. This gradual progression from relatively simple to increasingly more complex tasks is the system by means of which every method is learned. Do you think you have applied this procedure? You have not. Most likely you do not even know the name of the method I have in mind.

P: I don't think I know it.

E: I mentioned it frequently in past interviews. It is the Method of Attack on the Weakest Point. I shall refresh your memory by quoting examples. If a patient suffers from an explosive temper it will be easier for him to control it where the temperamental deadlock is mild than where it is in full blaze. At home with his wife and children whom he loves the deadlock is milder than with the boss whom he may hate. Should he check his explosions more or less regularly whenever his little daughter irritates him he would attack the chain of his temperamental flares at their weakest point. He might then transfer this practice to his wife, then to his friends and lastly to his boss who represents the strongest link in the chain. You may be inclined to doubt whether a method which works well with temper will also be effective with symptoms. Well, if you have read my books you will know that temper, exactly like symptoms, is initiated by an irritation or annoyance, that is, by sensations. To these sensations the temperamental person adds the ideas of either, "he is wrong" (angry temper) or the thought of "I am wrong" (fearful temper). You see here that in temper as in symptoms a thought is always linked to a sensation. Clearly the same method can be applied to both situations.

I shall give another example. You know that many of my patients suffer agonies because of their self-consciousness. They hesitate to address people, to offer opinions or to take part in conversations because they fear they might say the wrong thing or they may display a clumsy and awkward manner in speech, movement or carriage. Most of them are haunted by suspicions of being misunderstood or of being considered below par. Obviously there is here again a linkage between disturbing sensations and thoughts of insecurity. The sensations are those of discomfort on meeting people, and the thought is that of the danger of compromising oneself. In order to check the idea of insecurity the first step to be taken by the self-conscious person will have to be to practice in an environment in which the chances of being misunderstood or underrated are at their lowest. This is one of the reasons, as you know, why I insist that my patients associate with their fellow-sufferers in Recovery. There they have an opportunity to attack their fears and suspicions where they are weakest. I hope you realize now that if you wish to get rid of your troubles you will have to adopt this well tried method which means that you will have to attack those of your symptoms first which form the weakest links in the chain of your ill-balanced sensations, feelings and impulses.

P: It seems to me my symptoms are all pretty strong. It would be quite a job to find weak sensations among them.

E: I cannot agree with you on this point. You said your main difficulties are now (1) blurring of vision, (2) poor memory, (3) headaches, (4) pain around the heart, (5) fatigue with heaviness and numbness in the legs. It might be difficult for you to persuade yourself that the first four symptoms are without danger. The moment you experience the pain in the region of the heart the thought of a stroke or sudden collapse shoots into your brain, and it will not be easy to shut it out by means of a simple procedure or formula. You may also find it difficult to believe that your blurred vision, your poor memory and your headaches are harmless and devoid of danger. But this is altogether different with your fatigue. You think that your muscles are in danger of exhaustion should you continue to tax their fading strength. This thought of danger can be thrown out of your brain instantly if, accepting my authoritative knowledge, you conclude that yours is a psychological feeling of tiredness and not a physiological condition of exhaustion. If you do that you can decide to step out vigorously and to walk on for dozens of blocks. The sheer act of brisk and steadfast walking will give you the conviction that your muscles can easily perform a good sized piece of labor without withering or caving in. If you continue the walking practice day after day the conviction will gain strength and become unshakeable. The thought of muscular weakness and physical infirmity will give way to the idea of health, vigor and resistance; or the thought of security will replace the idea of insecurity. After you will have broken the link of fatigue in the chain of your symptoms you will know that when your body spoke of danger in connection with the fatigue it lied to you. Why should you believe the other symptoms if they voice threats and sound alarms? It seems to me that if the one symptom has been exposed as a liar the other symptoms can no longer escape the same kind of exposure.

I shall make one more point: what you call nervous fatigue is a condition that has its highest intensity in the morning, dwindling in strength in the afternoon and disappearing in the evening. You know that this is the case with your own so-called fatigue. Now if your muscles were weak to the point of exhaustion why should they regain their strength after a day's exertion? This alone ought to convince you that your fatigue is a feeling and nothing else. Moreover, this feature of the afternoon decline gives you an added opportunity to practice replacing the thought of insecurity with the idea of security. If after a day's work you set out on an energetic evening walk of about one or two miles you can easily persuade yourself that fatigued muscles which are capable of doing strenuous exercise after a day's hard labor cannot possibly have been exhausted in the morning and early afternoon. If you carry on your practice in the evening your performance will not only be convincing but it will have the additional advantage of being easy of execution.

6

TEMPER AND SYMPTOM—PASSIVE RESPONSE AND ACTIVE REACTION

Peter told the story of his seven years of suffering. It began when one night he awoke and could not catch his breath. He rushed to the window, tried to draw in the fresh winter air but the "air-hunger" persisted for what appeared to him hours of never-ending torture. He feel asleep again but in the morning belched incessantly. Although the breath-holding spell did not recur he still shuddered when he remembered the ghastly experience of the preceding night. He was certain he had a heart ailment. His physician reassured him with the result that except for recurring belching reactions he managed to maintain a precarious adjustment for five years. Then the belching increased in intensity and became associated with a pain about the heart region. This time the physician's assurance that his condition was harmless failed to convince Peter. One day, while working in his shop, he jumped up and "couldn't breathe." Now he was sure he was in danger of a physical collapse. He became panicky and intractable and was taken to the hospital. He was given electro-shock treatment which added the suggestion of mental ailment to the fear of physical collapse. After discharge from the hospital he returned to work. He was now obsessed with all kinds of fears and tormented with suddenly rising violent impulses. The fears centered about lungs and heart, and the impulses were in the nature of indiscriminate aggressions, for instance, "to punch somebody in the face." The impulses were controlled but the fears spread. He became afraid of swallowing because eating might lead to belching. If he occasionally exploded in a temper outburst he felt wretched. If he controlled temper he "felt like a rat." Trigger symptoms made their appearance. He thought of getting a spell of air-hunger, "and presto I got it." His concentration suffered. At time he stammered. All of this made him feel confused, self-conscious, miserable. It was at this stage that he was seen in the office and assigned to classes. He made a fair improvement, got the belching, air-hunger and fear of swallowing under tolerable control but what disturbed him most was his lack of self-confidence and the inability to check his temper.

E—Examiner
P—Patient

E: What seems to trouble you most is the fact that your self-confidence is reduced to a level in which you are no longer as cocky, argumentative, conceited and intellectually snobbish as you used to be. If my sharp wording displeases you I shall remind you of the pertness with which you used to voice your political opinions, the intolerance you used to display in your tiffs with friends, wife and co-workers, of the delight you took in out-arguing anybody who might engage in an exchange of views with you. As I see it, you do not suffer from any lack of self-confidence. You merely resent the fact that your former vanity and inflated sense of importance are now gone. You consider that a loss, thinking you have become a dish rag; I regard it as a gain, thinking you are on the way to develop a measure of humility. What interests me is your failure to curb your temper sufficiently. As long as you continue to indulge your temperamental habits your symptoms will persist. Eliminate your temper and you will do away with your symptoms.

P: I have tried the hardest to get rid of my temper and it seems to me I accomplished a good deal. At home I have few arguments, and in the shop I keep quiet most of the time. But of course I fly off the handle once in a while. And, good Lord, once I let myself go there are the palpitations and the confusion and some air-hunger and belching. Can't I ever be natural and human like others?

E: I am not at all concerned with your being natural and human. My sole objective is to rid you of your symptoms. You seem to think it is your natural and human privilege to exercise your temper. It is just as natural and human to eat steak. But if a man is suffering from a gastric upset he'd better relinquish his "natural and human right" to steak dinners. Are you willing to give up your temper for the sake of your health?

P: I guess I am willing. But this thing got me licked. I try to be calm and I do pretty well most of the time. But if the boss is unreasonable and rides me the worst way I cannot hold back and tell him where to get off.

E: Give me an example of the manner in which the boss is

unreasonable. Tell me what he does to "ride you the worst way."

P: The other day when I came to the shop a tool was missing. I asked the boss whether he had seen it and he said, "You lost it and you will have to find it." That just burned me up. I came back with a saucy remark and he laughed out loud. That dirty laugh made me boil. I let loose and gave him a mouthful. It didn't take a minute and I had my belching and it took me hours to get rid of it.

E: From what I know about you it seems to me that this example is representative. It represents your customary habit of reacting to minor frustrations. You asked a question, and the boss returned a gruff answer. Instantly you became irritated to the point of "burning up." The next link in the chain of events was that you came back with a "saucy" remark. The boss, refusing to become temperamental, laughed and made your blood "boil." The final result was that you belched for hours. You will realize that what "burned" and "boiled" was your temper. You know, however, that temper will neither burn nor boil unless you form the idea that you have been wronged. From this we conclude that prior to releasing your temper you thought or decided that the boss was wrong and you were right. It was this temperamental thought in your brain that touched off the temperamental commotion in your body. This again led to the "saucy" remark and ultimately to the sustained fit of belching. Let me repeat: there was (1) the temperamental thought, (2) the temperamental commotion, (3) the "saucy" remark, (4) the belching. You will understand that the thought "he is wrong and I am right" can be rejected, suppressed or dropped. You will also understand that your "saucy" remark could have been checked. In other words in this fourfold series of incidents, two lent themselves readily for control. You could have rejected the thought of being wronged by the boss and could have prevented your muscles of speech from voicing the "saucy" remark. Do we agree on this point?

P: Of course. I heard you say that many times and I know that ideas can be rejected and that muscles can be commanded not to move. I know that but it doesn't seem to help me. That thing gets me and I explode.

E: What you say means that control of thought and muscles is theoretically possible as a general principle but practically impossible in your particular case. Which means that you are an exception. But I do not recognize exceptions, and what one patient can do another can likewise. We shall take it for granted then that you could have controlled the temperamental thought in your brain and the temperamental utterance of your speech muscles. How about the temperamental commotion ("boiling") and the belching? Do you think you could have stopped that?

P: I can only say what you told us in previous interviews. Temper runs its course and symptoms do the same.

E: Correct. Both temper and symptom run their course, and you cannot stop them by an effort of the will as you can do with thoughts and muscular action. And if you say that temper and symptoms run on of their own momentum that means that once they are set going they continue on, rising and falling passively without any possibility of arresting their progress until they exhaust themselves. For this reason they have been termed the *passive responses* of the body to a disturbing event. They are called passive because they cannot be actively influenced by the intervention of will. This is different with thought and muscular action. Your will can play on them as it chooses. If you now think that your boss emitted a "dirty laugh" you can in a second change your view and admit that the laugh was perhaps not so dirty after all. If the thought strikes you that his remark about the tools was provocative and offensive there is nothing to prevent you from surmising that a more sympathetic explanation may be just as acceptable. And as concerns your muscles, well, that muscles can be restrained from moving is a commonplace fact that need not be stressed. And when you had the impulse to "let loose" and "tell the boss a mouthful" you could have decided to hold your tongue and to prevent your speech muscles from moving. Muscles and thoughts can be manipulated actively and for this reason are called the *active reactions* in contradistinction to the passive responses of temper and symptoms. If you really wanted to get rid of the belching all you had to do was to stop your speech muscles from voicing the "saucy" remark and to reject the absurd idea that you are the judge as to who is right and who is wrong. Had you done that your temper would have been reduced to a flicker of an inner stir and the belching would have been aborted. Do you understand now that your belching cannot be cured unless you control your temper and that the latter can only be checked if the brakes are applied to thought and muscles?

P: I understand that when I listen to you. But at the moment my temper gets me I forget what you told me.

E: Which means that in your opinion your temper is an overwhelming power that has you in its grip and leaves you helpless when it seizes you. But the grip is so tight only because you do not make the proper effort to loosen it. The time to make this effort is not when you are face to face with the boss. There a deadlock has developed between you and him, and the mere sight of the boss makes your temper flare. In order to get a hold on your temper you must practice control under circumstances which do not produce the situation of the deadlock. You must practice at home with your mother and wife and child. There is no deadlock at home, or if there is one it is mild and can be handled with ease. With the members of your family your temper rises slowly and perhaps never reaches excessive heights. There ought to be no difficulty rejecting the thought of "I am right and she is wrong" when your little girl irritates you with her childish pestering or when mother and wife ask annoying questions. These trifling impositions give you an opportunity for practicing temper control dozens of times each day. From your own account and from reports that come to me from other sources I know that you "let yourself go" in the morning before you leave for work and in the evening after you return from the shop. You permit yourself the expensive luxury of releasing wild thought and speech reactions. Once these active reactions are set off the passive responses of temper and symptom follow promptly in their wake. When you arrive at the shop in the morning you are already primed for the responses of temper and symptom because you failed to practice control of thought and speech reactions the evening before. On entering the shop you are disposed to explode and belch because you pre-disposed yourself to flare-ups in the paltry domestic squabbles of the previous day. Your temperamental disposition at the shop in the morning is the result of the temperamental predisposition cultivated in the evening at home. If you wish to get rid of your belching you will have to realize that the place to practice temper control is at home and not in the shop, and that the elements which have to be controlled are the active reactions of thought and muscles, not the passive responses of explosion and symptom.

7

INTUITIVE VERSUS DISCURSIVE THOUGHT IN TEMPER

E—Examiner
P—Patient

Lester had an accident five years ago in which he suffered a skull fracture. He recovered but was left with a persistent headache, spells of dizziness, and difficulty of remembering. In the course of the interview he made the following statement:

P: (Lester) After I returned to the office I expected the people I worked with to be understanding and considerate. Instead they did everything to irritate me and to make me feel sore.

E: What precisely did your co-workers do that showed they had no consideration?

P: Why, they slammed the doors and knocked against my chair and laughed and yelled when I was busy concentrating on my work. One fellow particularly made it a practice to brush against me whenever he passed me. When I told him to stop he made a sassy remark and then kept moving his chair and dropping objects and scratching the table with his pencil. Anybody could see that this chap just wanted to provoke me. That sort of thing went on all day. Do you wonder why I lose my temper?

E: Indeed, I wonder. Since you have persistent headaches, the best thing for you to do is to control your temper. The surest means of producing or aggravating your headache is to lose your temper. Why don't you make every effort to control it?

P: If anybody does something to irritate me, it gets my goat and I explode. I wish I could hold my temper, but I can't.

E: Have you been working in the same office all these five years?

P: I was transferred to another room but had quite a few battles there, too.

E: How are you at home?

P: I lose my temper at home, too. My mother pesters me, and my brother and sister wouldn't do a thing for me when I am suffering.

E: I know also that you have hardly any friends, because they did not give you the sympathy you expected and you threw tantrums whenever you did not have your way.

P: I think I am entitled to consideration. Can I help it if the headache drives me frantic and I explode?

Rhoda Joins the Interview

E: Rhoda, do you think Lester is unable to control his temper?

P: (Rhoda) You told us there is no uncontrollable temper; his temper is uncontrolled, but not uncontrollable.

E: What you tell me, Rhoda, is what you heard in previous interviews in which we reached the conclusion that tempers are frequently uncontrolled but never uncontrollable. But tell me, Rhoda, why does Lester leave his temper without control?

P: That's difficult for me to say.

E: Now, Rhoda, you remember the examples which Lester quoted. He becomes enraged when the man near him scratches the table with the pencil, or when somebody closes the door with more noise than Lester thinks proper, or when somebody else brushes inadvertently against his chair. You know that people do not, as a rule, "fly off the handle" because of such trivial irritations. Ordinarily, a person will go into a rage only if he is injured or insulted. I might be provoked and react with a violent emotion if I were addressed in rude language, or pushed off my chair with brute force. In an instance of this kind I would feel outraged because my right to peaceful living was infringed upon willfully and intentionally. Let me tell you, Rhoda, that nobody loses his temper unless he is or feels he is wronged or insulted intentionally. Your temper does not flare up if you hurt your foot against a stone. The pain and irritation which you experience may be just as intense as if somebody throws the stone on your foot deliberately. But in the one case the hurt was inflicted by accident and you do not feel insulted; in the other case, the hurt was caused by intention, and that makes you feel insulted and arouses your anger or your temper. If you understand that, you will realize that when the man near Lester scratched the table with the pencil, he did so by accident and not by intention; and if somebody slammed the door or brushed against Lester, the "irritating" act of behavior was again the result of an accidental happening and not of a deliberate intention to cause offense. Why, then, did Lester go into a huff because of such accidental trivialities?

P: I guess he thinks they are intentional and not accidental.

E: That's it. Lester thinks of intentions where there are only accidents. And since accidents may happen every time and in every place, he is provoked everywhere and on every occasion. Did you listen, Lester, and do you agree with what I said about your temper?

Lester Rejoins the Interview

P: (Lester) I listened and tried to understand what you said, but I am sure I don't think of intentions when I am irritated. I simply go off and don't think at all. The explosion comes before I have time to think.

E: In a sense, you are right, Lester. But in one sense only. The word "thinking" has two meanings, and I wish to explain to you the difference between the two kinds of thinking. Suppose I tell a story and in the process say, "A man approached me; he walked slow." Be certain I shall instantly catch my error and correct swiftly, saying, "I meant to say he walked slowly." Do you think I did a great deal of thinking when I offered the correction? Did I stop and reflect and deliberate whether the adverb "slowly" is better grammar than the adjective "slow?" Presumably I did not do any reflecting but noticed the error intuitively and felt likewise intuitively that my statement needed correction. But while doing this intuitive job of noticing and correcting the error I drew two discrete conclusions: I concluded (1) that "slow" was the wrong use, (2) that I had to correct to "slowly." In all of this I did not debate within myself and did not reflect on the words "correct" and "incorrect" or on the words "adjective" and "adverb." Had I done so, I would have discoursed (within myself) about the issue of the grammatical error, and my type of thinking would have been discursive. Instead, I drew the conclusions by way of intuition. Hence, my type of thinking was intuitive. I want you to understand this distinction between discursive and intuitive thinking. You see, children correct themselves frequently. At a certain stage of their development they may say, "I will go to kindergarten yesterday," and correct instantly to "tomorrow." We grownups could discourse in such an instance that the word "yesterday" connotes the past and clashes with the phrase "I will go" which connotes the future. If we do that our conclusions are drawn discursively. The child has not yet learned how to engage in discursive thinking of this sort. He must draw the same conclusions by a process of intuitive thought. I would perhaps tell you how we come to acquire discursive thought. It is done through school instruction mainly. How intuitive thought is achieved I am unable to tell. It is one of the mysteries of life which I, at any rate, am unable to explain.

I hope you will now understand, Lester, that in order to draw conclusions about the meaning of a situation, one does not have to reflect or to do an act of discursive thinking. One may reach the same conclusion by means of imaginative or intuitive thinking. That's what you do when your coworker scratches the table with his pencil. Intuitively you draw the conclusion (without having time to think by reflection) that he intends to irritate you. Once you reach this conclusion you interpret the situation as one in which an enemy attacks or provokes you, and instantly your anger (or temper) is aroused. You will now realize that the common variety of temper is a condition in which one person draws the intuitive conclusion that another person intends to offend him. The explosion and anger are merely the result of this preceding intuitive conclusion. Far less common is that variety of temper in which discursive conclusions are acted upon.

It was explained to Lester and the class that in order to gain control over his temper a person must learn through continuous practice to avoid the intuitive conclusion of a deliberate insult which precedes the temperamental outburst. Several more examples were given to illustrate the difference between discursive and intuitive thought. Finally the examiner asked:

E: Now, Lester, suppose your coworker will scratch the table with his pencil tomorrow; what will you do then?

P: (Lester) I will try not to draw the conclusion that he does that intentionally.

E: That would be fine. But I have reason to doubt whether you will be able to do that. You see, Lester, your temper has been with you for many, many years, indeed, since your childhood. True, it has become intensified and almost crystallized since your accident. But as such it has been with you practically all your life. Do you think you can change such a life habit just by making up your mind to drop it?

P: Of course, I'll have to practice.

E: That's it. You'll have to practice, and to practice hard. Can you tell me how you will carry out your practicing?

P: I will think of what you told me and will stop arguing.

E: I doubt whether that will be successful. You see, Lester, a temperamental outburst runs in stages. First, you explode and go into a rage. In a given instance, you may rave on for two or five minutes. During this time you are "out of your senses" and

will not be likely to exercise a great deal of thought. You will
certainly not stop to consult your memory recalling what I told
you about control of temper. So I take it that during this initial
stage of your explosion you will not think of the instruction I
gave you. You will simply rave on until your anger will subside.
I shall call this initial stage of your temper the "immediate effect
of the temper outburst." I hope you realize that when I want
you to practice avoiding intuitive conclusions, I do not ask you to
do that during this stage of the immediate effect. But after the
immediate effect is over, you enter a "cooling off" process which
may last some ten or fifteen minutes. This is the temperamental
after-effect. Once the after-effect sets in you begin to think,
perhaps not very clearly, but sufficiently so to be able to remember what I told you. Whatever thinking you do during the
immediate effect is intuitive, vague and dim. But in the after-
effect your thought becomes discursive again. You can then
reflect and meditate. The question is whether your type of
reflection will be rational or emotional. If it is emotional you
will continue to fume, will brood over the outrage of which you
were the "innocent victim." Burning with righteous indignation, you will justify the explosion which you released during the
immediate effect and will give it your endorsement. Once you
endorse your outburst as justified, you are primed for another
explosion; you fairly itch to "pay that fellow back" and thus keep
your temper boiling in anticipation of another bout. This is the
last stage of the uncontrolled temperamental cycle which we
shall call the stage of anticipation. It is called the stage of
anticipation because in this third phase of the temper outburst
you anticipate a renewed squabble in which you expect to come
out on top. You anticipate a victory which will wipe out the
"disgrace" of the present defeat. You will understand now that
the so-called temperamental cycle if left to itself without an
attempt to control it consists of three discrete stages; (1) the
immediate effect, (2) the after-effect, (3) the anticipation of a
renewed outburst. Can you tell me now which stage of this cycle
you must make use of for the purpose of remembering what I told
you in matters of control?

P: You said it can't be done in the immediate effect. So I think
it will have to be done after that.

E: That's correct. You will have to make use of the after-
effect. Of course, I do not expect you to succeed the first time,
nor do I expect full success the fourth, fifth and sixth time.

Instead, I presume you will become emotional in the first few beginnings of your practice and your after-effects will be spent in spells of fussing and fretting, with the result that the temperamental cycle will be run unchecked through its immediate effect, after-effect and the anticipation of the next temperamental "comeback." I hope, however, that after repeated practice you will finally manage to stop short at the end of the immediate effect and that henceforth the after-effect will be given over to a sane, rational appraisal of the situation in which you will refrain from endorsing your explosion, thus avoiding the anticipation of and preparation for the next outburst. This will come to pass if, after a few initial failures, you will not permit yourself to be discouraged and will continue practicing with solid determination. You will do that if you have the genuine will to remedy and check your temperamental habits. Do you think you will make the effort?

P: I sure will. After all, my temper didn't do me a lot of good.

E: What harm did it do you?

P: Why, I have lost all my friends, and I know I am a pest at home.

E: That is correct. Your temper made you lose your friends and has destroyed what peace and happiness was left in your home. But let me tell you, Lester, I am not so much interested in friendship and home life. My main interest is to get my patients to lose their symptoms. It is important, of course, to have friends, and to have peace in the home is a desirable aim, indeed. But the patient's first obligation is to get rid of his symptoms. I do not think you will make a strenuous effort to curb your temper if you merely have your eye on the damage it does to friendships and home life. This ought to be a strong incentive. But experience teaches it is not. The only thing that will make you bend all your energies toward conquering your temper is the realization that you cannot get well unless your temper is prevented from creating emotional upheavals in your body and producing an incessant train of symptoms. Mark this, Lester, I am not primarily interested in temper as a disturbance of social relations. I am interested in it mainly because it maintains and intensifies nervous symptoms. This is the reason why I insist that my patients cannot get well unless they learn to control their temperamental cycles.

8

THE PATIENT WANTS THE ENDS OF HEALTH, NOT ITS MEANS

Herbert had been in good health until four years ago, when waiting for a street car, he suddenly felt a "light-headedness" and was seized with the fear of "keeling over." The sensations passed quickly, and Herbert paid scant attention to the incident. But when three weeks later the sensations recurred in exactly the same fashion, again while waiting for a street car, the otherwise stolid man became alarmed. He feared he was suffering from a fatal illness. Henceforth, he was afraid of boarding street cars and experienced sweats and palpitations when in the morning he prepared to leave the house. The "lightheadedness" and "keeling-over" sensations became more frequent. He noticed they occurred in open places only. At home he was free from them. He also observed that he was never subject to spells on the street if he was in the company of another person. When first seen at the office he stated that for the past three years he has not left his home unaccompanied. He was compelled to give up his position, and his wife had to secure employment to provide for the family needs.

Two months after joining classes and acquiring membership in Recovery Herbert was able to take long walks without a companion. His "lightheadedness" did not disappear altogether, but he learned to dismiss the idea of danger and to ignore the symptom. Numerous disturbing sensations which had established themselves in the course of his ailment—palpitations, sweats, crawling and numbness in the arms, fatigue and blurred vision—were on the point of fading away. At the end of the third month he returned to work resuming his position as the breadwinner of the family.

He continued classes and stated in an interview, "I have been swell for the past six weeks. I worked and didn't have any of these symptoms, except that I felt some of the sensations for a short time occasionally. And they were very mild. I think you'd call them 'reminders.' But a couple of days ago I had a severe spell of light-headedness again. That sure scared me. And some of the other sensations came back, too. I tried to ignore them but it's not easy."

E—Examiner
P—Patient
E: When did you start on your new job, Herbert?
P: Six weeks ago.
E: Two months ago you told me that you were taking walks of three and four miles all by yourself. Have you done that lately?
P: No. I work hard and feel tired when I quit the job in the afternoon. I still walk the five or six blocks to the street car. But then I am all in.
E: How many hours per day do you work?
P: On some days it is four hours, on some seven.
E: I told you to take long walks every day. You did that until recently. Why did you not continue the practice? With an average of five to six hours of daily work you had ample time to take your walks. If you failed to do that you sabotaged my instructions.
P: I am on my feet all the time when I am at work, and it's always a rush. When I leave the shop I can hardly drag myself.
E: What you said is an excuse. You justify your failure to take long walks on the grounds of hard work, rush and fatigue. On this score you do not only practice sabotage; worse yet, you claim you were justified in practicing it. If this is so you will go on excusing and justifying, and the final result will be that the walks will cease and you will slip back into your condition of fear and helplessness. Is that what you want? Don't you want to get well?
P: Of course, I want to get well. I keep going to the shop and coming to classes. Would I do that if I didn't want to get well?
E: In a sense, you may be correct in stating that you want to get well. But I am just as correct if I say you do not want to get well. You see, Herbert, if a man who is out of work says he wants a job you will hardly deny that he really wants it. But then you observe that after he obtains the position he complains about the hard work and the poor pay. He loafs and stalls and makes excuses and finally absents himself frequently. Will you say that this man wants the job in the sense that he wants to do a good day's work?
P: But I do a good day's work and don't gripe.
E: I did not mean you when I spoke of the man who loafs on the job. And if you assumed that my remarks were aimed at you it merely shows that your conscience bothers you. That is a good

sign and indicates that you are by no means happy about your backsliding. But to return to the man with the job: he wanted it, no doubt. He looked for it, took it when it was offered and kept it although he didn't like it. What better proof do you need to conclude that he wanted it? But what precisely did the man want? He wanted the job, but he resented the things that had to be done on the job. In other words, he wanted the end but did not want the means that lead toward the end. Do you realize that the word "wanting" has at least two meanings? In the one sense it means that you wish to obtain an end; in the other sense, it means, you are ready to take every step to reach that end. In the first sense, you were correct when you said you want to get well. In the second sense, I was right when I objected that you did not want to get well. What I tried to make clear to you was that you wanted health as a shadowy, nebulous end but refused to employ the concrete means of hard application to accomplish that end.

P: I don't think I refused to work, and I certainly applied myself. If you ask my boss he will tell you that I was on the job all the time.

E: I told you that "wanting" can be used in two different senses. That applies with equal force to what you said about your being on the job. What you have in mind is the work on the premises only. In order to get to the premises where you work you must be able to take long walks; you must be able also to perform your task without being handicapped by "light-headed-ness," or fatigue, or palpitations, sweats and numbness. Obviously, if you do not manage to get rid of your sensations you will have to quit the job. If you want the job you must at the same time want to be in good enough health to carry on with your job. You will understand now that your health is a means toward the end of securing and maintaining the job. You want the job but not the means necessary to accomplish it.

P: Can I help it if the "light-headedness" comes back and I get those frightful palpitations and the sweats and the numbness?

E: I told you frequently that sensations come of their own account, not at your bidding. You are not responsible for their coming, but you are responsible for their persistence if you fail to handle them in accordance with my instructions. Every nervous sensation disappears after a short while if you refuse to get alarmed about it. If you permit yourself to become alarmed about the sensation you establish a vicious cycle. The more you fear the palpitations the worse they grow. The worse they grow the greater is your alarm. This vicious cycle can be cut through instantly if you refuse to think of the sensation as dangerous.

P: I know that and I have tried to be calm. I told myself that sensations are distressing but not dangerous but it didn't help me. The palpitations went on and the numbness got worse instead of better.

E: You repeated my formula but did not practice it. When your sensations started their rumble you should not merely have thought they were harmless; you should have demonstrated that to yourself. You should have demonstrated your indifference to the danger. This you could have done by walking on unhesitatingly in spite of the palpitations. You know numbers of patients who have conquered their sensations by the simple expedient of acting on them with indifference. The indifferent act demonstrates that there is no danger. Here is Jane, sitting two seats from you. You know that while walking on the street she had the frightful sensation that the pavement moved up toward her and the buildings were toppling over her. I take it you remember that several weeks ago when Jane was interviewed she told her method of dealing with these sensations. Do you recall what she did?

P: She walked on and disregarded the sensations.

E: Jane practiced the rules of fearlessness and got results. After three years of avoiding walks she now has no trouble and moves about as if she had never been sick. Had you practiced the rules instead of merely remembering or repeating them you would be well by now. You say you tried but did not succeed. Do you understand that what you tried was to achieve the goal without practicing the means? Jane had not only the goal in view but also the means that lead to it. If you really want to get well you will have to consider the practical means and not only the theoretical goal. Will you do that?

P: I shall certainly try.

E: That's not enough. You must want and not merely try.

The interview was then devoted to a discussion of the terms "trying" and "wanting." Herbert tried to walk long distances but relinquished his effort after an initial failure. The first failure discouraged him and he gave up. Jane, on the other hand, experienced the same initial failure but kept practicing until she succeeded. She showed will and determination, which means to want the end but also the arduous means that lead to its achievement.

9

MENTAL HEALTH IS SUPREME PURPOSE, NOT SUBORDINATE GOAL

E—Examiner
P—Patient

E: How are you, Helen?
P: I have been well for more than six weeks but last week I had a setback. It was during a card game. I didn't get my paralysis, but it was bad enough. I had a panic and couldn't shake it off for two days. Today I am much better, but I am still shaky.
E: You speak of paralysis. Can you tell the class what you mean by that? You are a young woman, and why should you have a paralysis at your age? Tell your story briefly and try to explain what you mean by "paralysis."
P: I have always been restless. After I got married I couldn't stand being alone at home in the evening, not even with my husband. We had to be in the company of people all the time. We either had people visit at our home, or we went out visiting. Usually we played cards. One day, three years ago, while playing a game of bridge, my hands suddenly went limp. I tried to move them and couldn't. Of course, that scared the wits out of me. I pretended to have a headache and excused myself. The moment I left the table my arms moved again. That was the first time I had that paralysis.
E: Did the condition return?
P: It did not for about three weeks. In between I played cards repeatedly and had no trouble moving the arms. I actually forgot the whole thing. But one evening I played again and the arms gave out. This time, I was so scared I didn't have the presence of mind to fish for an excuse but just ran out of the room. My husband called a doctor who said he couldn't find anything wrong with me. But I felt like in a daze, although I knew I could move the arms again. After that I could not get myself to play cards when I was out of the house. I was in terror when I thought that the arms would stop moving again.
E: Were you able to play cards at home?

P: Yes. I played without trouble at home, even when visitors were present. I was also able to visit people but I did not touch a card when I visited. I gave excuses, said I had a headache or felt dizzy and couldn't concentrate. That helped for a while but one evening the hostess was insistent and wouldn't take an excuse. I gave in and, sure enough, there was the paralysis. After that, I refused to accept invitations. I still had visitors at my home but they gradually petered out because I did not reciprocate.

E: Did the "paralysis" ever appear when you played cards at home, with only relatives present?

P: This didn't happen for a long time until, one evening, it finally happened. After that, there was no more card playing with anybody except my husband and my parents. With them, I never had the paralysis.

E: Did you have any other trouble aside from this "paralysis?"

P: For many months the paralysis was the only trouble. But then all kinds of other trouble came. The greatest trouble was meeting people. I hated their questioning me about my condition. I had to explain why I kept away from them, and it wasn't easy to find excuses. Finally I kept out of everybody's way, that means, I avoided going out as far as I could.

E: Did you continue seeing your relatives?

P: I did. But they became bothersome, too. When they came to the house the first thing they told me was, "Why, you are not sick; you just look the picture of health. You must be feeling fine." When I told them I still had my fears they said, "Oh, it's all in your mind." Or they told me to snap out of it, to use my will power. I knew they were right and the doctors had told me the same thing. But I hated their way of talking, perhaps because they were right.

E: That was an excellent description. I need not tell you, Helen, that what you just described was a very severe nervous condition. Had you continued avoiding people and shutting yourself up in your home your life would have been that of a helpless cripple, doomed to lead a useless and miserable existence. If this is so why don't you make an effort to get well?

P: If I had a setback does that mean I don't make an effort to get well? You told us so many times that setbacks are unavoidable.

E: That is correct. But I also told you that you must learn how to handle the setback. Do you think you handled it in accordance with my instructions?

P: I got over it in two days. Is that so bad?

E: It is bad enough. You said you were panicky and couldn't shake off the panic for two days. Then you added that you are still shaky today. Had you done what I asked you to do the setback would not have developed into a panic and would have lasted minutes or hours and not days. What did you do when you noticed the setback?

P: I remembered what you told me. I knew that sensations are distressing but not dangerous. Wasn't that what I was supposed to do?

E: You did very little. You merely "remembered" and "knew" something that I said. That's not what I call "doing." I shall ask you: Did you attend the Recovery meetings? Did you go to family gatherings?

P: No, I didn't. I was so fine the past six weeks that I was sure I was well and didn't need the meetings.

E: You spent three years in utter agony. Then you got well but were warned that the condition was likely to return unless you took part in classes and Recovery activities for at least six months. You attended my classes but neglected going to Recovery meetings. That means you made a half-effort. Why did you not make a total effort?

P: I did what I could. I had to come to your office twice a week. That took up two afternoons. The class took up an evening. Then I had to take care of the house and the children, and my husband is entitled to some of my time, I think. And you told me I should go and visit people which I did. All of this took plenty of my time.

E: You mentioned the home and the children and social activities. They are all very important. I do not deny that. You may call them the domestic, social and marital purposes. You took care of them and deserve all the credit that is due for the accomplishing of purposes, especially if they are as worthy as the ones you mentioned. You might have added that you had to attend a church meeting or meetings of a civic club. These would be the purposes of citizenship, community and church interest. All worthy and commendable purposes. But when you are ill your main and all-absorbing purpose must be the will to get well. All other purposes, no matter how inspiring and exalted, must be subordinated to the one leading and supreme purpose of getting well and keeping well. Unless you regain and maintain your mental health all other purposes will be frustrated. Only if you keep well will you be able to discharge your duties as mother, wife, friend, church and club member. I do not mean to say that health is more important than motherhood or religion. I merely say that motherhood, religion, citizenship and fellowship cannot function unless health is made to function first. To a patient his health must have unquestioned priority over all other purposes. Health must be the supreme aim to him, all other aims must be subordinated to the demands of health. You spent your effort on subordinated purposes and neglected that aim that ought to be supreme now. Instead of concentrating all your strength on the main issue, you frittered away your energies on a number of side issues. Why are you so careless of your welfare? Don't you want to keep well?

P: Of course, I want to keep well. I just shudder if I think of my suffering in the past.

E: You say you want to keep well. In a sense you are right. You would like nothing better than to have done with the "paralysis" and the awful difficulties into which it got you. That merely means that you wish to have your health. It does not mean that you have the will to health. I shall not enter into a comprehensive discussion of what is the difference between a loose wish and a determined will. This much I will say: A wish does not commit you to exercise all your energies toward attaining it. You wish to make a trip to a distant country. You may say you want the trip. But you don't want it hard enough to sacrifice other aims in its favor. You will not sacrifice your life savings or the welfare of your family for the sake of that wish. That wish is not directed toward a supreme aim. You do not give it priority over the family purpose. Should you for some foolish reason make that trip a supreme aim you might perhaps sacrifice all other purposes to it. Then you would pursue your aim with the force of a total effort. The trip would no longer be backed by a loose wish but would be insisted on with the vigor of a determined will. I hope that you understand now the difference between a supreme and subordinate purpose. Health was to you a subordinate aim, a loose wish, something that you thought you might be able to attain at the cost of a half-effort. You know better now. You know that health must take precedence over all other purposes and must be attended to with the energy of a total effort. If you keep that in mind you will not have to worry about your setbacks. You will be prepared for them and will shake them off in minutes instead of hours or days.

The examiner then pointed out that the real reason for Helen's failure to attend Recovery meetings was her sense of shame. Helen, he commented, is still harassed by the idea that her nervous ailment is a disgrace to her and her family. She still suffers from the pressure of stigmatization. To feel stigmatized means to be tense. The tenseness creates pressure on the nervous system and may produce or revive symptoms. As long as Helen continues to feel stigmatized she will be in danger of becoming "paralyzed" again. If she wants to prevent a return of the symptoms she will have to learn how to shake off embarrassment and stigmatization. One of the purposes of Recovery gatherings is to rid the patient of his feeling of being stigmatized. If Helen continues to shy away from the meetings she will have demonstrated that her will to avoid embarrassment is stronger than her will to get well. That will is a mere wish, not a solid determination.

10

SPONTANEITY AND SELF-CONSCIOUSNESS

Irene, a woman of 30 and mother of two children, developed a depression of mood which persisted for five years with only brief intervals of fair health. When she was first seen by the examiner she complained of a "complete absence of interest," difficulty of sleeping, lack of appetite, fatigue. She claimed she had no zest, pep or initiative. She could not plan, make up her mind, decide to get things started. In the morning it took her literally hours to get dressed, to choose the proper attire, to get started with cooking, dusting and cleaning. When she finally began to do her work she had to drag herself. Everything was done with extreme effort. Even such simple acts as turning on the faucet or lighting the gas range required her to use all of her strength. She could only do things if she forced herself to do them. A simple conversation was "hard labor," walking was an ordeal. On the other hand, sitting or lying down was intolerable because it made her restless. Because speaking and walking called for extreme effort she avoided going out and meeting people. After several weeks of combined office and group treatment she recovered her health and staged a comeback that surprised both her and the members of the family. When interviewed in class she reported that all her symptoms were gone and that she was as well "as anyone might wish to be."

E—Examiner
P—Patient

E: I have observed you closely for the past two months, and there can be no doubt that you have regained your health. But tell me, Irene, what do you plan to do for the purpose of maintaining your health?

P: I shall attend classes and Recovery meetings and I will study your books and the Recovery Journal. Isn't that what you want me to do?

E: Of course, I want you to do that. But the maintenance of health is a lifelong task and I do not expect you to attend classes all your life. And whether you will continue membership in

Recovery forever is questionable. So, what is your program for keeping well aside from your present activities in classes and meetings?

P: I certainly intend to take part in Recovery for good. I know that many members feel the way I do. They think they are in Recovery for keeps.

E: I like your spirit. But you cannot depend on Recovery exclusively. Suppose your husband will be transferred to an out of town branch of his concern. Then you will be separated from Recovery and will be thrown on your own resources. Are you prepared for a development of this kind? Are you ready to practice self-help?

P: I never thought of that. But it seems I'll be able to manage.

E: Look here, Irene, you have suffered for almost five years and have only been well some two months. In these two months you have heard me state repeatedly that every patient must be prepared for setbacks. You have listened to several interviews in which patients reported that they drifted into setbacks after months and years of good health. Last week you had an opportunity to listen to the interview with Emily who had enjoyed good health for three years in succession and then developed a severe spell that landed her in the hospital. You remember that when I criticized Emily for neglecting her participation in our after-care project she gave the excuse that three years ago she felt sure she was able to manage herself without the aid of classes or meetings. Emily paid dearly for her false sense of security. Now you also say you think you'll be "able to manage." Are you going to repeat Emily's mistake?

P: I don't know what more I can do than come to classes and work in Recovery.

E: Be certain I appreciate your loyalty to Recovery. But I must repeat what I mentioned before. Suppose some day you will be deprived of Recovery support. Are you prepared to practice self-help? Do you know how to go about it? Do you know which method to employ? You wish to keep well. That means you want to prevent a recurrence of your ailment. But prevention must be practiced correctly, methodically and systematically. Do you think you know the method which will help you maintain your health?

P: I don't know what to say.

E: You see, Irene, you told me that when you were ill you had no interest, zest or initiative. You could not plan or decide.

Making up your mind and getting things started was difficult or impossible. Simple tasks which are ordinarily done without hesitation, required extreme effort. All of this can be summed up in the statement that you lost your spontaneity. Do you understand now that if you are to keep well you will have to know (1) what is the nature of spontaneity, (2) what you can do to strengthen and preserve it? I shall try to tell you something about that. While I am speaking here before the class I have in mind a plan or intention. My intention is to express certain ideas and to make this class accept them. This intention must be carried out by my muscles. The muscles of my lips, tongue and cheeks must pronounce my sentences, the muscles of the throat must provide the proper intonation. The face muscles will have to mold and fashion my features in such a manner that they give adequate expression to everything voiced by my lips. Add the gestures of my arms, the carriage of my frame, all of them must fall in line with the central intention conveyed by my spoken word. In the space of one hour I shall have to set in motion hundreds of muscles in thousands of combinations and all the movements they will perform will be required to give expression to one intention, one plan, one idea. Let me tell you that what I described here is the pattern for every act of every description no matter what may be its meaning. You may say that *every act expresses one single intention through a multiplicity of muscular movements.* Suppose now that when I arrived tonight I felt tired, discouraged and dispirited, the reason perhaps being that I experienced a grave disappointment in the afternoon. If this is so, then, my intention may still be to plant certain ideas in your brains. But that intention will now be coupled with another intention: to go home and rest, to get this class out of the way, to be finished with it in record time. My mind will no longer be "made up" or determined by one single intention. Instead it will be torn between two intentions. The intention to continue this address will grapple with the opposite intention to go home and relax. The result will be that two sets of antagonistic impulses will reach my muscles of speech, intonation, facial expression and gestures, and the muscles will sometimes express the one group of impulses (to make a good and effective speech) and sometimes the other group (to be done with that speech that keeps me from taking a rest). The dual intention will distract my attention and will involve me in contradictions. Before long I will notice that I stray from the theme and that I do not hold the interest of the audience. The observation will scare me. I will lose my assurance and will be self-conscious. And once I become self-conscious I am not spontaneous. You will understand now that spontaneity is interfered with or destroyed by self-consciousness. You will also realize that self-consciousness is produced by the fact that two contradictory intentions endeavor to make the muscles express two different ideas at the same time. The muscles are thrown into disorder expressing portions of the one idea and fragments of the other with the result that the speech loses clarity and gives the impression of confusion. Do you understand, Irene, that when you lacked spontaneity your mind was the seat of two contradictory basic intentions and was not "made up" in favor of one single plan?

P: I know I was always self-conscious when I was ill. But when you speak of contradictory intentions I don't know whether that was so. I know I wanted to do something and felt I couldn't. I had to drag myself and when I forced myself to cook or clean I did it with great effort.

E: You say you wanted to cook but had to force yourself to do it. That means your intention or plan to cook met with resistance. You know that at present if you intend to cook you simply send an impulse down to your muscles and they perform the act. They do that with ease, without effort. You no longer drag yourself which means that strain is eliminated; you hardly think of and certainly do not reflect strenuously on what your muscles are doing which means that you are no longer self-conscious about your actions. Since your cooking proceeds without effort and without self-consciousness you can say that you are now spontaneous. Your spontaneity has reestablished itself because your impulse to cook is no longer resisted and thwarted by the contrary impulse not to cook. You will understand this situation better if you consider another example in which resistance hampers prompt and effortless action. I shall quote the act of buying necessities or conveniences. Should you want to buy a loaf of bread all you would have to do would be to have the proper intention and to impart the corresponding impulse to your muscles to walk out of the home, to cross the street, to enter the bakery shop, to pick up the bread and to pay for it. All these actions would be executed promptly, and without effort and without self-conscious hesitation. You would act spontaneously. In the afternoon of the same day you might want to purchase a coat. The question will be: cloth or fur? Now you will no longer just dispatch an impulse to your muscles, fetch a seal coat, pay for it and stroll home. Now there will be stalling, hesitation, plenty of thought and an abundance of reflection. You may want that sealskin very insistently but the intention to buy it will be crossed by the contrary intention to save the money. Your spontaneity will be gone because two antagonistic impulses will impinge on your muscles. I shall try to tell you what is at stake in situations of this sort. You see when it was a matter of securing a loaf of bread you were sure you needed it, you were certain that your intention was proper, reasonable, harmless. You knew with absolute assurance that after the purchase of the bread there will be no self-blame, no compunction, no threat to your moral ego. In other words, you felt secure with regard to carrying out the impulse once you conceived it. This sense of security was absent in the instance of your intention to buy a coat. You had the intention to acquire the cloth coat but it was not sufficiently dressy. Then the seal caught your eye and now you were uncertain whether you could afford it. The impulse to buy engaged in a running fight with the impulse not to buy, and the result was a sense of insecurity, strain and tenseness (effort) and stalling and hesitation (self-consciousness). In the end, you were left without spontaneity. You will now be in a better position to understand the factors which tend to do away with your spontaneity: (1) there is a conflict of intentions and impulses, (2) a sense of insecurity, (3) effort and self-consciousness, (4) inability to decide, plan and act. The inability to decide, plan and act is the outward expression of your defect in spontaneity; the conflict of impulses, the sense of insecurity and the self-consciousness are its inner causes.

In the subsequent portions of the interview it was explained that if Irene meant to preserve and strengthen her spontaneity she had to cultivate ideas of security and to reduce as far as possible her thoughts of insecurity. The examiner then demonstrated with suitable examples that patients can weaken their sense of insecurity if they learn to adopt the philosophy of averageness in preference to thinking in terms of exceptionality. Irene had been brought up as a perfectionist. Her ambition was to keep her home "perfectly clean"; to do a perfect job in the education of her children; to attain excellence as hostess, wife, friend, neighbor. Trivial errors, trifling mistakes and insignificant failures caused her to sweat and fret, to wear herself out with vexation and self-reproach. She worried, felt provoked at her fancied inefficiency, was perpetually flustered and confused. The confusion multiplied her record of bungled trivialities and botched irrelevancies. A vicious cycle developed: The more she was confused the more she bungled; the more persistently she bungled the more disturbing became her confusion. In the end, she lost confidence in her ability to do things "correctly," developed an exaggerated self-consciousness and lost her spontaneity. After joining Recovery she learned to be human and average, to permit herself to be "like others," to bungle as much or as little as people bungle "on an average." She rejected the grotesque idea of the "perfect job" and the "flawless performance," and imbibed the now familiar Recovery doctrine to "have the courage to make mistakes in the trivialities of everyday life." If Irene continued to practice these Recovery doctrines in her everyday activities, if she practiced methodically to laugh at the paltry consequences of her trivial mistakes, she was certain to develop self-assurance and to rout her self-consciousness. Then her muscles will not be wedged in between two sets of antagonistic impulses, her spontaneity will be established on the firm ground of self-confidence, and her solid habits of thinking in terms of averageness will prevent her from becoming discouraged, despondent and depressed.

An Important Book For The Patient And His Family

Lectures To Relatives of Former Patients
By Abraham A. Low, M.D.

The bulk of Dr. Low's Lectures to families have been gathered together in this book. It contains information of great value to patients and it is indispensible to those who seek to understand and help those patients.